ENGEN GUIDE TO

ADVENTURE TRAVEL

IN SOUTHERN AFRICA

ENGEN GUIDE TO

ADVENTURE TRAVEL

IN SOUTHERN AFRICA

Jennifer Stern

SOUTHERN
BOOK PUBLISHERS

ISBN 1 86812 669 2

First edition, first impression 1997

Published by
Southern Book Publishers (Pty) Ltd
PO Box 1303 Halfway House 1685

While the author and the publisher have endeavoured to verify
all facts, they will not be held responsible for any inconvenience
that may result from possible inaccuracies in this book.

Main cover photograph: Zambezi river white water rafting (courtesy of Shearwater Adventures)
Inset left: Horse safari in the Waterberg
Inset right: Bouldering
Back cover photograph: Bungi-jumping at Victoria Falls Bridge (courtesy of Shearwater Adventures)
Cover design by Alix Korte
Maps by Duncan Butchart
Set in 9.7pt Clearface Regular
Typesetting by Alix Korte
Printed and bound by Colorgraphic, Durban

This book is dedicated to the

memory of my parents, Jo and Doris Stern,

whose diverse histories resulted in my being born

in Africa, the most magical of continents.

Contents

CHAPTER 11

Get carried away

CHAPTER 12

The ultimate high

CHAPTER 13

Go jump off a bridge

CHAPTER 14

Catch a wave

CHAPTER 15

On the wild side

CHAPTER 16

Ride into the sunset

CHAPTER 17

Go underground

CHAPTER 18

Off the wall

Foreword

South Africa is extraordinarily rich in its natural and human resources. The characteristics of these resources are unique to us, and amongst the best to be found anywhere. Recently, South Africans have come to realise that they have within and around them an astonishingly valuable resource – ecotourism.

Environmentally balanced tourism development provides all South Africans with an opportunity of linking their own socio-economic progression with the ideal of protecting and nourishing the heritage of the natural resources of our land and those of our neighbouring countries.

Engen, as the leading supplier of fuel to the people of our country, is committed to the encouragement and support of ecotourism. We are proud to be associated with this work for it not only provides information to the traveller, the adventurer and the explorer, but it provides employment, investment, revenue and entrepreneurial opportunity. Most of all, it brings with it the dynamic of ecotourism, which in turn brings hope, prosperity and goodwill to the many diverse people of our great nation.

Rob Angel
CEO, Engen Petroleum Limited

Acknowledgements

I had a great deal of fun writing and researching this book but without the help and encouragement of a number of individuals and organisations, it would have been impossible. I'm sure I have forgotten at least one or two people, for which I apologise.

Many thanks to the following friends, family and Friends who assisted and encouraged me in many ways: Ansi Adams, Cait Andrews, Claire Bateman, Dani Craill, Mandy Drummond, Felicity Ellmore, D'arcy, Ross Gillett, Bill, Mary, Sam and Sarah Harrop, Clive Hassall, Leonard le Roux, Debbie McLean, Robbie McLean, Eric Miller, Carl Munson, Pamela Murray, Rose Pereira, Mary Roberts, Jeremy Routledge, Nozizwe Madlala Routledge, Vicky Rowlands, Rocco, Biddy, Dayne and Beyers Stern, Nadene Svirovsky, Anton van Druten, Pat and Don Wetzlar and Kallie Zwahlen.

Also thanks to Louise Grantham, Kate Rogan and Donna Sherlock of Southern, for cheerful and professional assistance and for putting up with my (not inconsiderable) idiosyncracies.

I am especially indebted to experts in many fields of adventure who gave of their time, knowledge and enthusiasm. Without the help of Tristan Behr (Lesotho paragliding), Paul Bewsher (hiking), Rowan Bouttel (cycling), Liz Boyes (climbing), Steve Craven (caving), Roger Ellis (caving), Rob and Julie Filmer (disabled access), William Gunning (Drakensberg paragliding) Mark Jury (surfing), Simon Larson (climbing), Suzy Mills (cycling), Jan Minnaar (Garden Route paragliding) Laura Nelson (paragliding), Mike Pascoe (gliding), Glen Patrick (gliding), Carol Schafer (disabled access), Kevin Schäfer (skydiving), Mike Tabelling (Eastern Cape paragliding), Euan Waugh (hiking) and Axel Zander (cycling) I would still be wandering around southern Africa trying to gather information.

The research was made easier by the generous tangible assistance of the following people and organisations:

Ken Lazarus, Cape Union Mart
Rod Murphy, Zimbabwe Express
Donald Pelekamoyo, Zambian National Tourist Board
Mike Rabbits, Digital South Africa
Sun Air

If it weren't for the generous sponsorship of Digital SA, this book would be no more than a whole lot of scraps of paper stuffed into a large plastic bag. The manuscript was written in the field on a Digital HiNote CS433, without which I simply could not have survived.

Last, but by no means least, I am immensely indebted to Engen Petroleum Limited for their generous assistance, their vision and their commitment to development and ecotourism in southern Africa. To Rick Robertson, Adhila Hamdulay, Gareth Griffiths and Tanya Hichert of Engen, Noel de Villiers and Leslie Shackleton of the Open Africa Initiative, and Tamra Veley and Enid Vickers of Corporate Image, a huge thank you for the time and effort you all personally put into the project and your continued faith in me when I was "somewhere out there in the bush" and you hadn't heard from me for months.

How to use this book

Although I hope it will be entertaining reading, this book is not written for armchair travellers. It is designed to enable you to most effectively plan an adventurous trip through the southern African region, or just one adventure experience (but the one most suited to your needs).

It should prove particularly useful if you are travelling in a group or as a couple. Each adventure described is followed by information on other activities, both adventurous and relaxing, in the area. In order to make the most of these suggestions, you should follow the many cross-references to other chapters. This is not nearly as tedious as it may sound, and it will ensure you get the most from your holiday. By using the cross-references you will ensure that you don't miss out on any exciting opportunities in the area and you'll be able to plan separate adventures close together for members of your party who have different interests, or plan one adventure while the rest of the party is secure in the knowledge that there is enough to do in the vicinity to ensure they won't get bored.

Unlike traditional travel guides, this book does not contain exhaustive lists of places to stay and eat because most of the adventures include accommodation and catering. The list of accommodation given towards the back of certain chapters is not comprehensive: it merely lists the most convenient places to stay before or after an adventure in cases where this would not be obvious. Restaurants are only listed in very rare instances in the "while in the area" section, and then only if they are pretty special.

Those on a tight budget can try to obtain a copy of the excellent little publication *BUG, the Backpackers Uptodate Guide*, published by Kirk Hall, Port St John's Backpackers. It is on sale in most backpackers' hostels.

You will find that the amount of information given for the various adventures differs considerably. This is not accidental. Some of the activities are quite dangerous if not done with knowledgeable guides so you will not find sufficient instructions to get you halfway up a mountain, down a river or into a cave. Rather, you will find enough information to enable you to make an informed choice as to what you would like to do and then who to contact. If you are an experienced adventurer, you will appreciate this attitude and would probably contact knowledgeable locals anyway before heading off on a self-guided epic.

In each chapter, details of the operator will be found in the alphabetical listing at the end. In the event that the name of the the operator or booking authority differs from the name of the trip it will be highlighted in **bold** in the text.

Most important, though, do not be intimidated. You are probably quite capable of enjoying most (if not all) of the adventures listed if you go about them the right way.

Get out there, have a great

time and return home younger

than you left.

CHAPTER 1

To whet your appetite

Overview of southern Africa

Tourism as an industry has the potential to generate a great deal of foreign currency, and also to redistribute wealth from the urban centres of southern Africa to the more outlying regions. This could enable rural people to earn a living close to their beloved homes and thereby save them from having to move to large urban centres to find jobs. Sensitive and responsible tourism is the only industry that can prevent much of the region from being taken over by the bland "international" culture that is slowly engulfing the world.

One of the reasons for producing this book is to publicise the wilder areas of southern Africa and to highlight the unique opportunities they present for adventure travel. Adventurers, as opposed to tourists, expect to rough it a little and to expend some energy in the pursuit of pleasure. They also expect to return from their adventure changed. The essence of adventure is to stretch yourself — maybe just a little, maybe an awful lot. This doesn't mean returning from your holiday with just a few calluses and a suntan, but altered in mind and spirit. Adventure is all about going further, faster, higher, deeper or wilder than you ever thought you could. It's not risking your life that makes it adventure; it's risking your comfortable preconceived ideas about life. After a week in the desert, a day on a wild river or half an hour under water the colour of the lounge suite or the size of your salary cheque seems less important, somehow.

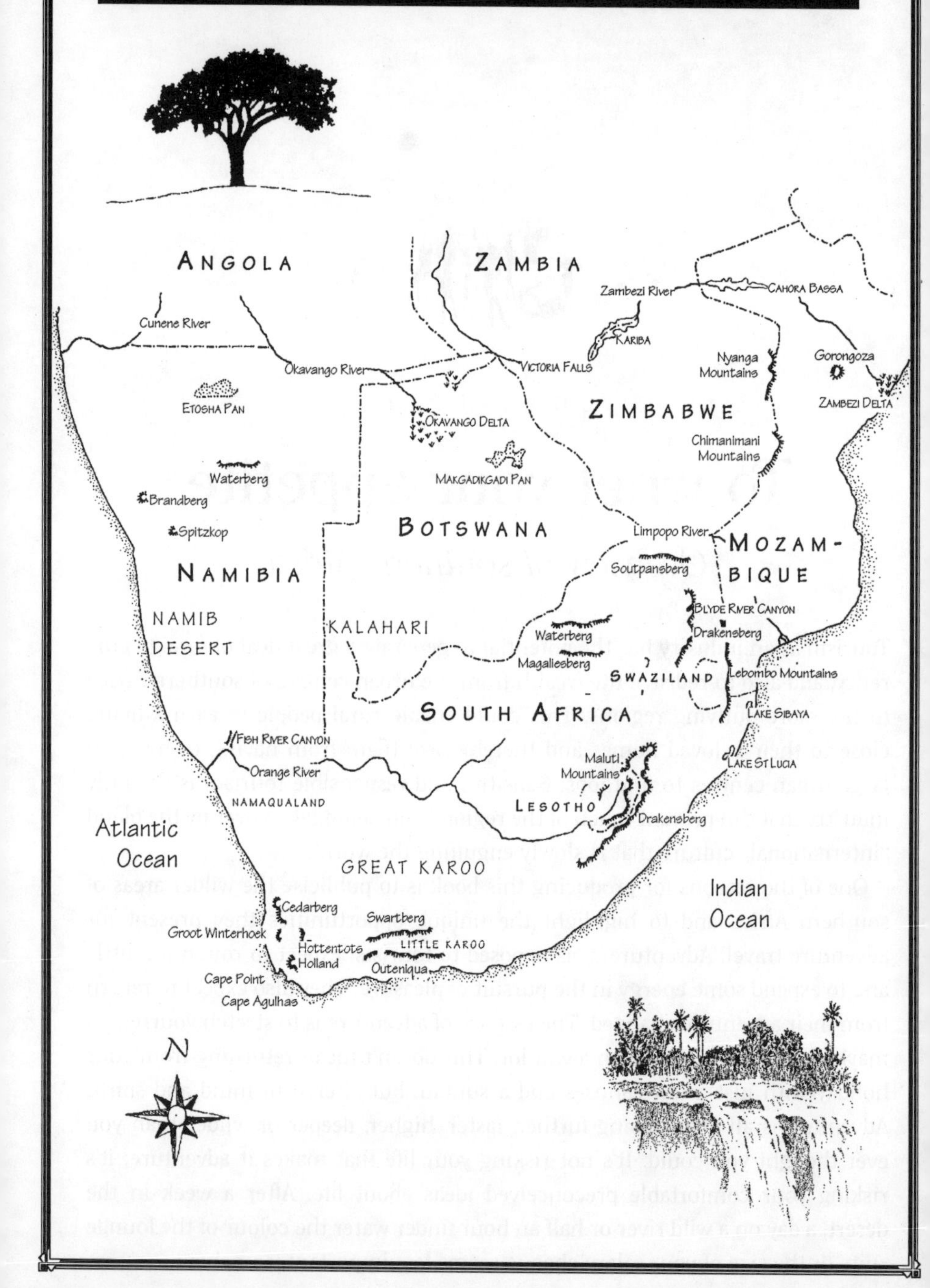
Southern Africa – Physical Features
ANGOLA
ZAMBIA
Cunene River
Okavango River
Zambezi River
Cahora Bassa
Kariba
Victoria Falls
Nyanga Mountains
Gorongoza
Zambezi Delta
Etosha Pan
Okavango Delta
Zimbabwe
Makgadikgadi Pan
Chimanimani Mountains
Waterberg
Brandberg
Spitzkop
BOTSWANA
Limpopo River
MOZAMBIQUE
NAMIBIA
Soutpansberg
Blyde River Canyon
NAMIB DESERT
KALAHARI
Waterberg
Drakensberg
Magaliesberg
SWAZILAND
Lebombo Mountains
SOUTH AFRICA
Lake Sibaya
Fish River Canyon
Orange River
Maluti Mountains
Lake St Lucia
NAMAQUALAND
LESOTHO
Drakensberg
Atlantic Ocean
GREAT KAROO
Indian Ocean
Cedarberg
Swartberg
Groot Winterhoek
Hottentots Holland
LITTLE KAROO
Outeniqua
Cape Point
Cape Agulhas
N

Climate and topography

At the tip of the most enchanting and mysterious of continents, southern Africa, with its many contrasts and surprises, is a most satisfying region to explore. Straddling as it does two vastly different oceans, embracing diametrically different cultures and supporting a hugely diverse range of life forms, the potential it offers for adventure is endless.

Most of southern Africa lies on a broad central plateau about 1 500 to 2 000 m above sea level with narrow coastal plains. The Indian Ocean, warmed by the Mozambique Current flowing down from the equator, brings subtropical weather and sea conditions much further south than would otherwise be expected. In fact, Sodwana Bay in the far north-east of South Africa has the most southerly coral reefs in the world, despite being well outside the tropics. Warm, moist air flows in from this ocean, rises as it reaches the escarpment and deposits its precious load of moisture as rain, supporting lush coastal forests.

Once on the plateau, the little remaining moisture in the air precipitates as rain in spectacular summer thunderstorms or is lost to evaporation as it moves westward, so the annual rainfall decreases steadily towards the Atlantic coast. Most of the plateau, where it has not been cleared to make way for agriculture or urban development, is covered with grassland or acacia savanna. The many river valleys and other low-lying areas in the north of the region have a very different climate, being almost subtropical or hot, dry woodland.

On the west coast, moist air blows in from the sea but it is cooled by the icy Benguela Current which flows northward from Antarctica, so it does not condense into rain. Instead it forms huge fog banks that roll in towards the land and support a unique and fascinating community of hardy plants and animals which have adapted to utilise this meagre water supply and thrive in the harsh desert or semi-desert conditions.

At the very tip of this marvellous continent, the Western Cape is quite anomalous. It has a Mediterranean climate, so its winters are cold and rainy and dominated by cold fronts originating deep in the Southern Ocean, while summers are hot and windy. Autumn is noted for good beach weather and balmy nights and spring, with its profuse display of wildflowers, is truly spectacular. In fact, this region is well noted for its immense floral diversity. It is also the region where the Indian and Atlantic oceans meet. The actual meeting point is subject to debate and, if such a thing actually exists, probably moves with the winds and seasons. Most experts insist the meeting point is Cape Agulhas, the southern-

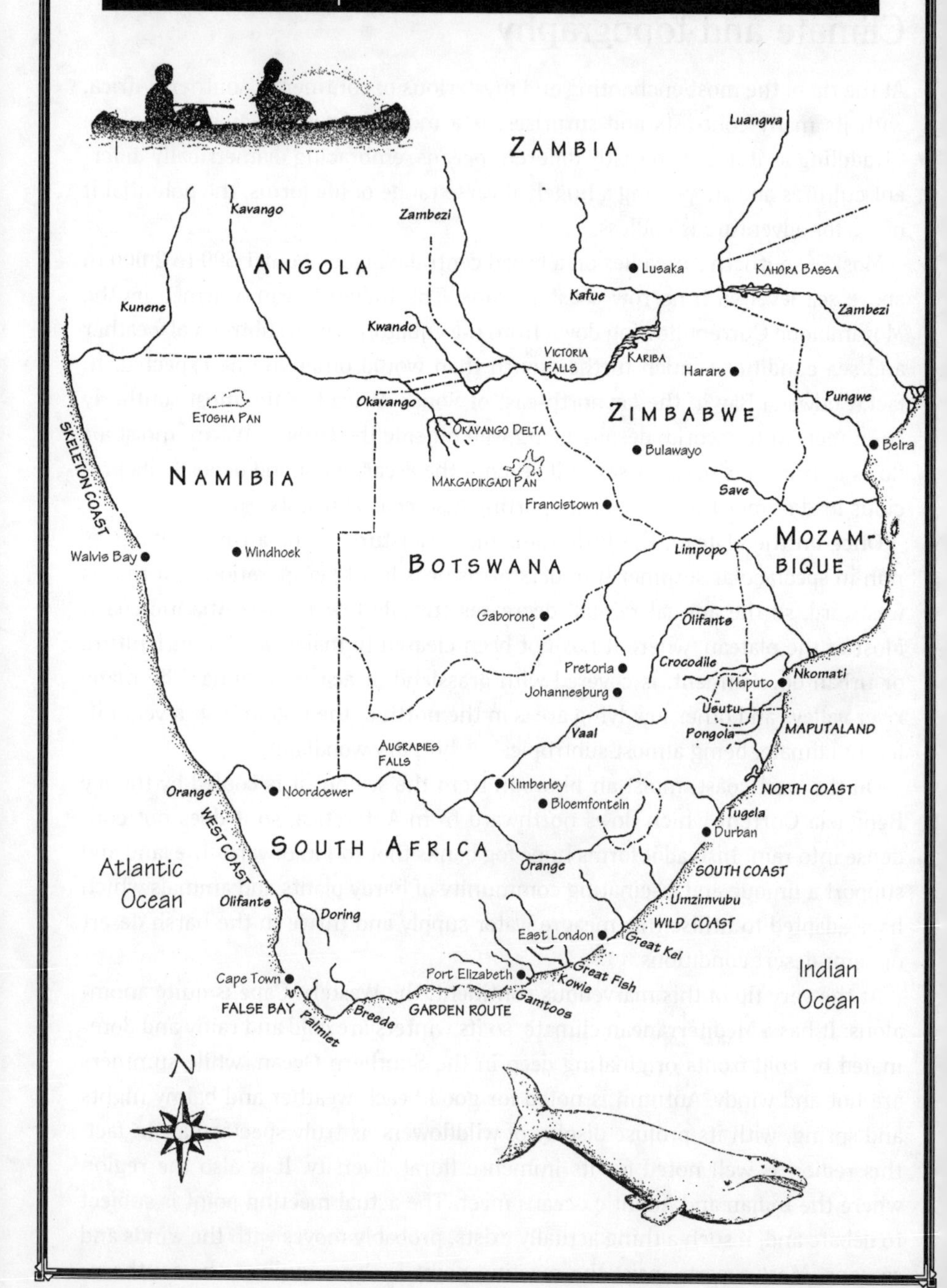
Southern Africa – Rivers and Coastline
ZAMBIA
Luangwa
Kavango
Zambezi
ANGOLA
Lusaka
KAHORA BASSA
Kafue
Zambezi
Kunene
Kwando
VICTORIA FALLS
KARIBA
Harare
Pungwe
Okavango
ETOSHA PAN
OKAVANGO DELTA
ZIMBABWE
Beira
Bulawayo
SKELETON COAST
NAMIBIA
MAKGADIKGADI PAN
Save
Francistown
MOZAM-BIQUE
Walvis Bay
Windhoek
Limpopo
BOTSWANA
Gaborone
Olifants
Pretoria
Crocodile
Nkomati
Maputo
Johannesburg
Usutu
Pongola
MAPUTALAND
Vaal
AUGRABIES FALLS
Kimberley
NORTH COAST
Orange
Noordoewer
Bloemfontein
WEST COAST
Tugela
Durban
SOUTH AFRICA
Atlantic Ocean
Orange
SOUTH COAST
Olifants
Umzimvubu
Doring
WILD COAST
East London
Great Kei
Cape Town
Port Elizabeth
Great Fish
Kowie
Indian Ocean
FALSE BAY
Palmiet
Breede
GARDEN ROUTE
Gamtoos
N

most tip of Africa, but Capetonians maintain it is really at Cape Point. Certainly this is a more dramatic site and one which will never be forgotten by anyone who has stood at the tip of that needle-sharp promontory and seen the line of foam "where the oceans meet" stretching away towards the end of the Earth.

Adventure activities

The vast range of climatic and vegetation zones, the many different geological formations and the encircling oceans make this relatively small region a veritable paradise for outdoor adventurers. If you plan your trip well and choose the right time of year you can enjoy almost any outdoor activity you like. This even includes snow skiing (although you will find the standard of this somewhat below the world's best). For almost any other adventure, though, you will look long and hard to find a better venue than southern Africa.

Because of the relatively low rainfall perennial rivers are few and far between, but they are spectacular. The Zambezi, one of the great rivers of Africa, wends its way through its subtropical valley offering, in various places, mind-numbingly wild white water rafting or gentle drifting through game-filled wilderness. The Orange is a sinuous oasis running through a desert wonderland, with fun white water and exquisitely stark scenery through which to paddle. Other rivers range from gentle, sluggish streams to spectacular, short-lived torrents and provide access to a huge range of scenery and locations.

There is some excellent climbing to be had on exposed granite domes, long mountain ranges of excellent quality sandstone and many incredibly beautiful spots just beckoning climbers and hikers. Myriad official hiking trails crisscross South Africa and Namibia and are very popular with an ever-growing body of outdoor enthusiasts. The many organisations that control mountain areas, ranging from local authorities through national parks boards to the various forestry administrators, are constantly opening up new areas for hikers and mountain bikers to explore, either independently as a group, or on an escorted trip. Organised horse trails, too, are operated in areas as diverse as mountain grassland, stark deserts and wilderness wetlands.

Local divers believe they have the best of both worlds, perched as they are between two oceans. Diving conditions range from icy kelp forests to tropical coral reefs with some unique environments in between, all of which have their own special attraction. At many points along the long coastline the huge rollers moving in from the open ocean meet just the right combination of bottom

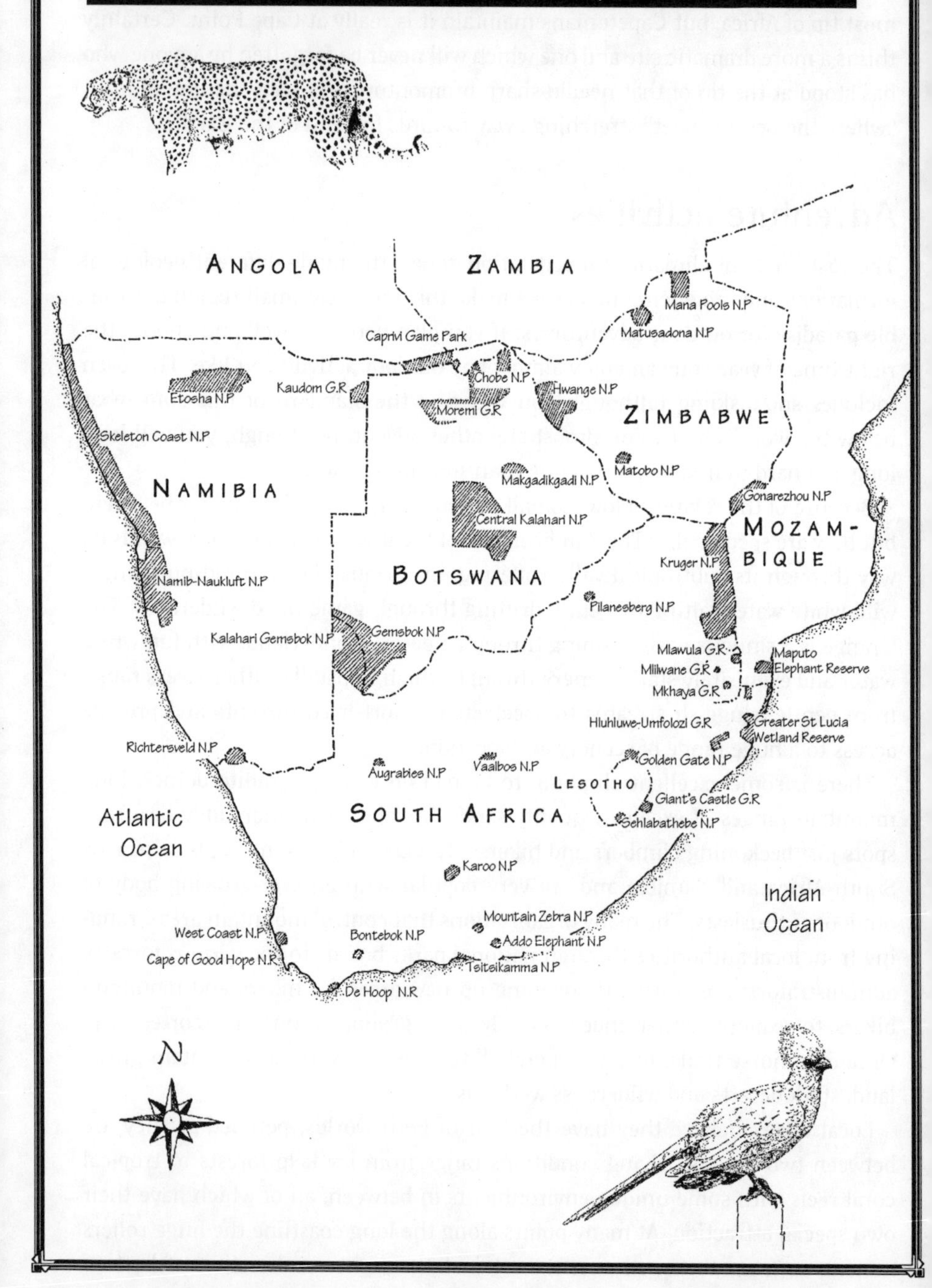
Southern Africa – Wildlife Reserves
ANGOLA
ZAMBIA
Mana Pools N.P
Matusadona N.P
Caprivi Game Park
Chobe N.P
Kaudom G.R
Etosha N.P
Hwange N.P
Moremi G.R
ZIMBABWE
Skeleton Coast N.P
Matobo N.P
Makgadikgadi N.P
NAMIBIA
Gonarezhou N.P
Central Kalahari N.P
MOZAM-
BIQUE
Kruger N.P
BOTSWANA
Namib-Naukluft N.P
Pilanesberg N.P
Gemsbok N.P
Kalahari Gemsbok N.P
Mlawula G.R
Maputo
Elephant Reserve
Mlilwane G.R
Mkhaya G.R
Hluhluwe-Umfolozi G.R
Greater St Lucia
Wetland Reserve
Richtersveld N.P
Golden Gate N.P
Vaalbos N.P
Augrabies N.P
LESOTHO
Giant's Castle G.R
SOUTH AFRICA
Atlantic
Ocean
Sehlabathebe N.P
Karoo N.P
Indian
Ocean
Mountain Zebra N.P
West Coast N.P
Bontebok N.P
Addo Elephant N.P
Cape of Good Hope N.R
Tsitsikamma N.P
De Hoop N.R
N

topography and wind working together to produce perfect waves. Some of these points are numbered among the top surf spots of the world.

The immense thermals that build up over the hot interior produce superb gliding conditions. A number of world records have been set at Bitterwasser, an exceptional flying venue in Namibia, and many long cross-country paragliding flights have been done in the hot skies above Kuruman in the Northern Cape. Dependable winds and steep mountains produce superb ridge soaring for hang- and paraglider pilots in many parts of the region, and there are skydiving clubs on the outskirts of most cities in South Africa as well as a few further north.

Of course, wildlife will be uppermost in the minds of most travellers in this region. You may visit a game park and observe animals at your leisure from your own vehicle or on an organised game drive. If you are a little more adventurous, though, you can do a safari on foot, on horseback, by bicycle, by quad bike, dugout canoe, floating over the veld in a hot air balloon or even on the back of a trained African elephant.

You will certainly never be bored. *Ex Africa semper aliquid novi.* Out of Africa, always something new.

CHAPTER 2

The nitty gritty

Essential information for travellers in southern Africa

The area covered in this book includes South Africa, Swaziland, Lesotho, Botswana, Namibia and the Zambezi Valley area of Zimbabwe and Zambia.

Getting around

The transport infrastructure of southern Africa varies from very poor to excellent. Although there are exceptions, South Africa, Namibia, Zimbabwe and Botswana generally have a more well developed transport network than Swaziland, Lesotho and Zambia.

DRIVING

The road infrastructure is extensive and varies from excellent to rudimentary. In all the countries in the region, motorists drive on the left side of the road and the wearing of seatbelts and, on motorbikes, crash helmets is mandatory. Speed limits and distances are shown in kilometres per hour and kilometres respectively. In order to cross borders you will need to be in possession of all the papers of the vehicle and, depending on your country of origin and destination, a temporary import permit, triptyque or *carnet de passage*; get details from the Automobile Association (AA) or from a diplomatic representative of the relevant country. Residents of the Southern African Common Customs Union (SACCU), i.e. South Africa, Lesotho, Swaziland, Namibia and Botswana, need only carry

Southern Africa – Transport Routes

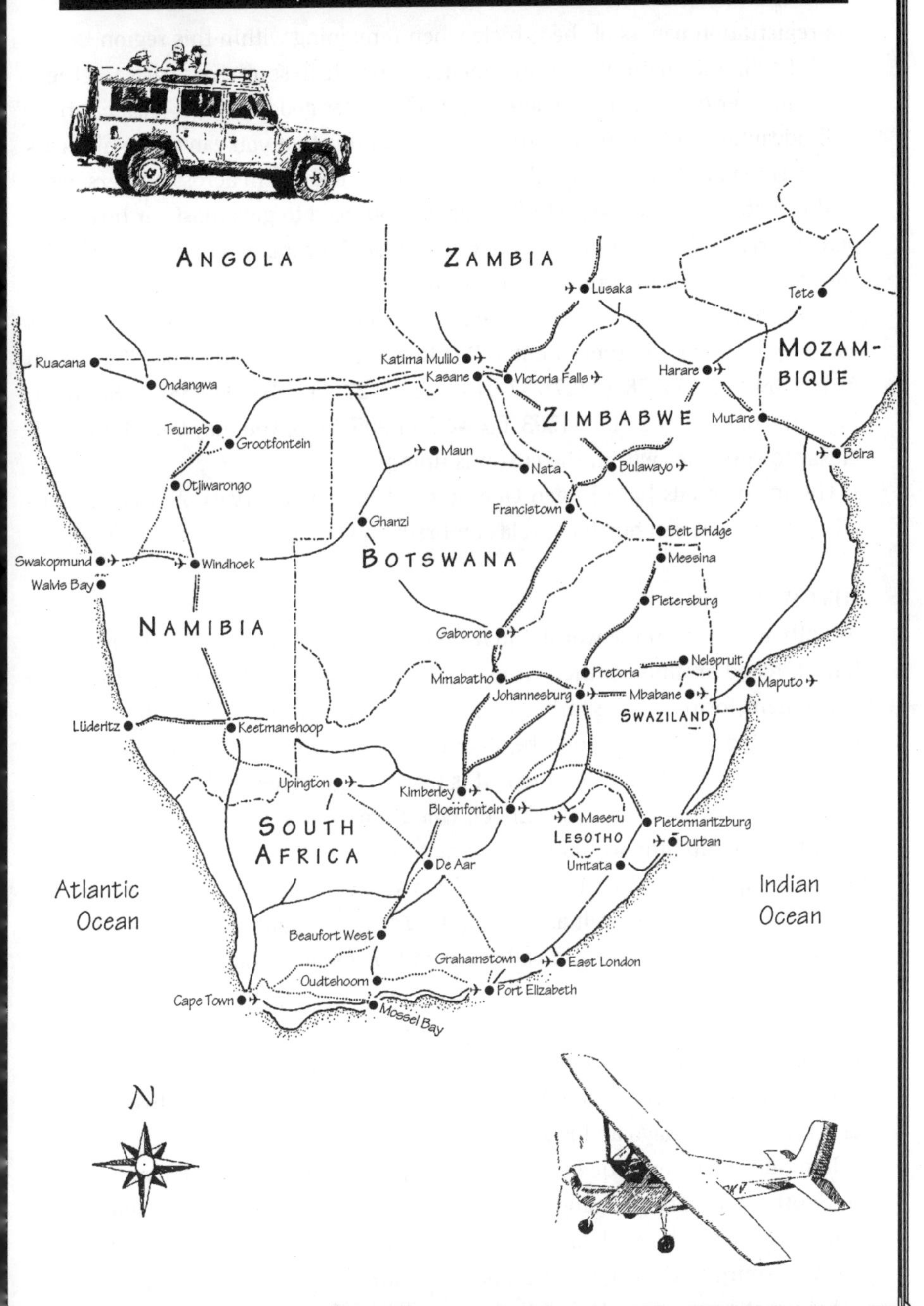
ANGOLA
ZAMBIA
Lusaka
Tete
MOZAMBIQUE
Ruacana
Ondangwa
Katima Mulilo
Kasane
Victoria Falls
Harare
ZIMBABWE
Mutare
Tsumeb
Grootfontein
Maun
Nata
Bulawayo
Beira
Otjiwarongo
Francistown
Ghanzi
Beit Bridge
Swakopmund
Windhoek
BOTSWANA
Messina
Walvis Bay
Pietersburg
NAMIBIA
Gaborone
Nelspruit
Pretoria
Maputo
Mmabatho
Johannesburg
Mbabane
SWAZILAND
Lüderitz
Keetmanshoop
Upington
Kimberley
Bloemfontein
Maseru
Pietermaritzburg
SOUTH AFRICA
LESOTHO
Durban
De Aar
Umtata
Atlantic Ocean
Indian Ocean
Beaufort West
Grahamstown
East London
Oudtshoorn
Port Elizabeth
Cape Town
Mossel Bay
N

the registration papers of the vehicle when remaining within this region.

All the big international car-hire agencies operate in southern Africa and there are a number of smaller companies that often offer good deals on local car hire. A disadvantage of this method of getting around is that you can't take hire cars across some borders. It is usually no problem to take them across borders within the customs union. To go to Zimbabwe, you need to give most car-hire companies a reasonable amount of time to organise the paperwork and none will let you take their cars to countries further north (from South Africa, anyhow). You can rent four-wheel-drive vehicles and campers from specialised companies such as Campers Corner Camper Rental, P O Box 48191, Roosevelt Park 2129, South Africa, tel: +27 11 789-2327/787-9105, fax: +27 11 787-6900/886-3187, or in Cape Town, tel: +27 21 905-1503, fax: +27 21 905-4493. You may take these vehicles into countries within the customs union.

The major roads have Engen One Stops at regular intervals. As well as refuelling there you can buy food, relax and refresh yourself.

HITCH-HIKING

As with anywhere in the world, hitch-hiking carries some risks but many people have hitched around southern Africa quite safely. If you choose this cheap and convenient form of transport, take some basic precautions. Don't hitch alone, don't hitch at night and don't hesitate to decline a lift if you have a bad feeling about the occupants of the vehicle. It is usually a good idea to hitch from a stopping point such as a toll gate, Engen One Stop or any other motorway stop. A safer form of hitching would be to contact Share-a-lift, tel: Pretoria +27 12 811-0115 or Cape Town +27 21 785-1893. This service is not free, however. You pay a fee to the agency as well as contributing a set amount to the driver for fuel costs. Obviously, you can also call this number if you are offering a lift.

BY BUS

Regular international bus services include routes between Johannesburg and Harare, Bulawayo, Gaborone, Maputo, Mbabane and Maseru and between Harare and Lusaka, Bulawayo and Francistown, Cape Town and Windhoek.

Long-distance domestic bus companies operate between all the major centres in South Africa, Namibia and Zimbabwe and offer relatively comfortable service but, because of the vast distances, the trips are very long. For example, the Johannesburg to Cape Town trip takes 18 hours.

Low-cost buses operate in all the countries of southern Africa and can be caught at the main bus or train stations in major towns. In South Africa, as well as a number of other companies, the Transstate buses run between industrial centres and "dormitory" areas in the rural areas. Basically they exist to transport workers to the mines and factories from their traditional homes in the country. The name is a hangover from when these areas were nominally independent states.

You can also take a long-distance minibus. This system is not formalised so you will need to do some detective work to find out where and when they run. You can start your enquiries at minibus terminals (usually near the main stations) or at backpackers' hostels. Because of overloading and indifferent maintenance, these do tend to break down and are, unfortunately, involved in accidents quite regularly.

Lately, a number of bus services have been started specifically to serve the backpacker market. They are cheap, convenient and fun. The Baz Bus travels between Cape Town and Johannesburg via Durban, picking up and dropping passengers at backpackers' hostels. They are very flexible, allowing you to hop on and off at various points along the way and, even more important, they have room for surfboards, dive gear, paragliders and the like. For bookings and information, contact: The Baz Bus, 8 Rosedene Rd, Sea Point 8001, tel: +27 21 439-2323 or fax: +27 21 439-2343. You can also book through most backpackers' hostels.

The Hopper Bus, tel: +27 41 55-4000, fax: +27 41 55-8402, a daily minibus, operates between Port Elizabeth and Cape Town in much the same way. It stops at even the out-of-the-way places such as Tsitsikamma and Nature's Valley.

BY RAIL

Standard international sleeper trains run between Johannesburg and Gaborone, Johannesburg and Bulawayo, De Aar and Windhoek and Francistown and Bulawayo.

Domestic train services operate in South Africa, Botswana, Namibia, Zimbabwe and Zambia. In South Africa, sleeper trains run between Cape Town, Johannesburg, Pretoria, Durban, East London and Port Elizabeth. The town of De Aar is very central and serves as a hub for the railways. The regular trains are very comfortable but, for a truly luxurious experience, try the Blue Train which runs from Pretoria to Cape Town via Johannesburg. In Zimbabwe, sleepers run between Mutare and Harare, Harare and Bulawayo and Bulawayo and Victoria Falls. In Botswana, sleepers run from Lobatse, through Gaborone to Francistown and back. Even the remote towns in the north of Namibia are served by an excellent rail service. Regular trains run between Windhoek, Swakopmund, Keetmanshoop, Tsumeb, Otjiwarongo and Grootfontein. There is no railway in Lesotho and the railway service in Swaziland is for goods only, although since the Swazi government set a precedent by repatriating Mozambican refugees by train in 1993 many people have travelled on trains in this country.

Rovos Rail run luxury steam trains between Cape Town, Johannesburg, Maputo and Victoria Falls. Union Limited Steam Safaris run luxury trips between Cape Town and Durban, Cape Town and Victoria Falls and along the Garden Route. These are not really a quick way to get to your destination but, if you have plenty of time, it is a pleasant way.

BY AIR

Southern Africa is well served by a number of airlines. South African Airways is the biggest. It flies between all the main centres in South Africa and connects with every country in the region. Other airlines that operate in the region include Sun Air, Zimbabwe Express, Air Zimbabwe, Royal Swazi Airlines, Air Namibia, Air Botswana, Zambezi Express and Lesotho Airways.

A number of smaller airlines cover niche markets, linking most of the medium-sized towns in South Africa.

Time zones

Central Africa Standard Time (CAST) is two hours ahead of Greenwich Mean Time and operates all year over the whole region except for Namibia in winter. Namibian Winter Time is one hour behind CAST. It starts at 2 am on the first Sunday of April and continues until 2 am on the first Sunday of September.

Seasons

It is important to have a general idea of the conditions in the various parts of the region before you plan your trip as some of the activities covered are very seasonal. The following can be used as a rough guide but more details can be obtained from the relevant chapter. For very seasonal activities, such as river rafting, dugout canoe safaris and flower-viewing, it is advisable to contact the operators or local tourism authorities closer to the time as conditions are not completely consistent from year to year.

SUMMER

Although October is the hottest month in much of the region, summer is usually considered to last from November to January. It is hot and, over most of the region, the rains start about the middle of November. In areas where malaria is endemic, this period is the most dangerous. Because of the new growth and standing water, this is not the best time for game-viewing as the animals are scattered and are difficult to see in the thick vegetation. The Tugela and Buffalo rivers in KwaZulu-Natal in South Africa should be runnable from about December to March or April, depending on the extent of the rains. The Batoka Gorge in Zimbabwe should be fairly low, thus offering exciting rafting, and the full trip should be runnable. In the Cape, summer is the dry period so the beaches are very popular and it is a great time for hiking. The Drakensberg and Lesotho are very pretty and green in summer, but it is not the best time for hiking there because of the very real danger of intense thunderstorms. The Namibian hiking trails are closed because of the intense heat, as is the Namib Horse Trail.

AUTUMN

Lasting from February to April, autumn is generally a time of cooling down and, especially in the northern part of the region, offers relief from the heat and rain of summer, as well as heralding a healthier climate. It is a good time for hiking, biking and horse trails in most of the region as it is cool and dry. In the Cape the days are warm and clear and the nights balmy and mellow.

WINTER

In the north of the region, winter is pleasantly cool and dry while in the Cape it is cold and rainy and there may be snow in the mountains, making this one of the worst times to hike in the Cape. In the more northerly high-lying areas, particularly the Drakensberg and Lesotho, there may be snow but it is the best time for hiking. This is an excellent time to do the Namibian hikes or the Namib horse trail.

Although winter is generally considered to run from May to July, a snow machine guarantees skiing from June to August at Tiffindel, South Africa's only serious ski resort in the Eastern Cape town of Rhodes. This is high season in the Okavango Delta as the water level is high, the weather cool and there is no rain so mokoro trips are at their best. Game-viewing over the northern part of the region improves throughout winter. The Western Cape rivers are at a high level and the Doring is runnable only for a short season, usually starting about July. The Zambezi should also be at a high level which indicates half-day trips in the Batoka Gorge, but the Sioma Falls should be runnable. Diving and surfing conditions are most consistent in winter, although there are good conditions somewhere in the region throughout the year.

SPRING

Spring is a time of joyous renewal in the Cape, which is noted for spectacular flowers in August and September. This is a great time to do mountain biking trails and hiking in Namaqualand and the Cedarberg, and the Doring white water season usually extends into August. In the northern part of the region, game-viewing improves as the vegetation continues to thin out and standing water becomes very scarce so animals are forced to visit permanent waterholes. In the north of the region October is known as "suicide month" as it is very hot and extremely humid. If you can deal with the heat, though, this is the very best game-viewing time and the Batoka Gorge on the Zambezi is virtually guaranteed to be at a very low level, thus offering a wild ride.

Money matters

The Lesotho Loti (plural Maloti), the Swaziland Lilangeni (plural Emalangeni) and the Namibian Dollar are linked to the South African Rand on a one-to-one basis, and you can use rands in these countries. Ensure that you change all your local currency back into rands before re-entering South Africa, though, as this arrangement is not reciprocal. The currency in Botswana is the Pula, in Zambia the Zambian Kwacha and in Zimbabwe the Zimbabwe Dollar. Major credit cards will be accepted by most hotels and travel agents and many adventure operators, but always check in advance with some of the smaller operators. Eurocheques are not accepted in Namibia. Fuel cards are not accepted at filling stations in Botswana, although some of the bigger ones will accept Visa or Mastercards (but not Visa or Mastercard fuel cards). In most of the region, banks are usually open around a core time of about 9 am to 3 pm on weekdays and on Saturday mornings. The black market is not very well developed and does not exist at all in South Africa, Lesotho, Swaziland, Namibia and Botswana. You may well be accosted by street financiers in Zimbabwe or Zambia, but they are quite likely to make an exorbitant profit by short-changing, or even robbing, you. It is advisable to stick to the legal methods of money changing.

TIPPING

If you are impressed with the service it is customary to tip in certain situations. Waiters usually receive about 10 percent, or up to 20 percent for very good service. It is usual to tip fuel attendants one or two rand if they offer to wash your windscreen, check your oil and water and are generally pleasant. At game lodges, it is usual to tip your ranger and tracker and to leave something with the manager for the cleaning and kitchen staff. This can range from about 10 per cent to 20 per cent of your total bill. Other adventure staff, such as river guides, are not that well paid and tips are greatly appreciated. In small operations, though, where the guide is also the owner of the business, it is customary to tip only the casual staff.

Languages

As well as English, which is spoken all over the region as a second language, most countries in the region have more than one local language. The exceptions are Swaziland and Lesotho, the citizens of which speak Siswati and Sesotho respectively. Most Batswana (citizens of Botswana) speak Tswana but there are speakers of other languages, e.g. Hambakushu, in the north and the many San (Bushman) dialects. Zimbabwe has two major languages, Shona and Ndebele, and Zambia has numerous languages but the most widely spoken are Bemba, Lozi, Nyanja and Tonga. Although South Africa has 11 official languages, the most common first languages are Zulu, Xhosa and Afrikaans.

Most of the African languages have common roots and many can be grouped together. For example Sesotho, Tswana and Lozi are very similar, as are Zulu, Xhosa, Ndebele and Ngoni or Angoni. Chichewa, as spoken in Malawi, is very similar to Nyanja, which is spoken in eastern Zambia.

English, as well as being the most common second language, is the first language of many people all over the region. Afrikaans is spoken by many people, black and white, in South Africa and Namibia and also by many whites in the rest of the region. German is spoken by many white Namibians and Portuguese is spoken by most Mozambicans.

If you are planning to spend a long time in one region, it might be a good idea to get a phrase book. If, however, your visit will be short or you are planning on moving from one area to another, it would be quite sufficient to learn the basic greetings and social gestures from the locals. Your efforts will be greatly appreciated and you are sure to have more fun.

Phones

The international dialling codes are as follows:

South Africa	+27
Lesotho	+266
Swaziland	+268
Botswana	+267
Namibia	+264
Zimbabwe	+263
Zambia	+260

For the sake of convenience, all the numbers in this book are given with the international codes. If you are phoning from within South Africa, Namibia or Zambia, drop the international code (27, 264 or 260) and add an initial zero (0). If you are phoning from within Zimbabwe, drop the international code (263) and add an initial "1". For calls within Swaziland, Lesotho and Botswana just drop the international code (268, 266 or 267) and dial the number direct.

Cellular phones operate in all the main towns and on the main arterial routes of South Africa. They can be hired from all the main airports or from GSM, tel: Johannesburg +27 11 789-7963, Cape Town +27 21 434-6565, Durban +27 31 469-2796 or Port Elizabeth +27 41 507-7370.

Power

Electricity is 220 volt and is supplied through round, three-pin 15 amp plugs (the old British system). Diesel and petrol (both leaded and unleaded) are available in even the smallest centres, although some service stations in cities may not sell diesel. Liquid Petroleum Gas (LPG) is available from fuel stations, hardware stores, camping stores and agricultural cooperatives and general dealers in small towns.

CHAPTER 3

Staying alive

Health, safety and fitness

If you decided to avoid all risks, you would have to refrain from driving (or even travelling in) a car, crossing roads, eating in restaurants, taking lifts, or even climbing stairs. Clearly this would be ridiculous, but these activities are risky. Most of us, though, have decided that we need, or want, to do these things and so have familiarised ourselves with the risks and minimised them by taking some commonsense precautions. You can do exactly the same with travel and adventure activities; by familiarising yourself with potential risks, you minimise them and so increase your chances of a safe and happy experience.

Infectious and parasitic diseases

If you are travelling far from home, you may be confronted with terrifying-sounding afflictions you have never heard of. Although you are unlikely to come into contact with any of them it is important to understand how diseases are spread in order to avoid being infected and also to know which symptoms may turn out to be serious.

Infectious diseases spread most rapidly under conditions of poverty, particularly malnutrition and inadequate sanitation, and so are endemic in many parts of southern Africa and virtually absent in many others. Use your common sense to distinguish between them. The best way to protect yourself against disease is to follow some basic rules of hygiene which you probably observe anyway. Always wash your hands before eating, keep food covered, wash all fruit and vegetables in clean water and try to avoid filthy environments. If you are injured, treat the wound with an antiseptic as even insignificant wounds can become badly infected, especially if you are malnourished or stressed.

The following information covers some of the most commonly encountered diseases, their modes of transmission and how to protect yourself against them.

AIDS (HIV)

The incidence of Aids in Africa is high so caution, but not hysteria, is called for. The accepted medical theory is that the HIV virus causes Aids and that it is transmitted in body fluids. In order to avoid infection, therefore, avoid exchange of body fluids in any way. Sexual intercourse (including anal and oral), fist-fights or assault, sharing of razors or toothbrushes and the use of recycled medical hardware such as needles, can all result in exchange of body fluids. In small, isolated villages medical facilities are run on shockingly small budgets so the horror stories of recycled needles do have a basis of truth. Carry your own set of needles, syringes, scalpel blades and other medical supplies. Probably the single most important precaution you can take, though, is to avoid unprotected sex.

Do remember that you cannot get Aids from toilet seats, eating utensils, hugging HIV-positive people or from mosquitoes.

BILHARZIA

One of the most common parasitic diseases you are likely to encounter in southern Africa is bilharzia (schistosomiasis). The bilharzia life cycle is complex. Bilharzia eggs are released into fresh water by humans who urinate or defecate into the water. They hatch into larvae which in turn infect a particular type of snail, in which they develop into flukes. These are then released into the water and can penetrate the skin of swimmers. If an infected person urinates into the water, the whole cycle begins again.

To avoid infection, boil or purify all drinking and washing water if you are in an endemic area and be careful where you swim. If you just have to swim in a doubtful area, avoid the shallow, warm water near the bank and, after your swim, dry yourself vigorously with a towel all over. This helps to dislodge the flukes before they can burrow in.

The symptoms include general lethargy and, in the later stages, blood in your urine. If you have any of these symptoms and have been in an endemic area, get a checkup immediately; bilharzia is reasonably easy to cure but, if it is left untreated, can do irreparable harm.

CHOLERA

Cholera is mostly a problem in areas of inadequate sanitation as it is usually spread by consuming food or water that has been contaminated by faeces. It becomes epidemic at the beginning of the rainy season in many parts of the region as, with the first rains, any faeces which have been deposited on riverbanks, hillsides or behind bushes are washed into the rivers and thus enter the drinking water. The most obvious symptom is very bad diarrhoea.

In order to avoid infection, boil all drinking water collected from doubtful sources, especially in the rainy season. Cholera vaccines are not required for any of the countries dealt with in this book, and in any case they are ineffective.

DIARRHOEA (NON-SPECIFIC)

Almost every traveller, at some stage, has a run-in with the dreaded "traveller's trots". This may be caused by a change in diet or drinking water, but may also be a symptom of some infection. (The mineral-rich water in places such as Namibia can produce diarrhoea in visitors for a few days; you can try filtering your drinking water if you are sensitive.) To avoid infection, boil all suspect drinking water for at least ten minutes and wash all fruit and vegetables in clean water. You may avoid all raw fruits and vegetables if you like, but the nutritional value of these foods makes it worth taking that little extra trouble.

Diarrhoea is one method your body has of ridding itself of harmful substances so, if at all possible, avoid taking medication. These just stop the diarrhoea and your body will simply retain the toxins. The best thing to do is to stop eating and drink only clean, boiled or bottled water, or even soda water, maybe with a rehydration powder. If it doesn't clear up in a few days, it might be something serious.

HEPATITIS

Hepatitis A is an acute viral disease and is transmitted by food or water that has been contaminated by faeces. It can live in the open air for quite a while so it can be transferred on improperly cleaned or shared eating utensils. Hepatitis B is transmitted in body fluids and can be chronic. It is extremely virulent and prevalent throughout Africa, so it should be considered a major threat if you are likely to be at risk. You can be vaccinated against both Hepatitis A and B.

MALARIA

This is one of the greatest killers in Africa. It is caused by a microscopic organism, called a plasmodium, which is transmitted by the bite of an infected *anopheles* mosquito. The symptoms usually occur between one and six weeks after being bitten and include any of the following: fever, possibly interspersed with chills, headaches, aches and pains, diarrhoea, nausea and dizziness. In other words malaria is a lot like flu, but much worse.

The only way you can be sure of not contracting this deadly disease is to avoid being bitten by mosquitoes. In endemic areas use mosquito repellent, always sleep under a net or in a mosquito-proof room or tent, wear a light coloured long-sleeved shirt, long pants and shoes and socks between dusk and dawn. You can also take a course of prophylactic drugs but consult a medical practitioner who is knowledgeable in tropical diseases before choosing which drug to take, as not all malaria drugs work in all endemic areas.

You may also choose not to take prophylactic drugs, but rather to carry the latest treatment with you in case of infection. Consult your doctor if you decide to take this route. Homeopathic malaria prophylaxis is also available and seems to be almost as effective as the usual drugs, but without the side-effects.

MENINGITIS

This is a serious, potentially fatal disease of viral or bacterial origin. The symptoms include a splitting headache, fever, nausea and a very stiff neck. If you have any of the above symptoms, try to put your chin on your chest and, if you can't, get medical attention immediately. Not only is this disease very dangerous, it is also exceptionally contagious so, if anyone you know has contracted it, stay close to medical help until you can be sure you will not succumb.

Creepie crawlies

Some things which may bite, sting or otherwise invade your space can have repercussions ranging from uncomfortable to life-threatening and it is important to be able to distinguish between them.

BEES AND WASPS

Certain African bees and wasps have a more painful sting than their European or American counterparts but, unless you are allergic, present no serious danger. If you are allergic, carry appropriate medication with you at all times.

MOSQUITOES

As well as being extremely dangerous, these are a major nuisance. Malaria is only transmitted by the *anopheles* mosquito; this is the sneaky one that doesn't whine. Avoid being bitten by mosquitoes if you are in a malaria area (see section on malaria, above). The very worst time is just before and after sunset, although they are active all night.

SNAKES

Snakes are not nearly as much of a threat as many people assume. In the first place snakes are generally shy creatures who go out of their way to avoid people, so snake bites are actually quite rare. If a snake does bite, it has to be poisonous to do you any harm, and it also has to inject venom into you. Poisonous snakes can bite without injecting venom. This can be because the snake has run out of venom, or it may be conserving it for a more threatening or edible target.

To avoid being bitten, keep your tent zipped up, especially when you are not in it. If you come across a snake while out walking, stop and slowly retreat or walk around the snake, giving it a wide berth (it will probably slither away when it hears you coming). Although they are not the most venomous snakes in southern Africa, puff adders are the most dangerous because they are very lazy. They lie in paths sunning themselves and, unlike more energetic snakes, won't get out of your way when they hear you coming. They are also very well camouflaged, so keep a beady eye out for them.

SPIDERS AND SCORPIONS

For healthy adults, spider bites and scorpion stings are usually more painful and uncomfortable than life-threatening, although they may produce a fever and general malaise.

To avoid being bitten or stung, use your common sense. Never walk around barefoot at night and be careful where you put your hands, particularly when gathering firewood. If you are camping, always shake out your shoes before putting them on and keep your tent zipped up.

TICKS

Ticks spend most of their lives in trees or long grass hanging around waiting for a passing animal from which they can suck a meal. If you are walking past, you will do just as well. Some ticks are infected with a rickettsia, which causes a disease called tickbite fever in humans. The symptoms include headache, chills, fever and aches and pains. This is a serious disease but is easily treated. After walking through the bush, always inspect your clothes and, once you get home or to your tent, inspect your body as well. If you are bitten by a tick, watch that space. If the bite swells, itches and goes dark in the middle after a few days, the chances are that you will develop tickbite fever.

TSETSE FLIES

These are only found in the northern part of the region. They can transmit sleeping sickness (trypanosomiasis), but many do not carry it. They are attracted to dark, moving objects, so wear light-coloured clothes in tsetse areas. A bite from a tsetse fly is very painful and you will know if you have been bitten so, if you subsequently develop a mysterious disease, tell the doctor treating you.

Wildlife

Your first sight of big game may lull you into a false sense of complacency, as wild animals will usually either ignore you or try to avoid you. If you are quiet, always approach from downwind and respond to any change in their behaviour. You can safely get quite close to most game but don't ever forget that animals in the wild can be unpredictable. (Even very experienced game rangers can be taken by surprise.) Always be alert and aware of your surroundings in the bush.

Never feed wild animals of any sort, even cute little vervet monkeys, and never wave your arms around, shout or get too close to an animal for that amazing photograph.

Most rivers in the northern part of the region harbour huge crocodiles in their murky depths, so be careful where you swim. It is usually safe to swim (wallow) in shallow, clean water where you can see for quite a distance around you and maybe have someone looking out for you as well. Be very careful collecting water from rivers; a crocodile can take a person from the bank if it is steep enough and the water is deep. Rather collect water from shallow areas and get someone to keep watch for you. (Even better, you keep watch and get the other person to collect the water.)

Crocodiles are so mean-looking that most people don't have to be encouraged to avoid them. Hippos, on the other hand, look cute, fat and clumsy — but don't be fooled. They are extremely fast, powerful, unpredictable and dangerous animals and are responsible for more deaths than any other mammal in Africa (humans excluded). They are very territorial so locals usually know how to avoid them. They also take refuge in deep water so never get between a hippo and deep water. When paddling, stay close to the bank and, if you are near a spot where they are known to hang out, make a noise so they can hear you coming and escape to deep water. Incidentally, hippos do not yawn because they are tired; yawning is an aggressive display meaning "get out of my space". You are advised to take this advice. On the subject of aggressive displays, elephants do a mock charge in which they spread their ears and advance at about half pace. Do not ignore this either, it also means "get out of my space".

Never get between an animal and its young or corner an animal in any way. Even the cute, bambi-like impala can inflict serious wounds if it feels threatened and can't escape. When walking in the bush, don't peer down interesting-looking holes as warthogs, the most likely inhabitants, are known to rush blindly through, not over or around, anything or anyone in their way. Such holes could also be inhabited by a porcupine or a family of hyenas and they certainly won't welcome the intrusion.

The elements

You will be spending a lot of your time out of doors so you should take some basic precautions to protect yourself from harm.

ALTITUDE

Southern Africa's highest point is just over 3 000 m, high enough for people who have had little previous exposure to such altitudes, or who are predisposed to altitude sickness, to succumb to the mild form of this condition. At these heights, you are unlikely to experience symptoms more serious than headache, mild nausea, lethargy and shortness of breath. You should feel fine after a day's rest but if this doesn't help you may have to retreat to a lower altitude. If you experience extreme shortness of breath, return to a lower altitude immediately.

COLD

Don't make the mistake of thinking that it never gets cold in Africa. Some of the regions covered in this book can be exceptionally cold. Mountainous areas are subject to sudden violent storms, thick mist and snow, and even in good weather are colder than the lowlands. Deserts can be particularly misleading — although hot in the day, they are freezing at night. Take warm clothing wherever you go in winter and very warm clothing when hiking in the mountains.

HEAT AND DEHYDRATION

Heat exhaustion and dehydration are very real threats in hot weather, especially when exercising. Always make sure you drink enough non-caffeinated, non-alcoholic liquids and, if you start feeling uncomfortably hot, stop and rest in the shade. If you ignore these initial symptoms, you could develop heat stroke, which is a life-threatening condition.

SUNBURN

Sunburn can be very serious in this region, even in winter. Always use sunscreen outdoors, and wear a hat and a shirt with a collar. If you are black, don't be fooled into thinking you can't be burned. If you have travelled from a temperate or cold climate, expose yourself gradually to the sun and you will soon be able to depend on your genetic advantage. The sun is stronger at high altitudes, so be aware of the burn potential of those crisp, clear mountain days.

Human and institutional threats

Undoubtedly the most dangerous animal on the African continent, as elsewhere in the world, is the human being. Like dealing with any other threat, avoiding potentially dangerous situations is far more effective than bludgeoning your way out of them.

CRIME

Many travellers are worried about crime in strange places, particularly as most of the news you hear about foreign countries is negative. Most of southern Africa is no more or less dangerous than anywhere else in the world so you should take all the common-sense precautions you would at home, particularly in the major cities and when hitch-hiking.

Gold and diamond jewellery just serve to attract attention (usually the kind you don't want) so, to be on the safe side, leave it at home. Keep important items such as airline tickets, passport and traveller's cheques in a money belt under your clothes. Get into the habit of looping your leg through the straps of your bag in bars, restaurants or at bus stops and, without being paranoid, always be aware of who is around you.

Although most people are honest, helpful and friendly, some people aren't (obviously, or our jails would be empty). If you are driving at night and break down in a doubtful place, don't hang around by the car, waiting for the first person to turn up. Take anything of great value with you and walk a few hundred metres, find a secluded spot to spend the night and go to sleep. Deal with the car in the morning if it is still there. Similarly, if you find yourself with nowhere to spend the night in a densely populated area or in a city, don't wander around looking lost — you will simply attract attention to yourself. Either find a secluded spot where you can curl up for the night or be proactive and approach someone who looks friendly. The best would be to choose a house which seems to be inhabited by a family, knock on the door and tell them of your predicament. You will probably get a safe place to spend the night, a meal and a whole family of wonderful new friends.

STAYING ON THE RIGHT SIDE OF THE LAW

Another aspect of crime to bear in mind is that your helpful family lawyer is probably a long way away. If you are caught breaking the law in a foreign country don't expect friendly treatment. In all the countries covered in this book, trade in recreational drugs, other than alcohol and tobacco, is illegal. Other activities which could get you into trouble include conducting black-market transactions, smuggling, photographing military, state or police institutions, bilking and attempting to bribe officials. Poaching is probably far from the minds of most travellers but be warned that game scouts shoot first and ask questions later. If you are reprimanded by a police officer or some other official for some minor offence such as not wearing a seatbelt, don't argue. Apologise, thank him or her for pointing out your mistake and promise to comply with the regulation in future.

WEAPONS AND MILITARY EQUIPMENT

In most southern African countries it is illegal, and very foolish, to wear military or military-style clothing, especially camouflage. It is unwise, unnecessary and, in some places, illegal to carry firearms. They are, anyhow, likely to cause more problems than they solve as they greatly increase your appeal as a robbery target.

BRIBERY AND CORRUPTION

In all the countries covered in this book, bribery is not tolerated and is not particularly common. Zambia had a bad reputation in this regard but the problem has largely been solved in that country. If confronted by someone asking for a bribe, let them know you are not intimidated. Most officials know that they will lose their jobs if they are reported trying to extort bribes.

Mind and body

Adventure is about discovery; discovering places and facts you never knew before and discovering abilities and strengths you never knew you had. If you return from an adventure unchanged, it was not an adventure.

Despite the foregoing, don't be talked into attempting feats which you genuinely believe are beyond your capabilities. There is a fine line between extending yourself and your limits and being stupidly rash. Learn the difference. Also don't let impatience get the better of your judgement. Rather play frisbee or go out to tea if the conditions are doubtful. You can always paddle, dive, fly or whatever another day.

If you are going on an organised trip, tell your guide if you have any particular fears, allergies or disabilities. This is especially important if you are hard of hearing or can't tell your left from your right as, in an emergency, you may need to follow directions. Most commercial adventure activities in southern Africa are run by professionals who know their field, don't take unnecessary risks and are well trained in rescue and first aid. If, however, the person who is going to be guiding or instructing you in a potentially dangerous environment does not inspire confidence, go to another company or try another activity.

FITNESS

You can safely take part in the adventure activities described in this book if you are of average fitness and use your common sense. If you continue with the activity on a regular basis, you will develop the necessary fitness to improve and may at some stage, be influenced by your co-adventurers to do a bit of cross-training. Any exercise you get out of doors actually doing something, though, is worth twice the amount of time spent in the gym.

PEOPLE WITH DISABILITIES

You can take part in most of the activities outlined in this book if you are disabled, although you might need a willing and able assistant. Depending on your disability, you may be able to perform just as well as an able-bodied person, but if you have restricted mobility you will probably need to make some adjustments. Near the beginning of each chapter is a short section describing the options available. This information is by no means complete, since more and more operators are making their facilities available to the disabled and it is hard to keep up. Your best sources of information are Eco-access in Johannesburg, tel: +27 11 673-4533 and the Disabled Adventurers Association, c/o Carol Schafer, Department of Sports Science, University of Cape Town, Private Bag, Rondebosch 7700, tel: +27 21 686-7330 x 297.

Plan ahead

Before leaving on an adventure trip, especially if it is to be an extended one or if you are travelling to isolated areas, give a little thought to ensuring your safety and health.

INOCULATIONS AND MALARIA PROPHYLAXIS

Tetanus and hepatitis A are devastating diseases and are quite easily contracted, so inoculation against them is highly recommended for travellers in southern Africa and in the rest of the world. Hepatitis B is transmitted sexually or in blood so medical workers, for instance, are commonly inoculated. The hepatitis inoculations last for life, but each one involves three separate injections over a period of six months so you really do need to plan ahead. Yellow fever inoculations are not necessary in southern Africa but may be recommended if you are travelling further north. Cholera inoculations are widely regarded as useless. Depending on your point of origin and routing, you may need an inoculation certificate to cross borders so ensure you get a certificate if you are inoculated.

The use of chemical malaria prophylaxis is also subject to debate. No drug offers total protection from malaria but most of them do reduce your chances of contracting this terrible disease. Unfortunately, they also mask your symptoms if you do succumb and, according to some sources, make it more difficult to treat. They all have side effects, both for the person who takes them and the general population; the use of chemical prophylaxis has been implicated in the evolution of more and more deadly and drug-resistant strains of malaria.

Before you decide whether or not to have inoculations or take malaria prophylaxis, consult a health practitioner, a specialist in tropical or infectious medicine or an organisation such as British Airways Travel Clinics.

INSURANCE AND MEDICAL EVACUATION

If you become seriously ill or are involved in an accident, you may need to be evacuated to a hospital in a large urban centre. If you are not insured, this could be very expensive. Your travel agent could assist you in obtaining general travel insurance or you could contact a medical insurance company directly. Medical

Rescue International (MRI) is based in Johannesburg, tel: +27 11 403-6174, and covers the entire region.

Before parting with your hard-earned cash, though, check that you will be covered for diving, river rafting, skydiving or whatever activity you are planning.

ESSENTIAL ITEMS TO TAKE

Since prevention is always better than cure, it is advisable to take multivitamin tablets to counteract the effects of irregular meals, as well as plenty of sunscreen. Unless you are completely celibate or in a stable relationship, pack a few condoms. If you are travelling to remote areas where the medical services may be stretched to their limit, carry a pack of syringes, suture material and cannulas; ask your chemist to put one together for you. If you have allergies or some other drug-dependent condition such as diabetes or asthma, take the necessary drugs with you.

You should carry a small first aid kit, well-stocked with the items you know you use often. If you tend to cut yourself, or get headaches at home, the chances are you will do the same on holiday. A sample first aid kit could contain the following:

- Latex surgical gloves (to protect yourself in case you have to administer first aid)
- A viroguard, for administering artificial respiration (as above)
- Adhesive bandages
- A few small sterile dressings
- Paraffin-impregnated gauze dressings for burns and grazes (if you intend cycling, pack quite a few of these)
- Small pair of scissors
- Tweezers
- Rehydration powder
- Aluminium sulphate solution (e.g. Stingose) for bites and stings
- Mycota powder or cream, for treatment of athlete's foot
- Painkillers
- Antibiotic powder, for treatment of wounds
- Antiseptic cream
- Antihistamine cream and tablets, for insect and spider bites
- Anti-diarrhoea tablets
- Anti-inflammatory tablets and gels, for sprains and bruises
- Eyedrops and an eye patch

Essential information for women

Women are often a bit nervous about travelling on their own, but there is no real need to be. It can be a wonderful experience, as you make all your own decisions and the people you meet are invariably nice and touchingly concerned about you. If you overlook the undercurrent of chauvinism this exposes, you will find it easy to get lifts, families in camping sites will offer you meals and local women and children won't be intimidated by you. There is of course an element of risk, but probably no more than we face every day in our city streets, homes and places of employment.

MENSTRUATION

It is a well known fact that travelling plays havoc with your cycle, so be prepared for surprises and don't panic or celebrate prematurely if you miss a period. You can take part in any of the adventures covered in this book while you are menstruating but you will enjoy yourself more if you can plan your trip for some other time of the month. If you really don't want to have your period on a trip and you know that it is due, you can obtain drugs which will delay it. Consult someone knowledgeable before taking this step as there are bound to be side-effects.

PREGNANCY

If you are fit and healthy, there is no reason why you can't take part in most of the adventures outlined in this book while pregnant. This is not a good time to learn a new sport, though, and be careful of activities such as horse riding and mountain biking, which can result in nasty falls. Bungi jumping or scuba diving are out of the question. If you are pregnant avoid malaria areas as most of the more effective prophylactics are contra-indicated in pregnancy and a dose of malaria will almost certainly result in a miscarriage.

If you are taking malaria prophylaxis and are thinking of trying to conceive, consult a doctor or pharmacist as some anti-malaria drugs may have side-effects which make it inadvisable to conceive for a significant period after discontinuing use.

CHAPTER 4

Tread lightly

Environmentally responsible travelling

Regardless of how long you stay in the region, your presence will have an effect, either positive or negative. The following information should give you some guidelines on how to make it a positive one.

Wildlife and the wilderness

Probably one of the reasons you want to travel in Africa is to see and/or interact with wildlife. This can be a safe and exhilarating experience. Bear in mind, though, that wild animals are just that — wild. And free. This means that they are not there for your amusement, as may be the case in a zoo or circus.

ON LAND

The worst thing you can do for wild animals is to feed them. If you do, they come to regard humans as an easy meal-ticket and start mugging unsuspecting tourists, always with fatal results. Usually the tourist survives but the animal has to be killed by wildlife authorities.

Try to restrict your driving to daylight hours in the wilder parts of the region as many animals tend to walk, or even lie, on the roads at night. A collision with an animal would be equally disastrous for you, your vehicle and the animal.

AT SEA

The oceans around southern Africa are rich in mammal life, including whales, dolphins and seals. The whales, particularly, are a great attraction as they come close to the shore along the Cape coast between June and October to mate and calve. As they are involved in these intimate activities, they are protected from excessive voyeurism by law. It is a serious offence to approach within 300 m of a whale anywhere along the South African and Namibian coast. The penalties are severe: a fine of R2 000, six months in jail and, for foreigners, deportation.

Avoid harassing seals or dolphins by respecting their space if you are travelling by boat. Although both these animals may play and jump in your bow wave, they should not be chased if they seem to have their own agenda. If you intend diving, snorkelling or fishing, obey all the regulations regarding closed seasons and size and bag limits of all seafood. The South African and Namibian Sea Fisheries inspectors are very alert and know all the tricks.

Dolphins, and sometimes whales, are occasionally stranded along the South African coast. If you find one of these animals in distress, contact one of the following organisations: Dolphin Action Protection Group, Cape Town, tel: (021) 782-5845, Sea Fisheries, Cape Town, tel: (021) 402-3911, Port Elizabeth Museum, tel: (041) 56-1051, or the Oceanographic Research Institute, Durban, tel: (031) 37-3536. There are large breeding colonies of penguins and other seabirds on offshore islands and in many places on the mainland. If you find a sick, injured or oil-coated bird, phone one of the above numbers, or contact SANCCOB, tel: (021) 557-6155.

EROSION

Avoid taking short cuts in mountainous regions as these become well-worn paths which, in the rainy season, channel water and further exacerbate the already severe erosion problems experienced in much of the region. If you are travelling in a four-wheel-drive vehicle, resist the temptation to thunder along unspoilt stretches of dune or bush as you could do lasting damage. This is particularly the case on dunes as, contrary to appearances, they are not just lifeless piles of windblown sand. Dunes of all kinds, but especially coastal dunes, support a large diversity of plant and animal species, many of which are very delicate and can be harmed, killed or even toppled over the precarious brink of extinction by careless trippers who destroy their habitat. If you must drive along a beach, first check that driving is permitted on that particular beach, observe any specific local regulations, and then drive very slowly and carefully.

FIRE

If you think how hard it can be to light a campfire when you want to, it is amazing how easily bushfires start. This is particularly true in the long dry periods experienced in summer in the Western Cape in South Africa and in winter in the rest of the region. If you smoke, be sure to extinguish all matches and cigarettes totally and to dispose of them properly. Take great care when burning toilet paper. Do not make fires in any places where they are prohibited and, if you are camping in undesignated areas, be careful to extinguish fires completely, preferably by smothering them, and remove any trace of your fire by digging a hole and burying the ash. Another problematic aspect of fire is that vast areas of southern Africa are rapidly being deforested as trees disappear under the cooking pot. Try to avoid contributing to this major environmental disaster. Carry a small camping stove and save open-fire cooking for areas where you can easily collect or buy firewood from dead or fallen trees. Also look out for charcoal which is locally made from alien trees. Once an area has been stripped of its natural cover by fire, it is very susceptible to erosion.

LITTER

Don't. If you could carry it in, you can carry it out. Remember, cigarette ends, used matches and toilet paper are all litter, even if buried. Even orange peels, commonly regarded as biodegradable, should not be discarded as they can take months to decompose.

PHOTOGRAPHY

If a subject is worth photographing, it is also worthy of respect and conservation. When photographing birds or animals do not interfere with their activities. Never disturb birds at their nests or animals at their den so that you can get a better shot, as you may cause the parent to abandon its young. If you spend a lot of time around a nest or den, or move a few rocks or plants to enable you to photograph the animals, you may be advertising their presence to predators and could cause their death. Do not offer food to wild animals to encourage them into your viewfinder; this is both extremely dangerous and bad environmental practice.

PERSONAL HYGIENE

Most of southern Africa experiences periodic drought, some areas more than others, so try to use as little water as possible when washing, even in cities. In wilderness areas, take extra special care. Never wash in streams, springs or lakes, even with biodegradable products. Rather take water in a bowl and wash away from the source of water. You can then pour the soapy water into the ground where it has a better chance of degrading harmlessly before entering the groundwater. Even better, instead of washing with soap, just take a swim and rinse the sweat and dust off. You will find that your hair, particularly, will benefit from a few days' or even weeks' rest from chemicals.

In order to prevent fouling of water supplies, defecate at least 50 m from springs, lakes or rivers and, despite their obvious convenience, avoid defecating in dry riverbeds. In dry areas bury faeces no deeper than 25 cm, but in well-watered areas you may bury them deeper. Toilet paper is not biodegradable and, if buried, will be exposed by wind or dug up by baboons, so it should be burned after use. This is not as difficult as it may at first seem and is an essential skill. First waft it around so that it dries out a little, then put it on a spade, rock or bare sand and light a dry part. Turn it around with a stick so the wet bits are always above the flame; they will dry out and eventually burn. Bury the ashes. Remember to dispose of your matches properly and take great care to avoid setting the bush alight. If you are in a very dry area or it is very windy, rather wrap your toilet paper and pop it in the general garbage to be disposed of later. Failing all that, if you have to bury it, dig a new hole and bury it deeply. That way it is less likely to be dug up.

Tampons are not biodegradable and are almost certain to be dug up if buried. The best way to dispose of them is to burn them but you need a very hot fire so you will probably have to wait until evening. Carry a small opaque plastic jar in which you can keep them during the day. Once the fire has been lit and is burning well wrap them in toilet paper and/or a used food packet and pop them in the flames. Tampons do not burn easily so don't put them into half-hearted fires. If you are in an area where fires are not allowed, you will have to carry them out with you. Plan ahead, take a number of little jars and pop them in the garbage every night or wrap them, put them in the garbage and wash and re-use your jar.

People and culture

When hiking, paddling a river or diving an offshore reef, your actions are bound to affect the people who live in the vicinity. If they found your visit a pleasant and positive experience, you are likely to be welcomed back time and time again, and so will other adventurers. The opposite also holds true.

When travelling through southern Africa, you can simply move from one river or rockface to the next and still have a wonderful experience. The region has much more to offer than that, though. If you take time out to speak to people you meet on the road and chat to vegetable sellers or taxi drivers, you may gain an insight into the way other people live and think. How you process this information and whether it affects your life is then entirely up to you.

COURTESY

You will find people in the rural parts of southern Africa very friendly and polite. For example, it is almost impossible to conduct any business, or even ask directions, until you have exchanged information about, and concern for, each other's health. Many rural people are very conservative and, if you want to have a meaningful exchange with them, you will gain nothing by disregarding their values and flaunting your own. This applies to dress, politics, religion and general lifestyle. Don't be hypocritical, just be tactful. In black African cultures older people command a great deal of respect, purely by virtue of their age, so always be very polite to the aged. Depending on your temperament, you will probably find local children either absolutely charming or a total nuisance. Like children everywhere, they are inquisitive, energetic and mischievous and may be totally intrigued by you.

Unless you are very skilled at "shooting from the hip", always ask permission before photographing someone. If they ask for payment, that's only fair.

ROCK ART

These beautiful paintings are the cultural heritage of a gentle people who were hounded to extinction by empire-builders in the pursuit of glory, and are as unique and precious as the Mona Lisa. Do not touch or scratch them. Some rock paintings have become a little faded with time and it is tempting to wet them to see them better or photograph them. This causes further fading and should not be done.

A positive impact

Tourism has the potential to be a powerful tool for development in this region. Like all tools, though, it can be used to build or to destroy. Try to ensure that your presence encourages positive, sustainable growth thus contributing to the continued well-being of local communities.

BLACK-MARKET TRANSACTIONS

Many travellers regularly change money on the black market. This does make your money go further but it is a practice fraught with risks and complicated moral issues. The risks are obvious. You are dealing with people who are prepared to risk breaking the law in one way and they may well short-change you or pass off forged notes. If this happens, you can hardly report them to the police as you, too, will have broken the law. The wider moral issue is trickier. It may seem that a little black-market trading does no one any great harm, but you will probably be helping some fat-cat expatriate to avoid paying taxes and to steal legitimate foreign exchange from a country forced to ransom its natural resources to pay off its foreign debt.

HOW YOU SPEND

Without becoming fanatical, try to support local businesses rather than international ones and support enterprises that seem to respect the cultural and environmental integrity of the area in which they operate. For example, rather eat at a small local restaurant than a McDonalds. Try, where possible to avoid buying pre-paid package tours in your home country; rather spend the money locally, preferably with companies who have a stated policy of ploughing profits back into the region. Also remember that the people of southern Africa are its greatest asset but, at the same time, potentially its greatest liability. Many skilled and qualified people are unable to find jobs in the formal sector and are starting their own businesses — a surprising number in adventure and tourism. Support these local entrepreneurs, black and white, as far as possible as they have a vested interest in ensuring that their enterprises are sustainable.

Use the above advice wisely and avoid making snap judgements; many international companies have a strong commitment to the area in which they operate. If they do, they will not be offended by your asking about their policies and will gladly show off any positive benefits to the region.

In the unlikely event that you come across unscrupulous operators who are obviously exploiting local communities or are operating in a clearly destructive manner, boycott them and, in serious cases, report them to the police or local tourist authority.

AND EVERY DAY

It is all very well to be a concerned traveller and avoid littering, polluting streams and burning trees but, if you are truly concerned about the wild areas of the planet, you need to consider the consequences of your lifestyle and everyday actions, all of which have far-reaching implications for the environments you'll be travelling in. Consider carefully the source of the things we, who live in cities, take for granted. Power comes from coal, oil, nuclear fission or the damming of rivers. Water is a finite resource and paper comes from trees which use up an inordinate amount of water. Our cars are fuelled by oil, which is transported in tankers that may be wrecked and destroy whole marine ecosystems. The food we eat may have been produced in a manner destructive to the planet, in which case it will probably also be destructive to our bodies, and the nice, colourful packaging which entices us to take things off the supermarket shelf is only so much wasted raw material and only so much more solid waste to dispose of.

Don't let all of the above get to you, though. Let's face it, you can't spend your whole life worrying about the planet and still get on with the business of living. Maybe that is why it seems to be easier to be green when on holiday, you have the leisure to reflect and you may be in a pristine environment, so it is easy to see the fragility, beauty and value of our planet. When you return to your daily grind, though, try to retain a little of the magic. You don't have to give up your job, donate your car to a recycling plant, buy a bicycle, wear recycled newspapers and join Greenpeace. Just try to make informed decisions and, where possible, choose to live in such a way as to conserve our precious resources.

CHAPTER 5

Take the plunge

Diving and snorkelling

Diving is a very popular pastime in South Africa but obviously not big in the landlocked countries. Namibia has a small diving community although most of the diving in this country is in deep sinkholes and caves, definitely not for beginners. Mozambique has some excellent diving but is outside the scope of this book. See *Guide to Mozambique* by Mike Slater, Struik, Cape Town, 1994 for more details. There is no live-aboard diving in the region at present.

Getting started

Before taking the plunge, do a recognised dive course. Diving is really easy and safe, but only if you know some basic rules and skills.

The major training institutions in the region are SAUU (South African Underwater Union), which is affiliated to CMAS (world underwater federation), NAUI and PADI, which are American agencies with representatives worldwide. PDIC and SSI are also represented, but to a lesser degree. The most important thing to know about these institutions is that the certification you receive from any one of them will be recognised in most parts of the world.

The most important choice is therefore not the agency, but the instructor. There are good and bad instructors in every organisation so ensure that your prospective instructor has a good track record and seems likeable (learning to dive is a long process and it may as well be fun). Once you have chosen an instructor, shop, school or club with whom to do your course you can expect the following. You will be asked to undergo a medical examination and sign an indemnity form. You will then attend lectures on the theory of diving, followed by a number of pool sessions where you will learn simple but counter-intuitive skills which require a great deal of practice. Depending on which organisation you choose, you may have to do a practical pool test. You will then do five open-water dives, during which you will repeat some of the skills.

At this point you will be a qualified open-water or one-star diver. This is a relatively basic qualification and, if you intend diving deeper or diving at night, on wrecks or in other unusual environments, you are advised to obtain a further qualification.

Equipment

Diving equipment is expensive. You will probably use rental gear on your diving course. When you buy your own, get advice from your instructor as you use different equipment under different conditions.

For visitors to South Africa, the water temperature ranges from about 8 to 25 °C. If you intend staying in the warmer water, you can get by with a 3 mm wetsuit but, if you intend diving in the cold water off the Cape, you will need at least a 5 mm wetsuit with hood, preferably attached. Most Cape locals dive in a 7 mm long-john and jacket with attached hood and no zips.

The very best suit if you want to dive the whole coast is a 3 mm long-john, a 3 mm jacket with zipped hood (for warm water) and a 7 mm jacket with attached hood and no zips (for cold water). This is what the author uses and finds it ideal. Women, particularly, will appreciate the use of a 3 mm long-john as your legs don't get that cold and the added flexibility of a thinner suit is useful if you have hips and a waist. A good compromise suit for all conditions would be a 3 or 5 mm two-piece or one-piece full suit and a 3 mm, or preferably a 5 mm, chicken vest (vest with attached hood). You can then wear the suit on its own in warm water and wear the chicken vest in the Cape. In the Cape, you will probably want to wear neoprene gloves and booties or "sockies" (soft neoprene boots). If you are doing shore dives, you will need to wear hard-soled booties for walking over rocks and will, consequently, be better off with open-heeled fins.

Other than the above, there is nothing special to know. Both "A" clamp and DIN fittings are used quite widely. You can fill high-pressure cylinders (300 bar) at some air stations, but not all. Air stations may be found at dive shops and dive operators. If you don't want to bring gear, you can rent all you need from one of the bigger dive operators.

Options for people with disabilities

Many people with varying degrees of disability have dived all over the world. As long as your heart, lungs, sinuses, ears and mind are fine, you should be able to dive. There are a number of qualified divers in South Africa who are paraplegics. Obviously their mobility is severely restricted and, for safety, they need to dive with at least two able-bodied divers. Scuba Explorers Society, in Johannesburg, offers courses for disabled people and welcomes disabled people on their diving excursions to various parts of the region.

KwaZulu-Natal

Most of this coast offers tropical or subtropical diving. Water temperature rarely drops below 20 °C, and then only in the south, and the visibility is usually 10 m or more. There can be good diving all year but the conditions are most dependable in winter.

MAPUTALAND

In the far north of the east coast, this area constitutes South Africa's only true tropical diving. Temperatures in excess of 20 °C and good visibility make diving on the offshore coral reefs a pleasure.

Kosi Bay is the most northerly resort in South Africa. Neither scuba diving nor boat launching is allowed but the snorkelling from shore is very rewarding. As the region develops the diving might open up, but it will be strictly controlled.

Sodwana Bay is the most popular dive destination in South Africa. The most southerly coral reefs in the world are found here, thanks to the presence of the Mozambique Current which brings warm tropical water far south. The reefs are named for their distance from Jesser Point, the only launch site, hence Two-mile reef, Five-mile reef, etc. The launch is from the beach through sometimes quite big surf — an exhilarating experience. There are three concession holders who have camps in the park and offer dive/accommodation packages. They are **Triple 'S'**, **Blueprint Diving** and **Coral Divers**. **Odysea Diving** is based near the Sodwana Bay Lodge, outside the park, and runs a smaller but more flexible operation. You may camp anywhere in the park and just take dives out with the concessionaires, or even bring your own boat and do your own dives. Surf launching is not a skill learned in a few days, though, and the reefs are not that easy to find, so consider this option only if you really know what you are doing.

WHILE IN THE AREA

The Hluhluwe-Umfolozi National Park, the site of the rescue of the white rhino from extinction, is close by and offers an excellent wilderness experience. Slightly further afield, the Greater St Lucia Wetland Park is renowned for its birdlife, boat trips to view crocodiles and hippos, fishing and magnificent walks through coastal forest (see chapter 7). This whole area has been the subject of much controversy as mining of the coastal dunes for titanium has been mooted. Local environmentalists and the international community caused a huge outcry as the wetland is very sensitive and the coastal dunes unique. It seems, at time of writing, that the mining project has been shelved. Also see chapter 15 for further attractions.

DURBAN

Beachfront attractions such as amusement parks, snake parks and an aquarium clearly identify the city of Durban as a popular seaside resort. The diving in Durban Bay is pretty but the visibility is often poor due to the runoff and the influence of the huge harbour. You'd be more likely to come here for the excellent surf or some other reason than specifically to dive but if you're in the area you may get in a good one. **Trident Diving** and **Underwater World** offer charter dives in the Durban area as well as further afield.

WHILE IN THE AREA

Durban is Disney by the Sea. The beachfront is highly developed with any number of touristy attractions including an aquarium. There is great surf, some nice restaurants, good theatre and vibey clubs, so you shouldn't get bored here. Best of all though; the surfing is superb (see chapter 14).

SOUTH COAST

Aliwal Shoal, off the mouth of the Umkomaas River, is a rocky reef with spectacular coral growth and myriad tropical fish. In spring, ragged-tooth sharks (*Carcharias taurus*) congregate on the shoal to mate and may be observed if you obey some commonsense safety and courtesy rules. Further south, Lander's Reef also offers excellent diving.

The dive sites are quite far from shore; all are boat dives and all launches are through the surf. Because of the strong current, they are all drift dives. There is a range of dives on both sites, some of which are suitable for novices but some should only be attempted by experienced divers. Wreck divers may want to dive the *Nebo*, a wreck more than 100 years old, or the *Produce*, a much more modern wreck of a bulk tanker. Both lie in about 30 m near Aliwal Shoal. The *Produce* is becoming a little unstable, so take care if you dive it.

Situated 8 km out to sea from Shelley Beach and in the Mozambique Current, Protea Banks is almost always clean. With the top of the reef at 36 m, a four- or five-knot current and plenty of big sharks, such as ragged-tooths, great whites, Zambezis and hammerheads, it is for experienced divers only but it is a spectacular site and an exhilarating dive. You are also likely to see a great variety of game fish at this site.

Andy Cobb Ecodiving do charters to all the dive sites along the South Coast and Andy himself has dived this area for many years. **African Dive Adventures** run charters to Protea Banks and some shallower dives close to Margate. They operate in conjunction with the Kenilworth-on-Sea guesthouse and offer reasonably priced dive-accommodation packages. The area is becoming very popular and many more companies have started operating here.

WHILE IN THE AREA

The South Coast is a well-developed holiday destination. As well as the excellent surf you may be lucky enough to encounter, you can do all the usual touristy things. There is golf, tennis and bowls if your tastes run that way. The beaches are long and lovely, the restaurants many and varied and the scenery pretty. The nearby Oribi Gorge Nature Reserve is a great place to spend a day or two. It has pretty waterfalls, day walks and many attractive picnic sites.

Eastern Cape

This is a long and varied coastline. The water is usually between 15 and 18 °C and it is exposed to the incoming waves from the open ocean, so is much rougher than the KwaZulu-Natal coast. As a rule, the conditions are much less ideal, with visibility usually around 5 to 10 m, and sometimes less. On occasion the Agulhas Current moves close inshore, bringing warm, crystal clear water. This is cause for celebration and diving to the limits of the tables, but it doesn't happen often.

WILD COAST

This is the coast of the formerly nominally independent territory of the Transkei. The name is apt. It is a beautiful, wild piece of coastline and, although it offers excellent surfing and spearfishing for those tough enough to brave the harsh conditions, it is not a great scuba diving destination. The long, lonely beaches are ideal for hiking (see chapter 7). If you decide to dive some isolated spot along this coast, travel in a large party as thefts and muggings have occurred.

EAST LONDON

A sleepy little city, East London is best known for its excellent surf (see chapter 14). The diving is reasonable, too, and there are a number of shallow wrecks that can be reached from shore. Some of the deeper dives which are only accessible by boat are much more interesting and display a unique faunal assembly, being somewhere between the cold-water system of the Cape and the tropical KwaZulu-Natal waters. **Dive Africa Tours** offer local charters, as well as organising countrywide dive tours, and **Pollock Sports** offer local charters.

WHILE IN THE AREA

The surfing is great. The East London Museum is interesting and the nearby Hogsback mountains offer excellent hiking (see chapter 7).

PORT ALFRED

At the mouth of the Kowie River, this little town has some remarkably good diving but the conditions are, unfortunately, quite erratic. You can have crystal clear water one day and then zero visibility for two weeks. The coast is also very exposed and, when the sea is running high, it is virtually impossible to launch a boat. Don't plan a diving holiday here, but if you visit the area for its many other attractions, take your dive gear and you may be lucky enough to have a great dive. **Kowie Dive School** operates from the Halyards Hotel.

WHILE IN THE AREA

There is an interesting canoe trail (see chapter 6). The fishing is excellent and the surfing great (see chapter 14). Not too far away is the very comfortable and somewhat upmarket private game reserve, Shamwari (see chapter 15 for details of wilderness walks, or you could just relax there and go on the odd game drive). The small town of Bathurst, on the way to Grahamstown, is pretty and has many interesting old buildings, including a very quaint pub, the Pig and Whistle. In the first ten days of July the university town of Grahamstown bursts at the seams as tens of thousands of people flood in to the annual festival of the arts.

PORT ELIZABETH

This medium-sized city has a number of dive schools, shops and clubs. Roman Rock, Devil's Reef, Philip's Reef and Slipway are all fun sites in Algoa Bay which can be dived by experienced and novice divers. The *Haerlem* is an interesting wreck dive, also in the bay, but it is not suitable for novices. Sea life in the area includes sea fans, sponges and numerous species of nudibranch. Fish are plentiful but are more of the edible than the pretty variety.

Very exposed to currents, Thunderbolt Reef has a prolific growth of invertebrate life, but there is often a strong current so some of the sites are not suitable for novices. One such is the Pinnacles, one of the better dives in the Port Elizabeth area. It is very colourful and teems with fish. There are two interesting wrecks on the reef. The *Pati,* in about 8 m of water, is a good wreck dive for novices; there are many solidified cement bags lying around and a number of small fish and interesting invertebrate life. The *Kapodistrias* will attract divers who are particularly interested in modern wrecks, but it is in very shallow water and there is a tremendous surge and lots of jagged metal so it is only recommended for very experienced divers. **Scuba Ventures** and **Pro-dive** offer charters in the Port Elizabeth area, or contact **Mike's Dive Shop** for further information.

WHILE IN THE AREA

Port Elizabeth, affectionately known as PE, is an interesting town with a well-developed tourism infrastructure. It has a large museum, aquarium and many interesting old buildings. There is good mountain biking (see chapter 8), diving and many interesting day walks and short horse rides. The beaches are pleasant and the city has the usual range of hotels, restaurants and other urban attractions. The Addo Elephant National Park is close by, as is Shamwari (see chapter 15).

Western Cape

This region covers a very varied diving environment. The water is colder than in the Eastern Cape, and it gets colder as you move towards Cape Town.

PLETTENBERG BAY

The best time for diving this area is between September and October but there are reasonably good conditions all year. The average water temperature is about 18 °C and visibility usually ranges from 5 to 10 m but can exceed 20 m on a good day. There are a number of pretty sites close to the Beacon Isle Hotel which are a quick boat ride away or can be done as a shore dive by moderately fit and experienced divers. Further out, there are good dives around the Island, at Robberg Peninsula, and some nice offshore pinnacles such as Whale Rock. **Indian Ocean Divers** is conveniently situated in the Beacon Isle Hotel.

WHILE IN THE AREA

Built around a beautiful bay and blessed with pretty lagoons and rivers, this seaside resort is one of the most popular along the entire coastline. In summer, hordes of people take up residence in very opulent holiday homes. There are numerous hotels, restaurants and coffee shops. Equitrailing Horse Trails are based near here and offer rides for a few hours or a few days through the forests. See chapters 7, 8, 13, 14 and 16 for more information on this interesting area.

KNYSNA

This lovely town is dominated by a huge lagoon in which, surprisingly, there are some good dives. Thesen's Jetty looks like an underwater tip but you are virtually guaranteed a sighting of sea horses among the rubble. In the mouth of the lagoon, known as the Heads, is the wreck of the *Paquita*, a German iron barque which sank in 1903. It is a lovely dive but has to be timed to coincide with slack tide as the tidal current can reach a speed of nine knots. Outside the Heads are some superb dives with spectacular invertebrate life; Bruce se Bank is one of the better ones. The conditions are fair most of the year but are more dependable in winter. In summer, though, there can be very good diving from time to time.

Waterfront Divers is situated in the parking lot at the Heads, convenient for a shore dive to the *Paquita* or for launching for a sea dive.

WHILE IN THE AREA

You can do a gentle canoe trip on the lagoon, go for a walk in the forest or do a mountain bike trail (see chapters 7 and 8). You can also take a boat across the lagoon to the Featherbed Nature Reserve for a walk or a picnic. The town itself is a bit of an artists' haven with scores of craft shops and a fleamarket. There are some excellent pubs and restaurants; Jetty Tapas, on Thesen's Jetty, and Cranzgots, at the Heads, are two favourites.

MOSSEL BAY

Most of the dives in this area are shallow and close to shore, so they can be dived in marginal conditions but will be rather murky except in good conditions.

WHILE IN THE AREA

Mossel Bay has historical significance as the site where Bartolomeu Dias and his crew first set foot on South African soil in 1488 and left letters under a flat stone at the foot of a tree. Amazingly, they were picked up by other sailors and delivered. The Bartolomeu Dias Museum houses exhibits relating to this period. Also see chapter 13 for bridge and bungi jumping.

The deeper dives offshore, such as Windvogel Reef, can only be dived in calm conditions but are spectacular. **Mossel Bay Divers** at the Protea Santos Hotel offer all dive services.

GANSBAAI AND HERMANUS

These two towns are on the western side of Cape Agulhas and the water here is significantly colder than Mossel Bay, often going as low as 12 or 14 °C but still reaching the high teens or even hitting 20 °C at times. Kelp, although not as prolific as further west, is seen in this area.

WHILE IN THE AREA

Gansbaai is a very small but not particularly picturesque fishing village. The harbour is interesting, though, and the nearby cave system of De Kelders is fun to explore (see chapter 17). In spring and winter southern right whales come into Walker Bay to calve and can be seen to great advantage from shore in both Gansbaai and Hermanus. There are many other attractions in Hermanus such as the Fernkloof Nature Reserve, a lovely clifftop walk of 12 km, a golf course and quaint shops and coffee shops.

Gansbaai is a little fishing village with two spectacular but little-dived sites. The wreck of the *Birkenhead* is an interesting dive as well as having great historical significance. It is relatively deep, about 30 m, and there is a strong current so it is only for experienced divers. This is not an easy wreck to find and you will have to ask around for someone to take you there. A salvage permit has been granted so, if you remove even the tiniest thing from the site, you will probably be sued (the permit holders have spies).

The other dive is at Dyer Island, home to numerous huge white sharks. This is a popular site for cage diving but at the time of writing it appears that it may be in danger of being overdived. This is of great concern as the white shark is a protected species and, as this is the only tourist industry where operators regularly feed wild animals, it is possible that this practice may be detrimental to the white shark population. It is also uncertain how regular baiting may affect the sharks' behaviour, and therefore the long-term safety of continuous, regular cage diving has still to be assessed. For information about chartering cage dives, enquire from divers or dive operators in Cape Town.

The nearby but much bigger town of Hermanus has a number of pretty dive sites. There are a couple of pleasant shore dives which can be reached by swimming out of the old harbour and some very pretty boat dives. **Scuba Africa** and **BS Divers** operate out of Hermanus.

FALSE BAY EAST SIDE

This steeply sloping shore offers good diving in summer after the south-easter has blown for a few days. Tougher local divers do favourites such as Percy's Hole and Kruis as shore dives, but they involve a steep walk and a moderately tricky entry and exit. Novices can enjoy these sites as a boat dive with **Ocean Divers International** in Gordon's Bay. Just around the corner from Percy's is a resident group of seals who may come to play if they are in the mood.

WHILE IN THE AREA

The area between Hermanus and Gordon's Bay is very pretty; the Harold Porter Nature Reserve in Betty's Bay has a magnificent display of flowers in spring and offers gentle scenic walks at any time of year. The sand dunes of Betty's Bay are the accepted beginners' slopes for Cape Town paragliders (see chapter 9), and are also very popular with dune surfers. You need a piece of polished masonite with a string on one side and you can almost fly down the slopes. This coast is also close to the winelands and the picturesque town of Stellenbosch.

FALSE BAY WEST SIDE

The diving here is best in winter, after a north-wester has blown for a few days. The diving is not tough at all but you need to steel yourself to think of diving in a cold, grey Cape winter. It's worth it, though. The reef life is spectacular with many brightly coloured sponges, soft corals, sea fans and smaller invertebrates, such as a huge variety of nudibranchs. Most of the dives can be done from shore but, if you haven't done entries off rocky shores before, go out with an experienced local the first few times. You can usually find the shore dives by driving along the road to Cape Point and looking out for the parked cars.

The wrecks of Smitswinkel Bay are very popular with experienced divers. They are deep, about 38 m on the sand, and are quite intact, thus offering a fascinating look at some modern wrecks. There are two frigates, two fishing boats and a diamond dredger, all of which were deliberately scuttled. Another, newer, artificial reef is the *Pietermaritzburg,* which was scuttled in 1994. History buffs will be interested to know that this boat took part in the D-Day invasion of Normandy in the Second World War under its previous name of HMS *Pelorus*. If you would like to dive with seals, the best spot along the whole coast is the little reef just off Partridge Point, as the colony there is very friendly. The seals will probably come and play if you just hang around in the vicinity and let them take the initiative. It is a short boat trip from Miller's Point slipway.

There are no operators specialising in this side of the peninsula. All Cape Town operators go where the conditions are best (one of the best things about Cape Town diving is that at least one side should offer reasonable diving at any given time) so check under Western Seaboard for operators.

WHILE IN THE AREA

This area is part of metropolitan Cape Town and so has no lack of attractions. More locally, though, there are interesting caves in the mountains above Kalk Bay, lovely mountain walks and good surfing (see chapters 14 and 17). The whole area from Muizenberg to Simon's Town is quite fascinating and you can spend a day or two visiting harbours, coffee shops, antique and craft shops, pubs and doing pleasant walks right along the coast. You can also visit the penguin colony at Boulders Beach. The road from Simon's Town to Cape Point is very pretty and is a lovely gentle cycle.

WESTERN SEABOARD

This chapter started with the warm water off KwaZulu-Natal and has moved south. Once you have rounded Cape Point, the water gets really cold: between 8 and 12 °C. In summer, after the south-easter has blown for a few days, ice-cold, crystal clear Antarctic water moves in to replace the surface water which has been blown out to sea. There are a couple of popular shore dives, such as Justin's Caves and *Het Huis te Kraaiestein*. You can't miss these; just drive along Victoria Drive until you see a huge line of parked cars with hordes of divers kitting up. From the same entry point you can dive Geldkis, if you are fit enough; it is a swim of about 400 m each way in icy water. It is worth it, though, as very few divers make the effort. Charters are run to some very popular offshore dives, most notably Vulcan Rock, a spectacular dive for experienced divers and the *Maori,* probably the most-dived wreck in Cape Waters. There are a number of operators in the Cape Town area. **Orca Industries**, **Iain's Scuba School**, **Blueprint** and **Underwater World** are just a few.

WHILE IN THE AREA

Cape Town offers an endless variety of activities. Visit Table Mountain, Cape Point, Kirstenbosch Botanical Gardens, the Constantia and Stellenbosch winelands. You can surf, winsdsurf, sail, climb, hike, cave, ride, mountain bike and hang- or paraglide somewhere along the Peninsula. Or you can shop till you drop and then go to the opera and dinner, if you prefer. In summer, the Sunday afternoon sunset concerts at Kirstenbosch Gardens are very highly recommended. Take a picnic basket, a bottle of Cape wine and chill out to the sounds of anything from a full symphony orchestra to a marimba band.

WEST COAST

As a rule, this coast does not offer good diving as it is very rough and very cold and the visibility is usually about one metre. There is some fun snorkelling in Langebaan Lagoon, though, and there are some interesting but not very well preserved wrecks further up the coast (**Orca Industries** occasionally run charters to these). They are not suitable for beginners as they are all shallow and in the high energy surf zone, and will only be enjoyed by divers who are absolutely fascinated by anything to do with wrecks.

Namibia

The Namibian coast is not ideal for diving. It is a shallow, high-energy coast so the visibility is usually less than one metre and the water is cold. The crayfishing in season (1 November to 30 April) is very good, though.

Most Namibian divers dive in one of two spectacular sinkholes. They are Otjikoto and Lake Guinas, both of which are deep and at altitude. Lake Otjikoto has an "underwater museum" of sorts as the Germans dumped vast quantities of ammunition, including large guns, here when they were retreating from the Allied troops in the First World War. Some of these have been salvaged and are on exhibition in the nearby Tsumeb Museum. The largest known underground lake in the world is in Namibia, in Dragon's Breath Cave. Diving there involves organising a huge expedition, though. For contacts, see chapter 17.

Zimbabwe

Surprisingly, there is a BSAC (British Sub-Aqua Club) branch in Zimbabwe. They dive mostly in Chinhoyi, which is a crystal clear sinkhole with a large cave section. It is deep, at altitude and is a cave so it is not a suitable dive for beginners. It is set in a lovely campsite with good birdwatching and a pleasant hotel nearby for a drink or a meal. Local divers also spearfish in Kariba for tigerfish, barbel and other freshwater fish. There are lots of huge crocodiles, though, so consult the locals before attempting a dive. They all seem to survive.

Listings

OPERATORS AND RETAIL OUTLETS

African Dive Adventures, in the Kenilworth-on-Sea Guesthouse, Margate, tel: +27 39 377-3255 or 377-5342, fax: +27 39 377-5504, take charters to Protea Banks off the Natal South Coast.

Andy Cobb Ecodiving, 10 Marion Road, St Winifreds 4126, South Africa; tel: +27 31 96-4239, run charters to Aliwal Shoal and Lander's Reef and conduct shark speciality courses.

Blueprint Diving, tel: +27 11 432-2573, run a dive camp inside the Sodwana Bay National Park in KwaZulu-Natal and have a branch in Cape Town, tel: +27 21 418-5806.

BS Divers, tel: +27 283 2-1376, operate part-time and run charters off Hermanus in the Western Cape from time to time.

Coral Divers, tel: +27 331 45-3076, run a dive camp inside the Sodwana Bay National Park.

Dive Africa Tours, P O Box 2444, Beacon Bay 5205, East London, South Africa; tel: +27 431 40-3101 or +27 82 892-5513, take charters to East London dive sites and will organise dive trips countrywide.

Dive Nautique, tel: +27 31 561-1139, are not mentioned in the text but they run charters north of Durban.

Iain's Scuba School, P O Box 1331, Sea Point 8060, Cape Town, South Africa; tel: +27 21

439-9322, is based at Atlantic Underwater Club, runs courses and takes charters to dives off Cape Town.

Indian Ocean Divers, Beacon Island Hotel, tel/fax: +27 4457 3-1158, run charters from the Beacon Isle Hotel in Plettenberg Bay.

Kowie Dive School, in the Halyards Hotel, tel: +27 464 24-4432 or +27 83 261-4786, fax: +27 464 4-2466, runs charters off Port Alfred and offers all services.

Mike's Dive Shop, 63 Western Road, Walmer 6070, Port Elizabeth, South Africa; tel: +27 41 55-3367 offers gear sales, service and air.

Mossel Bay Divers, Santos Protea Hotel, Santos Road, Mossel Bay 6500; tel: +27 444 91-1441, run charters in Mossel Bay as well as offering full dive facilities.

Ocean Divers International, Kine Park, Rink Street, Walmer 6070, Port Elizabeth, South Africa; tel: +27 41 51-5121, offer all dive facilities.

Ocean Divers International, tel: +27 21 856-2952, run charters to dive sites on the eastern side of False Bay and offer all services.

Odysea Diving, tel: +27 83 255-5717, run very flexible charters for smaller groups at Sodwana Bay in KwaZulu-Natal. They do not operate from within the park but are based across the road from the Sodwana Bay Lodge.

Orca Industries, cnr Bowwood and Herschel Rds, Claremont 7700, Cape Town; tel: +27 21 61-9673, fax: +27 21 61-9733, are based in the southern suburbs of Cape Town and offer all dive facilities. They also sometimes dive the West Coast wrecks and have run dive courses for paraplegics.

Pollock Sports in East London, tel: +27 431 5-8486, take charters off East London and offer full dive facilities.

Pro-dive, tel: +27 41 583-5316 or +27 83 659-2324, is situated on the beachfront and takes charters to all the Port Elizabeth dive sites.

Replay Sports, tel: +27 21 25-1056 or +27 21 64-4222, sell and rent all sports equipment.

Scuba Africa in Hermanus, tel: +27 283 6-2362, runs charters off Hermanus.

Scuba Explorers Society, 243C Louis Botha Ave, Orange Grove 2192, Johannesburg; tel/fax: +27 11 485-1158, run courses for disabled (and able-bodied) people and welcome disabled people on their multi-day diving excursions.

Scuba Ventures, tel: +27 41 51-5328, operate in the Port Elizabeth area.

Trident Diving, 80 Point Rd, Durban, tel: +27 31 37-8295, runs regular charters into Durban Bay and at Aliwal.

Triple 'S', tel: +27 35 571-0055, runs the dive shop in the lodge at Sodwana Bay and has a dive camp in the National Park.

Underwater World, Zero House, Wicht Close, Cape Town 8001; tel: +27 21 461-8290 or +27 21 462-1674, offers full dive facilities.

Underwater World, 251 Point Road, Durban 4001; tel: +27 31 32-5820, offers all facilities.

Waterfront Divers, Bottom Car Park, Knysna Heads, tel: +27 445 2-2938, run charters from the Heads.

ACCOMMODATION

As diving is not a live-in activity in this region, except for Sodwana Bay, accommodation has been listed near most dive sites.

KWAZULU-NATAL

Durban

The Royal Hotel, tel: +27 31 304-0331, is one of the smarter hotels in Durban and is priced accordingly.

The limited service Holiday Inn Garden Court, tel: +27 31 37-3341, offers good value.

Tekweni Backpackers Hostel, tel: +27 31 303-1433, offers basic, friendly rock-bottom budget accommodation.

South Coast

The Kenilworth-on-Sea, Marine Drive, Margate; tel: +27 39 377-5342, is an attractive and comfortable guesthouse. It has lovely sea views and offers dive/accommodation packages in association with African Dive Adventures.

The Wild Coast Sun, tel: +27 11 780-7800 (Central Reservations), is a rather more upmarket casino and resort, for those who prefer a little glitz.

EASTERN CAPE

East London

The Kennaway Protea Hotel, tel: +27 431 2-5531, is a comfortable three-star establishment with a view over some of the inshore dive sites.

Roeberts Holiday Resort, tel: +27 431 36-6381, has self-catering chalets.

East London Backpackers, tel: +27 431 2-3423, and Sugarshack, tel: +27 431 2-1111, are typical backpackers' hostels for those on a tight budget.

Port Alfred

The Halyards Hotel, tel: +27 464 4-2410, is a comfortable three-star establishment set on the Royal Alfred Marina.

Rugged Rocks Beach Cottages, tel: +27 464 4-3112, are self-catering cottages and wooden chalets right on the beach.

There are two campsites: Riverside, tel: +27 464 4-2230, and Medolino, tel: +27 464 4-1651.

Port Elizabeth

Hacklewood Hill Country House, tel: +27 41 51-1300, is a small exclusive guest house for those who are prepared to pay for a little luxury.

Summerstrand Inn, tel: +27 41 53-3131, is a comfortable three star hotel near the beach and with great facilities for families.

The City Lodge, tel: +27 41 56-3322, is a limited-service hotel offering good value for money and comfortable accommodation.

Jikeleza Lodge, tel: +27 41 56-3721, is a typical backpackers' hostel offering friendly, cheap, dorm accommodation.

WESTERN CAPE

Plettenberg Bay

The Beacon Isle, tel: +27 4457 3-1120, is a comfortable RCI (Resorts Condominiums International) affiliated timeshare resort and hotel. It is conveniently situated just opposite some of the inshore dive sites, has a dive operation on the premises and a launch site at the bottom of the lawn.

Robberg Holiday Resort, tel: +27 4457 3-2571, offers caravan sites, camping and self-catering accommodation.

The Albergo, tel: +27 4457 3-4434, will appeal to divers on a tight budget. It is a casual, friendly backpackers' hostel, with a good vibe and interesting guests.

Knysna

Ai Due Camini, tel: +27 445 82-5339, is a comfortable upmarket bed-and-breakfast, right at the Heads, close to the dive shop, launch site and the *Paquita.*

Under Milkwood, tel: +27 445 2-2385, is a self-catering chalet development, also at the Heads.

Overlanders, tel: +27 445 82-5920, is a cheap and friendly backpackers' hostel.

Mossel Bay

The Santos Protea Hotel, tel: +27 444 7103, is a three-star hotel right on Santos Beach and has a dive shop on the premises.

The Santos Express, tel: +27 444 91-1995, is a real train carriage parked right near the beach. It is cheap, different and fun.

Mossel Bay Backpackers, tel: +27 444 91-3182, offers comfortable dorm accommodation. It is round the back of the slightly more upmarket Huis de Marquette and is run by the same people.

Die Bakke/Santos Holiday Resort, tel: +27 444 91-2915, is right opposite some of the inshore dives and offers self-catering chalets, caravan and camping sites.

Hermanus

The Windsor Hotel, tel: +27 283 2-3727, is a comfortable hotel, conveniently placed for the launch site at the harbour or for some of the shore dives.

The Marine Hotel, tel: +27 283 2-1112, is a more upmarket, three-star hotel perched on the cliff overlooking the sea. It is not far from the old harbour, where there are a few nice shore dives.

Zoete Inval, tel: +27 283 2-1242, offers comfortable self-catering accommodation and backpackers' accommodation.

Cape Town

There are so many hotels in this popular resort city that your best bet would be to contact Captour, tel: +27 21 418-5202, for information and hotel bookings. Those on a tighter budget can phone Hostelling International South Africa, tel: +27 21 419-1853, for information on youth hostels and backpackers' hostels.

CLUBS AND SOCIETIES

BSAC Branch 63, P O Box ST391, Southerton, Harare, Zimbabwe.

Namibia Underwater Federation, P O Box 40003, Windhoek, Namibia.

NAUI, Africa Branch, P O Box 1228, Estcourt 3310, KwaZulu-Natal, South Africa.

South African Underwater Union, P O Box 557, Parow 7500, Cape Town; tel: +27 21 930-6549.

CHAPTER 6

Go with the flow

River rafting, canoeing and kayaking

The whole southern African region is relatively arid so there are only a few perennial rivers suitable for year-round paddling. They are the Orange, the Vaal, the Breede, the Great Usutu and the Zambezi. The Kunene is runnable almost all year except for a month or two at the end of the dry season (usually September and October). These form the mainstay of the local river running industry but they are supplemented by smaller rivers and the seasonal white water rivers which are run at specific times; usually in winter in the Western Cape and in summer in the rest of the region.

The commercial river running industry is well developed and you should find an escorted trip to suit almost every taste and budget. They range from mostly scenic and social with only a few rapids, if any, to serious white water adventures.

White water kayaking, as a sport, is rather underdeveloped and under-represented in southern Africa and, in terms of numbers, takes a poor second to flat water and marathon racing. Surf paddling is popular and is good training for white water paddling but is covered in chapter 14, as is sea kayaking.

Basic information

Rapids are graded from one to six. Grade one is nice moving water with no obstacles and grade two is a little bigger, possibly with a few relatively easily avoided obstacles. Grade three rapids usually have more volume, a greater drop and either some moderately tricky obstacles or turns. Grade four rapids are characterised by a considerable drop, big water and difficult turns or obstacles which need to be accurately read and negotiated to avoid injury or loss or damage of equipment. Grade five rapids are big and technical with only a very small margin of error. Grade six rapids are run only by adrenalin junkies or people who have no other means of proving their manhood. Grade seven — you go to heaven. If there is a waterfall or a crocodile pool below the rapid, it immediately scores a higher grade.

Commercial trips are run in one of the following: open, semi-Canadian style fibreglass canoes, closed klepper fibreglass canoes, inflatable rafts or "crocs", which are locally made and designed two-place inflatables. Canadian canoes are easy to paddle and steer but, because they can ship water in rapids, are used only up to about grade two. Kleppers are a little more stable, don't ship much water and so can be used up to grade three, but they are a little harder to manoeuvre. Crocs are robust, self-bailing and reasonably manoeuvrable so they can safely be used on grade three rapids but they are rather sluggish on flat water. Rivers with grade four or five rapids are commercially run only with rafts, which may be rowed by the guide, using oars, or paddled by the passengers under the supervision of a guide.

The Southern African Rivers Association (SARA) regulates safety and environmental standards and controls the training and registration of river guides in the region. Ensure that the company you use is registered with SARA.

Getting started

You will learn all you need on an escorted trail in a canoe, croc or raft while on the trip. If you intend to kayak, however, you should pick up some extra skills.

Before attempting anything in a kayak, ensure that you know how to get out of it — it's not difficult but neither is it completely straightforward. You will, of course, need to know how to steer it (not too tricky) and, before venturing onto even the mildest rapid, learn how to brace (using your paddle to prevent you from falling over). At some stage you will also need to master the Eskimo roll.

This can be tricky and you are well advised to learn it in very quiet water, even a swimming pool, with experienced supervision.

Although there are no formal courses, except for the **SARA** programmes which are only for aspirant guides, there are a few semi-formal training opportunities. The clubs will help with basic skills but they do tend to concentrate on competitive paddling. A number of river guides supplement their meagre earnings, from time to time, by running paddling courses. These ephemeral training organisations spring up and disappear according to the weather, whim, or other employment opportunities so you may need to do some detective work to track one down. Enquire from clubs, river trip operators or SARA.

The Zambezi International White Water School, at Victoria Falls, offers three-day and five-day kayaking courses as well as full-time guide training. **Adventure Runners** offer a kayak instead of a canoe as a standard option on their Black Eagle Trail below Augrabies on the Orange River, and will teach you some of the basics. After five days on the river, you should have a reasonable idea of what's going on. You can try to negotiate with one of the other companies to allow you to do a similar thing if you have your own kayak. Not all will be willing to do this (and not all the rivers are suitable) and you will probably pay the same price as you would if you were using one of their boats.

Equipment and clothing

Commercial operators usually supply all paddling equipment, including lifejackets, and, if necessary, helmets. If you have delicate hands you may like to bring some paddling gloves (sailing, cycling, or even gardening gloves are fine). Except for the Doring River in the Western Cape, the most comfortable paddling gear is a swimming costume and a pair of light synthetic shorts which can dry quickly. (Some of the river companies sell great shorts with zip-up pockets for sunscreen.) Your legs are likely to get sunburned, so bring a kikoi (or sarong) to cover them, or a pair of leggings. You will need a hat, and a light-coloured shirt with a collar is advisable. Sunglasses are a good idea but make sure that they are securely fastened. Do not bring your new designer clothes on the river (especially "brown" rivers such as the Orange) as they will never look the same again. Rather stick to comfortable, old, even slightly torn or stained clothes.

As the Doring is paddled in late winter/early spring it can get very cold, so it is advisable to do this river in a wetsuit or specialised paddling thermal gear (if you can borrow some). Almost any wetsuit will do but the most convenient is a long-john or sleeveless shortie of about 3 mm. This can be worn with a polypropylene or wool jersey, which will keep you warm even if it is wet. The next layer would be a light windbreaker which will be worn under your lifejacket. It can get quite warm during the day so you'll want to strip down, but you should wear the wetsuit in case you fall into the icy water.

It is necessary to enquire about other equipment as trips span the spectrum from completely self-catered to luxuriously appointed.

Options for people with disabilities

The shorter day trips, such as those on the Breede, Riviersonderend and Kavango, should not be a problem. Do, however, inform the operator of the extent of your disability when booking and emphasise your abilities. Obviously, though, to do trips with minimal facilities you will need one or two willing and able helpers.

Impaired vision or hearing, even to the extent of total blindness or deafness, should not prevent you from enjoying a river trip, as long as you have a partner who can look or listen out for you.

Restricted movement would not be a major constraint, either, on condition you can lift your legs in the water. This is essential as, if you capsize or fall out in a rapid, you need to float in your life jacket with your legs out in front of you. If you cannot do this, your foot (or feet) may get trapped in rocks on the riverbed. This could easily and quickly lead to drowning. Surprisingly, one of the safer river trips for paraplegics is the Batoka Gorge on the Zambezi River in Zimbabwe. This is because of the huge volume of water, the depth and hence the very small chance of foot entrapment. A number of paraplegics and double amputees have done this river. You need to book well in advance and the operator will organise a stretcher and porters to transport you in and out of the gorge at no extra cost. People with very limited use of their legs, and at least one paraplegic, have done other river trips in southern Africa. They were watched carefully at all times and, if they had fallen in, would have been assisted by a guide immediately. This is, however, a risky venture.

For experienced kayakers

There are a number of white water kayaking enthusiasts in the region, mostly concentrated around Cape Town (in winter), KwaZulu-Natal (in summer) and the Zambezi. There are canoe clubs in most of the major centres but they tend to concentrate more on racing than fun tripping. If you are an experienced kayaker and are visiting, or new to the region, you can contact any of these clubs for information about suitable rivers. You could also enquire from SARA or one of the local trip operators, who should be able to point you in the right direction.

Regular events

There are a number of races during the year. Except for the Zambezi White Water Challenge, they are all in South Africa. Probably the two best known are the Berg River Marathon in the Cape and the Duzi Marathon, starting in Pietermaritzburg in KwaZulu-Natal.

The Berg River Marathon is 228 km long and run over four days in July. The first two days offer some smallish rapids, tricky weirs and many confusing channels which can lead unwary paddlers way off track. From day three it broadens out and day four is on absolutely flat water, often with a very strong headwind. The race starts in the winelands at Paarl and ends at Velddrif, a small but very picturesque fishing village.

The Duzi, a three-day race, is paddled on the Umsinduzi and Umgeni rivers in January. (The Umsinduzi is a tributary of the Umgeni and joins it 50 km into the race.) It is only 130 km but is one of the toughest races around as it involves numerous compulsory portages, some of which are up to 10 km long. This is more of a biathlon than a straight canoe race. It is run as either a K1 or K2 race in alternate years.

Also in KwaZulu-Natal, the Umkomaas marathon is run in late February or early March, usually to coincide with the highest water. Run over two days, this is a rough-water race, testing paddlers and racing kayaks to the limit.

Other popular races include the two-day Breede River Marathon, predominantly a K2 race, in the Western Cape, and the Fish River Marathon in the Eastern Cape. The Vaal River Marathon, run in December, is particularly popular with inland paddlers.

In a slightly different vein, the annual White Water Rodeo is run near Hopetown in December. There is a slalom race and a surfing competition where serious waveriders strut their stuff. Although competition can be stiff, this is primarily a fun event.

The classic of the region, though, is the Zambezi White Water Challenge, run on the Batoka Gorge in October or November. This usually consists of a rafting race and a white water kayaking race. This event is becoming more and more popular with paddlers from all over the world as word of this first-class paddling venue spreads. The whole town of Victoria Falls is in a party mood for the duration and commercial trips are still run.

The Kavango/Okavango River

Starting in the highlands of Angola, the Cubango River crosses into northern Namibia, where it is broad and flat and is known as the Kavango River. Once it crosses the border into Botswana it is called the Okavango River. The broad, flat section near Shakawe is known as the panhandle, with the Okavango Delta the pan. The delta is formed when the vast amount of water being carried in the river dams up behind an almost imperceptible fault line and the water starts to fan out into many limpid channels and lagoons. These support a spectacular variety of plants, animals and birds and the area is one of the world's premier safari destinations. Mokoro (dugout canoe) safaris in the delta are covered in chapter 15. This is not really a paddling river but there are two sections on which interesting trips are offered.

POPA FALLS CANOE TRIPS

Ngepi, a small, rustic lodge on the river in Namibia, offers half-day trips in Canadian canoes from the very scenic Popa Falls back down to the camp. It is a totally flat-water trip and you are likely to see many birds, crocodiles and hippos. This is not very formal; you can just arrange it the day before if you happen to be in the area.

WHILE IN THE AREA

The Popa Falls are worth a visit, even if you don't do the paddling trip. You can spend hours swimming in the pools among the rapids as it is the only section of the river which is free from crocodiles. The Mahango Game Reserve must be crossed en route to the Botswana border and offers some good game watching, especially if you take the longer road, down by the river. Not too distant by Namibian standards, is Kaudom Game Reserve, a truly wild and remote destination for a real four-by-four safari.

PANHANDLE RIVER TRIPS

Over the border in Botswana, the panhandle section of the Okavango River offers excellent fishing and is worth doing a short trip on for the incredible birdlife. There are a number of rare or endemic species such as the whitebacked night heron, Pel's fishing owl, Cape parrot, African skimmer and blackfaced babbler. From September to October you can observe carmine bee-eaters nesting in the banks while you drift downstream.

You can choose to go out in a rowing boat, small motorboat or even in a mokoro. The latter is a bit dangerous in this deep water, though, so be careful if you take this option. You are not expected to paddle or anything like that, so this trip is suitable for anyone. Be aware that there are many hippos and crocodiles in the river and that they can be very dangerous. Trips are run from **Drotsky's Cabins** or **Shakawe Fishing Camp**.

WHILE IN THE AREA

Most people come here to fish, especially between September and December when the barbel run may occur. The other major attraction is the renowned fighting fish of Africa, the tigerfish. Close by is Drotsky's Caves, an extensive and beautiful limestone cave formation (see chapter 17) and the Tsodilo Hills, a mysterious rocky outcrop in the sandy Kalahari. A visit to either or both of these places can be arranged at Drotsky's or Shakawe fishing camp. The nearby town of Etsha Six has a basket-weaving collective where you can see and buy beautifully crafted baskets at a reasonable price.

Kunene River

The Kunene River forms the border of Namibia and Angola and runs through an area largely undeveloped on both banks. This section consists of quite long stretches of quiet water interspersed with rapids ranging from grade one to four. Being downstream from the Ruacana hydro-electric scheme, the water level fluctuates daily with the opening of the sluice gates and, obviously, also fluctuates annually.

The scenery is spectacular, with dramatic gorges and waterfalls and lovely stretches of open water. The vegetation is dominated by large acacia thorn trees and towering Makelane palms with flowering shrubs overhanging the river in many places. Birds are plentiful and varied with the Cinderella waxbill and the rufoustailed palm thrush being endemic to the river bank.

With few exceptions, only the semi-nomadic pastoralist Himba live here and can often be seen on the banks herding their cattle and goats. They are a proud nation and have preserved much of their tribal identity, particularly their fascinating dress, unique jewellery and elaborate hairstyles. They are, as a rule, very friendly people and, although few of them speak any language other than Ovahimba, they are willing to communicate and trade.

For most of the 1970s and early 1980s this area was a war zone and, although peace has returned, the scars, in the form of abandoned and bullet-marked buildings, can still be seen along the banks in a few places.

The river is usually runnable between November and August. When the water level is very high, usually in midsummer, the river is fast-flowing, the birding is good and the rapids are fast and big but not too technical. As the level drops, in winter, there are more rapids so the general paddling is more fun but the summer migrants leave so the birding is less rewarding. As the river drops still further, towards the beginning of spring, the rapids become more technical and some of the more rocky ones may have to be portaged. The weather is most pleasant during winter or early spring. Summer can be very hot indeed and the threat of malaria is consequently much greater. Optimum times change from year to year as the rainfall is not totally dependable.

KUNENE RIVER EXPEDITION

This is a five-day paddling trip from just below Ruacana Falls to just above Epupa Falls. This river is very remote and trips usually start in Windhoek. You then drive to the Etosha Pan National Park, where you spend two nights and one day. Another day's drive gets you to the Kunene, just below Ruacana hydro-electric scheme, where you bush-camp before setting off the following morning. The trip from the take-out point to Windhoek takes two and a half days. You can join the trip in Cape Town in which case you will spend two days, each way, driving to and from Windhoek.

This is a full-service, fully catered trip. Tents, inflatable mattresses, all paddling equipment, crockery and cutlery, etc., is supplied and you are not expected to assist in cooking, cleaning or setting up or breaking camp. Some nights are spent at organised campsites and some bush-camping (this means no running water and no toilets). All supplies, personal gear and equipment are taken from camp to camp in a four-wheel-drive back-up vehicle. You need only bring your own sleeping bag, personal gear and alcoholic or other favourite beverages. This is a malaria area and relevant precautions should be taken. There are crocodiles in this river but, because they were mercilessly hunted during the war, they are very shy and hide if they sense the approach of humans. You should, nevertheless, swim only in the immediate vicinity of rapids where you stand less chance of encountering a croc. The sun is very harsh at all times and the air in winter very dry, so bring plenty of sunscreen, moisturiser and lip balm. A sunhat is essential.

This trip is suitable for reasonably fit people who are happy in water. Both Epupa Falls and Ruacana can be reached by two-wheel-drive vehicle in the dry season, but the track along the river is negotiable by four-wheel-drive only. If it proves viable, fly-in trips may be introduced in the near future.

The trip is run by **Felix Unite River Adventures**. A local company has started running trips on this stretch and below Epupa Falls. For more information, contact **Eben Delport**.

The Orange River

Contrary to popular belief, the Orange was not named for its colour (it is a muddy orangey-brown) but was named after Prince William of Orange. It has an older name, though. The original inhabitants of the region, the San, called it the !Gariep, meaning the great river, and in this dry region it is truly great — a lifeline through the desert, creating a long green oasis.

Starting high in the mountains of Lesotho, bubbling streams leap down the escarpment in a number of spectacular waterfalls and then join together to form the Orange which winds its sinuous way to the sea at Oranjemund, some 2 000 km from its source. Along the way it picks up a precious load of diamonds which it deposits in the sea, forming the basis of the South African and Namibian offshore diamond mining industry. Just downstream from the spectacular Augrabies Falls, the river forms the border of South Africa and Namibia.

There are some serious white water sections on this river, especially Thunder Alley near Hopetown and the Orange River Gorge, near Onseepkans. These were run commercially in the past but these trips have ceased to be profitable. If there is sufficient demand, though, a trip can be organised at a price. The best companies to approach if you have an interested group would be **Walker's**, **Intrapid**

Rafting, **Adventure Runners** or **Which Way Adventures**. The kayaking, as one would expect, is excellent and the annual white water rodeo near Hopetown attracts many kayakers.

For the whole length of the river on which there are commercial trips, it runs through a desert region. The sun is very harsh at all times and the air in winter very dry, so bring plenty of sunscreen, moisturiser and lip balm. A sunhat is an essential. There are no dangerous animals and the area is free from tropical diseases. Trips are run all year round but it can be very hot in late summer. In winter the days are pleasantly warm and the nights decidedly crisp.

AUGRABIES RUSH (ABOVE AUGRABIES)

This is a scenic and exciting half-day trip above Augrabies Falls. The rapids are fun and, depending on water level, quite tricky and definitely bigger than those on the section below the falls. There are pretty stretches where you can relax and look out for birds such as the Goliath heron, fish eagle, cormorant, kingfisher, etc. Although the risk is negligible, the knowledge that the falls are just downstream from the take-out adds a certain spice to this trip.

Participants on this trip meet at the Augrabies National Park campsite, from where they are transported to the put-in. The trip ends back at the campsite where there are full ablutions, a restaurant, bar and shop.

The rapids are grade two or three and the paddling is not too strenuous, so the trip is run in crocs. It is suitable for beginners but you must be reasonably well coordinated, moderately fit and happy floating in a life jacket.

The trip is run by **Walker's Augrabies Canoe Trails**. You can book the day before if you are staying at Augrabies, but it is better to book in advance.

BELOW AUGRABIES

This is a scenic five-day trip with some fun rapids, but the emphasis is on relaxation. Birdlife is prolific with fish eagles, black eagles, herons, cormorants, swallows, kingfishers and many others. The scenery is spectacular with plenty of greenery on the banks and, immediately behind that, stark arid mountains towering over the river. The lack of vegetation on the mountains exposes many interesting geological formations.

This section is operated by **Walker's Augrabies Canoe Trails and Adventure Runners.** The meeting point for Adventure Runners is at their base camp, which is a short drive from the park on a good gravel road. There is a sleeping shelter, showers and flush toilets. Walker's meet at the Augrabies National Park and transport you to the put-in by minibus. The Walker's trails start and end about 10 km below Adventure Runners.

All paddling gear is supplied. Both trips are fully catered but you must bring your own cutlery and crockery and no camping equipment is supplied. There are no washing facilities. Walker's supplies a portable chemical toilet. In winter, Walker's spend one night camping beside a natural hot spring. On the Adventure Runners trip you are expected to help with the preparation of meals. You may choose to do only part of the Adventure Runners trip as one half of a "two ships trail" (two days in a canoe and two days on a camel; see chapter 16).

The rapids are mostly grade two but may be grade three, depending on the water level. The trips are both run in Canadian canoes and are suitable for beginners. Children from the age of about six may do the trip if accompanied by a parent. There are some stretches where you need to paddle for quite a while and if there is a headwind it can be a bit strenuous. For those who would like to learn some of the basics of kayaking, Adventure Runners offer the option of doing the trip in a kayak, but you must book this in advance.

Booking for the **Adventure Runners** trip is through their Johannesburg office and for **Walker's** through their Cape Town office or their base at Augrabies.

WHILE IN THE AREA

Before or after the Augrabies Rush or the multi-day trail you could spend some time at the Augrabies National Park. The falls themselves are spectacular as they plunge into a long, deep granite gorge and exploring them can fill at least half a day. There are black rhino in the park and a unique day trip is run by the park operators. You spend the morning exploring the gorge in an inflatable boat and the afternoon on a game drive where you are almost guaranteed to see black rhino. Also run by the park, the Augrabies three-in-one consists of a short paddle towards the tail end of the gorge, a hike out of the gorge and a mountain bike trip back to the camp. The Klipspringer hiking trail (see chapter 7) leaves from the park. The fascinating kokerboom or quiver tree can be seen in abundance in the area (see description in Klipspringer Trail entry). For more information about this remote and fascinating area, contact Walker's who also organises hikes and trips into Bushmanland.

NOORDOEWER TO AUSENKEHR OR VISRIVIERMOND

This stretch of the Orange River is very popular for multi-day trips so you are almost sure to see other parties, but only in passing. You can choose between a four-day and a six-day trip and, after a few days, the peace of the Orange just seeps in through your pores — you could be on another planet.

If you are hoping for peace and quiet, avoid this trip during the Easter weekend, Christmas, New Year and Cape school holidays as every operator is booked up with families who have young children.

The river runs through the Richtersveld, a spectacular desert mountain range. The scenery is similar to that below Augrabies but is somehow more dramatic. The mountains are higher and seem to go on further and both the river and the sky seem to be wider. Long scenic stretches are interspersed with some moderately challenging rapids.

There are optional walks to an old diamond mine, a fluorite mine and way up the hill to see the "halfmens" (*Pachypodium namaquanum*), which is so named as according to local legend these succulents are half human, half plant. It is not difficult to see how this legend arose; the plant, usually about 2 m high but reaching 3 m, stands alone on rocky hillsides with its long, thorny, tapering trunk leaning towards the north, inclined always at an angle of between 20 and 30 degrees. Its leaves are large, slightly hairy and clustered at the top of the single stem, looking very much like the head of a human from a distance. They produce beautiful red and green flowers between September and December.

You meet at a base camp near Noordoewer, where you spend the first night and then put in in the morning. The camps are quite rustic but have showers, flush toilets and cooking facilities. On the river there are no washing facilities and a portable chemical toilet is supplied. You will need to bring your own crockery, cutlery and camping equipment. You are transported back from the take-out on the back of an open truck.

There are some pleasant grade two rapids separated by long scenic stretches where you can relax, swim or raft up and chat. The trips are run in Canadian canoes, crocs or rafts (enquire on booking). Canoe trips are suitable for children from the age of about six, if accompanied by a parent, and even very small children may accompany a parent on a rafting trip. This trip is suitable for beginners and reasonably nervous people as you can walk around all the rapids if you like. The paddling is quite gentle but may be strenuous if there is a headwind.

Felix Unite River Adventures, **Orange River Adventures**, **Wild Thing Adventures** and **River Rafters**, all based in Cape Town, run this stretch of river.

WHILE IN THE AREA

The river forms the northern border of the Richtersveld National Park, through which you can do a four-wheel-drive trail. Booking should be done through the Warden, Richtersveld National Park, P O Box 406, Alexander Bay 8290, South Africa; tel: +27 256 506. There is also a guided or unguided hiking trail (see chapter 7). The nearby town of Keetmanshoop is the centre of another four-wheel-drive trail, administered by the Southern Tourism Forum, Private Bag 2125, Keetmanshoop, Namibia; tel: +264 631 2-2095, fax: +264 631 2-3818. There is an impressive kokerboom forest near Keetmanshoop where you can camp. The hot springs at Ai Ais are less than a day's drive from Noordoewer and are the end point of the Fish River Hiking Trail (see chapter 7).

The Vaal River

The Vaal, which is one of the main tributaries of the Orange River, is the primary water supply for Gauteng. Although it flows through a heavily industrialised region, it is a haven for watersports enthusiasts from the nearby urban areas. There is an annual two-day race from below the Vaal Dam to Parys.

There are two different but similar trips run from near the small town of Parys, just over an hour's drive from Johannesburg. This is a fun-filled, gentle day trip, and offers a quick and easy escape from the big city. Scenic stretches are interspersed with some small rapids and the scenery is a lot prettier than most people would imagine, being so close to a major industrial centre.

This is a particularly popular river for corporate breakaways and team-building trips, so it is often booked up. The season runs from September to May as it gets extremely cold in winter. If you have a group of eight or more, you can book a trip to your specifications. You can choose to include hiking and abseiling in weekend trips. Both operators have attractive riverside camps with extensive catering facilities, hot showers, flush toilets and comfortable chalets or tents.

The trip is not strenuous and is suitable for beginners. The rapids are grade two and the river is run in crocs. When the water level is very high the trip is run in paddle rafts. This can be very exciting but it only happens every few years, at most.

The trips are run by **Sunwa Ventures** and **River Tours and Safaris**.

Doring River

Running through the spectacular Cedarberg Mountains in the Western Cape, the Doring offers beautiful mountain scenery and some exciting rapids. It is runnable only for a short season after the winter rains, usually August and a week or two into September.

Most trips are run over a weekend; you meet on Friday night and return on Sunday afternoon, but all the companies will offer trips during the week if there is sufficient demand. There are two sections which are run, both of which are only a few hours' drive from Cape Town.

The lower section is very popular and is run by virtually all the river companies in Cape Town and as a result can be very crowded over weekends. The upper section is much less crowded as access to this part of the river is restricted and there is usually only one company on the water at a time.

The Doring is a very popular river with local kayakers, many of whom spend a few days or weeks in the area, accompanying their friends who run the organised rafting trips.

If the river is very high, the rapids are quite large and very fast. As the river level drops, they become less wild but more technical. At the lowest runnable level, the trip consists more of dodging rocks than running rapids, but this, too, can be fun. If the river is running high there may be time to marvel at the extensive rock art and interesting flora on the banks. Although the rapids must, obviously, be treated with respect, this is a relatively benevolent river with no major risks. As the name suggests, though, thorn trees grow profusely on the banks and care should be taken to avoid them and other trees through which the river may flow at high water. Even though this is theoretically winter, always take sun precautions.

UPPER DORING

The upper section is run by **Which Way Adventures** on paddle rafts. They supply all equipment, crockery, cutlery, tents and mattresses. This is a full-service trip and you are not expected to help in food preparation. The first night is spent in comfortable chalets with hot showers and flush toilets. On river, there are no washing facilities and a chemical toilet is supplied.

Intrapid Rafting also run this stretch of river which is much less crowded than the lower section. They also supply tents, mattresses, crockery or cutlery and run the trip in rafts or crocs.

WHILE IN THE AREA

This is a lovely area with spectacular mountain passes, beautiful streams and interesting little towns. Ceres, near the start of the upper section trip, was on the old route to the diamond fields and keeps this link alive in the Transport Riders Museum, which describes the role of transport riders in the development of the interior of South Africa. The Gydo Pass links the Warm Bokkeveld to the harshly beautiful Cold Bokkeveld. This pass was originally built by the famous road builder Andrew Geddes Bain in 1848, but has since been partially rebuilt and is well worth seeing.

LOWER DORING

Almost all the Cape Town river companies run the lower section of the Doring. Prices, levels of service and facilities vary so enquire from the operators listed below until you find a trip which suits your tastes and budget. All the operators have a base camp, invariably a somewhat rundown farmhouse, where you spend Friday night. There is some form of toilet — pit, chemical or flush — and either showers or, at least, taps. You are then transported to the put-in point by truck or minibus. Saturday night is spent camping. While on the river, there are no facilities for washing. A portable chemical toilet is supplied.

WHILE IN THE AREA

The nearby town of Clanwilliam is renowned for its flower show in August, when the whole region bursts into bloom, happily at about the same time the river is runnable. Rooibos tea (a herbal tea with many claimed therapeutic benefits) is grown and processed in the area and you may take a tour through the factory and taste the tea and other by-products (such as liqueur). There is a small museum in the Old Gaol building, where you will also find the tourist information centre.

Felix Unite, **River Rafters**, **Wild Thing Adventures**, **Intrapid Rafting** and **Orange River Adventures** run this section. It is not necessary to bring crockery, cutlery, tents or mattresses on the Felix Unite trip and deckchairs are supplied. On all the others you can choose between a fully catered or a self-catered trip but you must bring all your own cutlery, crockery, sleeping bag and some form of camping mattress in either case. River Rafters' base camp is right at the put-in and on the second night they camp in a huge cave.

The Riviersonderend (Enchanted River)

The Riviersonderend is literally translated "river without end", so named as it peters out in a wetland near the town of Riviersonderend (appropriately enough) and does not reach the sea. It starts in the Hottentots Holland Mountains where it plunges through a pretty gorge and is a very popular kloofing venue, especially the section known as Suicide Gorge (see chapter 7).

Where the Riviersonderend passes close to Greyton, it has a reasonably shallow gradient and is densely overgrown with reeds and trees, resembling a Tolkienesque Middle Earth landscape, hence "the enchanted river".

WHILE IN THE AREA

This is an easy day trip from Cape Town but you will regret it if you don't plan to spend more time in this delightful area. The small village of Greyton is quite charming and filled with excellent guesthouses, coffee shops, restaurants and antique and craft shops. The nearby Greyton Riding Centre, tel: +27 28 254-9009, offers two-hour rides in the picturesque Riviersonderend Mountains. There is a 16 km hike across the mountains to the equally charming village of McGregor. This can be done on an "out and return" basis, spending the night at McGregor. Contact Cape Nature Conservation, tel: +27 2353 621/671. You can rent mountain bikes from Rory, tel: +27 28 254-9559, who will point you in the right direction but does not escort trips.

This is not so much a paddling trip as a waterborne obstacle course. The meeting point is at the Greyton municipal campsite, which has hot showers and flush toilets. A light breakfast is served and you are then transported to the put-in point. The trip ends back at the campsite. You negotiate overhanging trees and laughingly navigate narrow palmiet channels, all the while looking forward to the extensive picnic lunch and fine Cape wines that form the focus of the excursion. There are a couple of tiny grade one rapids and some reasonably fast channels. The rest is really laid back paddling on flat water. There is hardly ever a headwind and the whole trip is incredibly relaxed. The trips are run in crocs.

Intrapid Rafting runs this section and plans to run two-day trips upstream.

Palmiet River

This is a beautiful, typically Cape river running through the Koggelberg Nature Reserve. It is fast flowing, rocky and very technical with some really fun grade three rapids. This is a one-day trip, starting in the reserve and ending in the lagoon, just near the mouth. Usually, you start off with tea or coffee, paddle from start to finish and then break for lunch, after which you do the whole trip again.

The trip described above is run by **Energy Tours** as part of a pilot project to ascertain the environmental sustainability of commercial trips on this beautiful and sensitive river. Four-place inflatable rafts, specifically designed for the river, were used. At the time of writing the outcome of the pilot project was uncertain, but it seems that the project will go ahead. **Felix Unite River Adventures** and **Intrapid Rafting** may also run this river, probably in crocs.

WHILE IN THE AREA

The Koggelberg Nature Reserve is spectacular. Only 30 000 ha in extent, it is home to more than 1 600 plant species, of which about 150 are endemic. There are numerous pleasant day walks on which you may marvel at the rich floral diversity or just admire the views of sea and mountains. A permit is essential.

Breede River

The Breede starts off high in the Groot Winterhoek mountains near Ceres in the Western Cape and is well worth kayaking in its upper reaches. The Dwars, a tributary of the Breede, offers kayakers exciting grade four and five rapids, also in winter. A two-day K2 race, usually from Robertson to Swellendam, is the second biggest of the Cape races.

Once out of the mountains, the Breede (which means "broad" in Afrikaans) spreads out to live up to its name. It meanders through the Worcester Valley where it nourishes the flourishing vineyards and where the Wine Route Adventure is run. From Worcester, the river flows through more farmland to Swellendam. It then flows through a large wheat-growing area and past the once prosperous hamlet of Malgas, which used to be a depot for the steamships that sailed up from the sea before the mouth silted up (probably as a result of bad farming practices). Its main claim to fame now is as the site of South Africa's last working hand-operated pontoon. From this point downstream, the river is broad and tidal. It enters the sea at Infanta, a popular fishing and spearfishing spot.

BREEDE WINE ROUTE ADVENTURE

Both **Felix Unite River Adventures** and **River Rafters** run "wine-tasting" trips on the upper section near Worcester. These are very gentle one-day canoe or croc trips with the emphasis more on the extensive picnic lunch and fine wines than on the paddling.

WHILE IN THE AREA

Worcester is a medium-sized town with many museums, the most interesting of which, the Kleinplasie Living Open Air Museum, portrays the type of farming activities which occurred in the area up to about 1900. Either on your way there or back, take the long way around the Du Toit's Kloof Pass, avoiding the tunnel. The views are spectacular and there are lovely picnic spots along the way. If you decide to spend some time in the area, the charming little village of McGregor is a great place to base yourself. It boasts a country hotel and a number of bed and breakfast establishments. This town is considered to be one of the best-preserved examples of a 19th century Cape town. There is a 16 km hike over the mountains to the equally charming town of Greyton (see entry on the Riviersonderend).

BREEDE RIVER RAFTING

Downstream from Swellendam, this is one of the few river trips which is not strictly linear as two groups do the trip simultaneously. You each paddle one section of the river the first day and then swop around. It is more a fun experience than an expedition as you return to one of two base camps every night. There are beds, hot showers, flush toilets and a full bar. These trips are fully catered.

The rapids are grade two and the trip is run in crocs. It is not particularly strenuous and so is suitable for beginners. This is a very popular venue for corporate breakaways and team-building trips.

The trip described above is run by **Felix Unite River Adventures**. **Which Way Adventures** run more usual excursion trips on the same section of river.

WHILE IN THE AREA

Swellendam has some beautifully restored buildings and an interesting museum. The Bontebok National Park (see chapter 15) was established in 1930 (in a different but nearby setting) to bring the then remaining 22 bontebok back from the brink of extinction. It has since been stocked with other antelope as well and is worth a visit. It is worth planning your trip to include crossing the river by the pontoon at Malgas. You can even attempt to help the ferrymen pull it across — not as easy as it looks.

Kowie River

There is a scenic, flat water trip which can be done over one or two days on this pretty river near the Eastern Cape town of Port Alfred. The trail passes through the small Kowie Nature Reserve, which does not have much in the way of game but is an excellent birding venue with areas of attractive indigenous bushveld dotted with thorny acacias, succulents and big tree euphorbias. It is not a formal trail, so you basically do your own thing. If you plan carefully, you can go upstream with the flood tide and then come down with the ebb. You can book the trip through and rent canoes from **Riverside Camp Site** in Port Alfred.

WHILE IN THE AREA

There is a pleasant day ride over the dunes and along the beach (contact Three Sisters Horse Trails, tel: +27 464 71-1269). There is a two-day walking and paddling trail nearby, also contact Three Sisters for information. See entries on Port Alfred in chapters 5 and 14 for details of other attractions in the area.

The Great Fish River

This river, which runs through the Eastern Cape, is an interesting one for paddlers. Much of its water is obtained from the Orange River through a regulated interbasin transfer scheme and is released at regular intervals for irrigation. Although this obviously has its negative effects, it is rather useful if you are planning a paddling trip as, if you liaise with the Department of Water Affairs, you will know when the best time is. For example, the Fish River Marathon is run every year on released water, making it one of the most dependable and therefore popular races in the country. Run as a K1 and K2 race in alternate years, it is the venue of the South African Championships.

There is a 28 km, two-day escorted, self-catered trip below the Elandsdrift Dam near Cookhouse. The banks are mostly covered with Karoo scrubveld and the birding is good. The trip is enlivened by a few fun grade one and two rapids.

Bookings are through **Berg Sports** in Port Elizabeth.

WHILE IN THE AREA

There is some nice sport climbing near Cradock (contact Berg Sports for details) and Olive Schreiner's home in Cradock has been converted to a museum. There is an interesting hiking trail in the nearby Mountain Zebra National Park (see chapter 15).

The Tugela and Buffalo rivers

These two KwaZulu-Natal rivers (the Buffalo is a tributary of the Tugela) run through the Tugela Biosphere Reserve, which consists of a number of private farms that have been consolidated to form a huge area for trophy hunting and general safaris.

The name "Tugela" means "the startling (or frightening) one" in Zulu and it is apt. Neither of these rivers is for the faint-hearted and they are generally considered to be the finest commercially run white water within South Africa's borders. They are also very popular with local kayakers, and many Cape kayakers travel up here for the season. As KwaZulu-Natal is a summer rainfall area, both rivers are only runnable in summer and are a mere trickle in winter, when the area is used for trophy hunting.

TUGELA WHITE WATER ADVENTURE

Participants in this adventure meet just outside the town of Weenen, in central KwaZulu-Natal, where you can relax with a drink while you wait for stragglers. You are then transported to Zingela Camp by four-wheel-drive vehicles; this trip may be a little rough and crowded, but is an adventure in itself. The trip is fully catered and you need bring only your personal clothing and a sleeping bag. You sleep on beds in comfortable safari tents. There are communal hot showers and flush toilets.

WHILE IN THE AREA

There is plenty to do close by before or after the rafting. This area is steeped in violent history as it was the site of many battles — between Zulus and British, Zulus and Boers and Boers and British. You can obtain a map to the KwaZulu-Natal battlefields by writing to The Secretary, Private Bag 2024, Dundee 3000, South Africa, or phoning +27 341 2-2654. It will give you some of the history and guide you to burial sites and small museums, one of which can be found in the appropriately named town of Weenen, which means "weeping". Although this name officially refers to one incident — the killing of a party of Boers — it is descriptive of the whole era. Not too far away is the Hluhluwe-Umfolozi National Park and the Greater St Lucia Wetland Park (see chapter 15 for more details).

This is a white water trip with a number of big rapids, grade four or even five. It is usually run over two days but is not an expedition as you are based at the camp for the whole period. The trip is run in crocs or paddle rafts, at the discretion of the guides. To do this trip you must be reasonably fit and, preferably, able to swim or at least not frightened of moving water. Although this may change to accommodate changing water levels, you are usually transported upstream on the first day and then paddle down to camp. On the second day, you start paddling at the camp and are transported from the end point, usually back to your meeting point in Weenen. You can choose to do some abseiling or even a short walk to see game.

The river water is not safe to drink, so try to keep your mouth closed if you fall out. All drinking water should be obtained from camp. Although this area is not considered a malaria area, the disease is endemic not too far away.

The trip described above is run by **Sunwa Ventures**. **River Tours and Safaris** also run a similar trip downstream, in the Tugela Gorge, and **Isibindi River Adventures** run a similar trip on the Buffalo.

The Great Usutu River

A tributary of the Pongola, the Usutu is the biggest river in the kingdom of Swaziland. Its source is in the highlands of Mpumalanga in South Africa and its tributaries drain most of the western part of Swaziland. It is usually runnable all year, but may get a little low towards the end of the dry season in a year of poor rainfall.

This is a fairly intense one-day trip of good white water. It is a fast-moving river; rapids follow one after the other with only short flat sections in between. There is one compulsory portage, a waterfall, and, depending on water level, possibly a few more. You may abseil next to the waterfall if you like.

Clients staying at Mkhaya Game Reserve are transported from the reserve to the Sipophonene police station, where they will meet up with other paddlers. Transport to the put-in is in open, four-wheel-drive safari vehicles. A very simple lunch is served on the river and at the take-out you are met by the same vehicle, which will transport you back to the police station.

Most of the rapids are grade three or two and there are a couple of grade fours. This is a fun, technical river but it can still be attempted by novices if they are reasonably fit, competent and confident in water. In medium to low water the trip is run in crocs and in high water in paddle rafts.

The trip is run by Mkhaya Game Reserve and all bookings are through **Big Game Parks of Swaziland** Central Reservations.

WHILE IN THE AREA

While you are in the area you may plan a day trip or overnight stay at Mkhaya, which is highly recommended. They offer escorted game walks and mountain biking trips through the reserve (see chapters 8 and 15). Also in Swaziland is Mlilwane Game Reserve, which offers biking and horse riding, and Malalotja, which has some of the best hiking in southern Africa (see chapter 7).

The Pungwe River

Starting high in the Eastern Highlands of Zimbabwe, the Pungwe rushes down the escarpment and, first feeding a huge mangrove forest, enters the sea at Beira, the second largest port in Mozambique. This little-known river is runnable between December and April when one-day white water rafting trips are offered. They are suitable only for fit and capable people and are run by **Far and Wide**.

WHILE IN THE AREA

This area is an adventure traveller's paradise. Nyanga National Park has some small game and pine plantations and sections of grassland through which you can hike. There are many lovely streams in which to swim or catch trout, as well as some specially stocked dams. You may also do a one-day horse trail through the park and see some game. The Chimanimani Mountains, not too far away, are covered in beautiful montane grasslands which offer excellent hiking (see chapter 7), and the Bvumba Mountains are shrouded in misty, mysterious forests through which you can wander for kilometres.

The Zambezi River

The Zambezi is one of the great rivers of Africa. It starts in the highlands of Zambia and, showing great disdain for artificial borders, skirts through Angola before re-entering Zambia. Near Katima Mulilo it forms the border between Zambia and Namibia — a geographical peculiarity that came about because of colonial Germany's insistence on having access to the Zambezi through the Caprivi Strip. Still with Zambia on the left, it forms borders with Botswana and then Zimbabwe before flowing into Mozambique and then to the sea at Quelimane.

Huge, powerful, beautiful and wild, it varies from vast and placid through wild to just utterly spectacular. The Mosi-oa-Tunya (smoke that thunders), better known as Victoria Falls, is the greatest waterfall on earth in terms of volume. A mile wide and only 100 m high it carries, at high water, over 500 million litres a minute over a sheer precipice into its spectacular gorge. Spray is visible for about 20 km and there is a constant rainbow and, at full moon, a lunar rainbow.

You would have to be a very jaded traveller indeed not to be deeply impressed by this spectacle.

As well as the trips described here, you can do a three-, four- or seven-day trip on the lower Zambezi which is described in chapter 15.

Hippos and crocs are a hazard on the whole river except the Batoka Gorge but, with the standard precautions which are taken, are not much of a threat. Malaria is endemic in the entire Zambezi Valley and, although the water is safe to drink upstream of Mlibizi, it is less advisable to do so in Kariba Dam. The sun is very harsh here at all times so bring plenty of sunscreen, moisturiser and lip balm. A sunhat is essential.

SIOMA FALLS

Sioma, or Ngonye, Falls are about 300 km upstream from Victoria Falls. They consist of a series of rapids with many channels flowing around a number of beautiful tree-studded islands. At high water (March to May or June) some of the rapids are runnable, about grade four or five.

This half-day trip starts just above the falls and is run in paddle rafts. You take one of the many channels to just below the falls, get out and walk back while the porters carry the raft upstream. You then try another channel. After trying them all, you can repeat your favourite a few times. In low water, the trip starts below the falls and is not nearly as exciting, but still fun.

Downstream from the falls, there are a few grade three rapids and a quick paddle past basking hippos and crocs back to the lodge. At the end of the trip it is just a few short steps to the bar where you can relive the experience as the rapids grow in size, directly proportional to your bar bill.

WHILE IN THE AREA

Also offered by Tukuluho, are tigerfishing excursions and game drives in the nearby Sioma-Ngwezi or Liuwa national parks. In the dry season (August to November) they offer full-moon excursions to watch herds of elephant as they come down to the river at night to drink and frolic in the water.

The trip is suitable for beginners but you must be reasonably fit and confident in water. Also on offer is a milder half-, one- or two-day canoe trip below the lodge.

There are a few grade one rapids, many species of birds, and hippos and crocs. You may be lucky enough to see game on the banks. The trip is run by **Tukuluho Wildlife Limited**, based at Maziba Bay Lodge. Booking is through their Gauteng agent.

UPPER ZAMBEZI

Half-, one- or two-day trips are offered on the Zambezi above Victoria Falls. There are a few rapids, lots of scenic stretches and the opportunity to see game. On day trips lunch, and sometimes breakfast, is served and the overnight trips are fully catered. The level of service offered and the stretch of river covered does vary somewhat depending on the operator. All the trips are run in Canadian canoes or crocs, except for Chundukwa, who run in kleppers.

Trips on this section are run by **Shearwater** and **Kandahar Safaris** from the Zimbabwean side and **Makoro Quest**, **Tongabezi** and **Chundukwa Adventure Trails** from the Zambian side. All the trips and activities in the Victoria Falls area can be booked through any of the agents or directly through your hotel or lodge and even through the backpackers' hostels.

ZAMBEZI WINE ROUTE/ROYAL DRIFT

This is a very gentle float down the flatter section of the upper Zambezi. You are paddled downstream in a three-seater Canadian canoe (one paddler to two clients). Drinks and snacks are served en route and the trip ends around sunset a few hundred metres above the falls. Although there are no vineyards on the Zambezi, you do get the chance to sample some Zimbabwean wine if you like; it's not comparable to Bordeaux, or even Cape wines, but it is quite palatable. Also on offer is some Cape wine, Zimbabwean beer (which is better than the local wine) and a range of other beverages, both alcoholic and non-alcoholic. There are no rapids and the trip is suitable for non-paddlers and non-swimmers.

These trips are run by **Shearwater**, **Frontiers** and **Kandahar**. All the trips and activities in the Victoria Falls area can be booked through any of the agents or directly through your hotel or lodge and even through the backpackers' hostels.

BATOKA GORGE

The Batoka Gorge below the Victoria Falls is reputed to be the best commercial one-day white water rafting trip in the world. That is debatable, but it is certainly an unforgettable experience. All paddling equipment, including life jackets and helmets, is provided and lunch is served on the riverbank halfway through the trip. You need to bring very little. Sunscreen and hat are essential. You need to wear non-slip shoes in which you can walk comfortably and which you don't mind getting wet. They must be secure because if you fall out you could lose them very easily. The most sensible clothing is a swimming costume, shorts (with a drawstring) and a shirt or T-shirt for sun protection. Everything you take or wear needs to be tied on. (Don't wear a skimpy bikini as you will probably lose at least part of it if you take a swim.) There are waterproof containers on the boats for very small essentials. You may take a camera which will be put in the waterproof container, but at your own risk.

You meet at a designated spot, usually in the grounds of one of the hotels in either Victoria Falls or Livingstone. You can arrange transport from your hotel and, if you are doing a trip from the Zambian side, you can arrange transport across the border from the Zimbabwean side.

This stretch is best run at low level (usually September to December or longer, with October and November being virtually guaranteed). At high level the rapids are not quite as wild and, when the level gets too high to safely negotiate the portage at number nine, the trips start at rapid ten. They are then only half-day trips; the Zambians take out at rapid 23 and the Zimbabweans at rapid 24.

From either side, the trip starts with a long and rather steep walk into the gorge. From the Zambian side, in low water season, you descend almost to the Boiling Pot at the base of the falls. If the water is extremely low you might even raft the "minus rapids", those right at the base of the falls. (This happens very seldom.) After a practice session you negotiate rapid one and float under the bridge waving to the onlookers and the bungi jumpers.

From the Zimbabwean side the trip starts at rapid four. For the best value for money, do the low-water trips from the Zambian side and the high-water trips from the Zimbabwean side.

Rapid five is the first really big one and after that you feel capable of handling anything. Between rapids you can relax on the leisurely stretches and look at the scenery, gazing up cliffs of over 100 m. If you like, you could even try your hand at rowing while your guide takes a rest. The rapids are very, very big and quite scary but really relatively safe. Because of the huge volume of water and great depth, if you flip or fall out, you will get very wet and possibly scared but not much else. There is, however, a possibility that you may have a few seconds of down time which will seem like hours. You stop for lunch after rapid ten and then continue to either rapid 18 or 23, for the Zambian trip, or rapid 19 or 20 for the Zimbabwean trip.

Remember that steep walk into the gorge? Now you've got to get out. No problem, you still have sufficient adrenalin surging through your bloodstream to keep you going and, if that doesn't do it, the thought of a cold drink at the top should encourage you. You are then driven back to your starting point in an open-sided truck with seats. A party atmosphere usually prevails en route.

This is a grade five river and is run only in rafts, either oar or paddle. Although you don't need any previous experience, you need to be reasonably fit, able to swim and fairly confident in water to enjoy this trip. The oarboats are not too strenuous, you just need to hold on and "highside", i.e. throw your weight to the front or side of the raft to stop it flipping, or you can choose to go in the back of an oarboat in which case all you have to do is hold on. If you choose to do the trip in a paddle raft, though, you have to paddle the boat the whole way and don't get to hold on in the rapids. This option is a lot more challenging but is not for the nervous.

WHILE IN THE AREA

There is no lack of attractions in the Victoria Falls area. See chapter 11 for microlighting and ultralighting, chapter 12 for skydiving, chapter 13 for bungi jumping and chapter 16 for horse trails. Game-viewing drives are on offer in both the Zambezi National Park on the Zimbabwean side and in the Mosi-oa-Tunya National Park on the Zambian side. The falls themselves are well worth a visit and you can walk down to the Boiling Pot or (at low water) to Livingstone Island from the Zambian side. Guided tours around the Livingstone area are run by **Mokoro Quest**. These may include the game park, the pioneer cemetery at the old drift, the museums and the cultural villages or can be tailormade to suit individuals.

Although the one-day trip is the standard, you can choose to do a half-day trip, in which case you walk out of the gorge before lunch. (Don't go for this option unless you have serious time constraints — some people have burst into tears, not wanting to leave the party halfway through.) You can also choose a two- or seven-day trip in the dry season. The first two days are as described above but then you continue down the river. For real adrenalin junkies, African Extreme offer the "Gruesome twosome". You bungi jump off the bridge, get lowered into a waiting raft and then, adrenalin pumping, head off downstream. This is only available from the Zambian side. Each trip is accompanied by professional photographers and videographers. You can view videos that night and photographs the next day, and you'll be hard pressed to resist the temptation to buy them.

The trip is run by **Shearwater**, **Frontiers** and **Safari Par Excellence** on the Zimbabwean side and **Sobek**, **Quest Rafting** and **Safari Par Excellence** on the Zambian side. All the trips and activities in the Victoria Falls area can be booked through any of the agents or directly through your hotel or lodge and even through the backpackers' hostels. There is a tariff agreement between the companies who run this stretch and there is no point trying to negotiate a lower price, regardless of where you book.

Listings

OPERATORS

Adventure Runners, P O Box 31117, Braamfontein 2017, South Africa; tel: +27 11 403-2512, fax: +27 11 339-4042, do five-day paddling trips on the Orange River and the Two Ships camel and canoe trip.

African Extreme, P O Box 125, Victoria Falls, Zimbabwe; tel: +260 3 32-4156, offer the Gruesome twosome, a combination bungi jump and rafting experience from the Victoria Falls bridge and then down the Batoka Gorge.

Berg Sports, tel: +27 41 51-1363, fax: +27 41 51-4548, is a climbing shop in Port Elizabeth. They take bookings for the Great Fish River Canoe Trail.

Big Game Parks of Swaziland, Central Reservations, P O Box 234, Mbabane, Swaziland; tel: +268 4-4541, 6-1591/2/3 or 6-1037, fax: +268 4-0957/6-1594, do all the booking for the Mkhaya Game Reserve white water rafting trip on the Usutu River.

Chundukwa Adventure Trails, tel/fax: +260 32-4006, offer one- or two-day canoe trips on the upper Zambezi, as well as walking and horseback safaris.

Delport, Eben, tel: +264 61 294-7468, +264 61 294-7466 or +264 81 122-0014, runs trips on the Kunene River.

Drotsky's Cabins, Private Bag 13, Maun, Botswana; tel: +267 66-0351, is primarily a fishing camp but also offers short trips on the Okavango River.

Energy Tours, all booking through Gopher Travel, tel: +27 21 685-4040, fax: +27 21 685-5409, run trips on the Palmiet River.

Far and Wide, PO Box 14, Juliasdale, Zimbabwe; tel: +263 29 2-6329, run one-day white water rafting trips on the Pungwe River in Zimbabwe.

Felix Unite River Adventures, PO Box 2807, Clareinch 7740, Cape Town; tel: +27 21 683-6433, fax: +27 21 683-6488, run trips on the Breede, the Orange, the Kunene and the Doring.

Frontiers, P O Box 117, Victoria Falls, Zimbabwe; tel: +263 13 5800, fax: +263 13 5801. Harare; tel: +263 4 73-2912/3, fax: +263 4 73-2914. Johannesburg; tel: +27 11 884-4185, fax: +27 11 784-2985, offer white water rafting trips in the Batoka Gorge on the Zambezi and canoeing trips upstream from Victoria Falls, as well as taking bookings for a range of other activities.

Intrapid Rafting, P O Box 16193, Vlaeberg 8018, Cape Town; tel: +27 82 555-0551, fax: +27 21 23-8585, offer trips on the Doring and the Riviersonderend River (the Enchanted River).

Isibindi River Explorers, P O Box 124 Dundee 3000, KwaZulu-Natal; tel/fax: +27 3425 620 or tel +27 11 403-2511, fax 11 339-4042, offer white water rafting on the Buffalo River in KwaZulu-Natal in South Africa.

Kandahar Safaris, P O Box 233, Victoria Falls, Shop 9, Sopers Arcade, Parkway Drive, Victoria Falls, Zimbabwe; tel: +263 13 4502, fax: +27 13 2014, offer half-, one- and two-day trips on the upper Zambezi. This is a small family-run operation and consequently their departure dates are less flexible, but they offer just that little bit more personal attention.

Mokoro Quest, P O Box 60420, Livingstone, Zambia; tel: +260 3 32-1679, fax: +260 3 32-0732, offer one-day trips on the upper Zambezi, as well as tailor-made day trips around Livingstone.

Mkhaya Game Reserve offers one-day white water rafting trips on the Usutu River in Swaziland. All their booking is through Big Game Parks of Swaziland, see above for address.

Ngepi is a rather informal camp on the Kavango River in Namibia. You can usually just turn up. It is signposted on the road. They run half-day canoe trips on the river.

Quest Rafting, P O Box 60420, Livingstone, Zambia; tel: +260 3 32-1679, fax: +260 3 32-0732, offer one-day white water rafting trips in the Batoka Gorge.

River Rafters, P O Box 14, Diep River 7856, Cape Town; tel: +27 21 72-5094/5, run the Orange, the Doring and the Breede.

Riverside Campsite, Port Alfred, tel: +27 464 4-2230, rent canoes on the Kowie River.

River Tours and Safaris, PO Box 474, Rivonia, 2128; tel: +27 11 803-9775, fax: +27 11 803-9603, run one- or two-day trips on the Vaal, near Johannesburg, where they specialise in team-building and corporate breakaways, and two-day white water trips on the Tugela River in KwaZulu-Natal.

Safari Par Excellence, P O Box 108, Victoria Falls, Zimbabwe; tel +263 13 4424/2051/3/4, fax; +263 13 4510. Zambia; tel: +260 3 32-3349/32-1432, fax: +260 3 32-3542.

Johannesburg; P O Box 1395, Randburg 2125; tel: +27 11 888-4942, fax: +27 11 888-4942, operate white water rafting on both the Zimbabwean and Zambian sides of the Batoka Gorge and canoe trips on the lower Zambezi, as well as taking bookings for a range of other activities.

Shakawe Fishing Camp, P O Box 12, Shakawe, Botswana; tel/fax: +267 66-0493, concentrates mainly on fishing but will offer short trips on the Okavango River.

Shearwater, P O Box 125, Victoria Falls, Zimbabwe; tel: +263 13 4471, fax: +263 13 4341. Harare; tel: +263 4 75-7831/6, fax: +263 4 75-7836. Johannesburg; P O Box 76270, Wendywood 2144, South Africa; tel: +27 11 804-6537, fax: +27 11 804-6539, offer one-day and multi-day white water rafting trips on the Batoka Gorge and multi-day canoe trips on the upper and lower Zambezi, as well as taking bookings for a range of other activities.

Sobek Expeditions, P O Box 60305, Livingstone, Zambia; tel: 260 3 32-3672, fax: +260 3 32-4289, run one- and multi-day white water rafting in the Batoka Gorge and canoe safaris on the lower Zambezi, as well as taking bookings for a range of other activities.

Sunwa Ventures, P O Box 313, Parys 9585, South Africa; tel: +27 568 7-7107, fax: +27 568 7-7362, offer one- or two-day trips on the Vaal River near Johannesburg, where they specialise in corporate team-building, and white water rafting on the Tugela River in KwaZulu-Natal.

Tongabezi, Private Bag 31, Livingstone, Zambia; tel: +260 3 32-3235, fax: +260 3 32-3224, run very upmarket trips on the upper and lower Zambezi.

Tukuluho Wildlife Limited run white water trips at Sioma Falls in western Zambia. All booking is through their agent, Pulse Africa, tel: +27 11 327-0468, fax: +27 11 327-0281.

Walkers Augrabies Canoe Safaris, 10 Park Island Way, Marina de Gama 7951, Cape Town; tel: +27 21 788-1715 or at Augrabies: +27 54 451-0177, offer multi-day canoe trips below Augrabies Falls on the Orange River and half-day white water rafting above the falls.

Wild Thing Adventures, tel/fax: +27 21 461-1653, tel: +27 21 461-9693 or +27 83 259-9997, offer trips on the Orange River and on the lower Doring River in late winter or spring.

Which Way Adventures, 34 Van der Merwe St, Somerset West 7130, South Africa; tel: +27 21 852-2364, fax: +27 21 852-1584, e-mail: whichway@africa.com.za, offer rafting trips on the Breede, the Orange, near Onseepkans, and the upper Doring in the Cape.

ACCOMMODATION

This list is by no means a complete accommodation guide. Victoria Falls and Livingstone, for example, have many entries as most people go there to spend a few days and accommodation is at a premium. Places close to a major city or trips with base accommodation may have no listings or, if they do, it will usually be because the establishment concerned is particularly convenient or suitable.

THE ORANGE RIVER

The Augrabies National Park, tel: +27 54 451-0050/1/2, offers camping and self-catering chalets. There is a restaurant, bar and basic shop. It is best to book in writing through the National Parks Board, P O Box 787, Pretoria 0001, or P O Box 7400, Roggebaai 8012.

The Bloudraad Café Backpacker @ Augrabies, tel: +27 54 451-0177, is run by the resident staff of Walker's Augrabies Canoe Trails and offers friendly rough and ready accommodation at a very reasonable price.

The Camel Lodge, P O Box 1, Noordoewer, Namibia; tel: +264 637 7171, fax: +264 637 7143, is the closest accommodation, other than the river camps, to the Noordoewer section of the river.

THE ZAMBEZI RIVER

Victoria Falls

Victoria Falls is a popular tourist destination and offers a reasonable range of accommodation but, except for the campsites and the backpackers' hostels, it is far from cheap.

At the top end of the luxury scale, the gracious Victoria Falls Hotel, P O Box 10, Victoria Falls; tel: +293 13 4203/5, is the oldest and grandest in town.

Close by, the Makasa Sun Casino Hotel, P O Box 90, Victoria Falls; tel: +263 13 4275, is very comfortable and has a bit of a buzz at night.

Further out, the Elephant Hills Hotel, P O Box 300, Victoria Falls, Zimbabwe; tel: +263 13 4793/7, could be considered a blot on the landscape but it is superbly luxurious inside. It has a golf course and is on the edge of the national park. It is suitable for large groups.

The Victoria Falls Safari Lodge, P O Box 89, Victoria Falls, Zimbabwe; tel: +263 13 4728/9, 4725, is a somewhat more tasteful but equally luxurious option, also on the edge of the national park.

Ilala Lodge, P O Box 18, Victoria Falls, Zimbabwe; tel: +263 13 4337/8, close to the falls and town, offers very comfortable accommodation at a slightly more affordable price.

The Sprayview Motel, P O Box 70, Victoria Falls, Zimbabwe; tel +263 13 4344/5, offers comfortable family accommodation and is widely regarded to be the best value in town. It is usually booked up six months in advance, though.

The A'Zambezi, P O Box 130, Victoria Falls, Zimbabwe; tel: +263 13 4561/4, and the Rainbow Hotel, PO Box 150, Victoria Falls, Zimbabwe; tel: +263 13 4583/5, are also in the lower price range.

Camping and chalets are available in the National Parks campsite, which is clean and comfortable and offers good value for money. Booking is through National Parks Central Booking Office, P O Box 8151, Causeway, Harare, Zimbabwe; tel: +263 4 70-6077/8. Be warned, though: there is usually a long waiting list and even confirmed reservations have been known to go astray.

The Victoria Falls Town Council Campsite, tel: +263 13 4210, is usually crowded and not very clean but is very conveniently situated and cheap. They also offer chalets and dorm accommodation.

There are two backpackers' hostels. You don't book for these; just turn up. There is one at 357 Gibson Road and one halfway along Courtney Selous Crescent.

Livingstone

In Livingstone you will find accommodation to match almost every taste and budget.

Wazawange Lodge, P O Box 60278, Livingstone, Zambia; tel: +260 3 32-4066, 32-4077/8, fax: +260 3 32-4067, is very conveniently situated close to town on the airport road and offers comfortable, air-conditioned chalet accommodation and unpretentious fare.

The Mosi-oa-Tunya Intercontinental, P O Box 60151, Livingstone, Zambia; tel: +260 3 32-1210/11, 32-1122/5, 32-1217, fax: +260 3 32-1128, is a typical Intercontinental hotel but its position, about five minutes' walk from the falls, affords it some individuality and there are African touches to the decor and menu that distinguish it from every other Intercontinental worldwide.

The Victoria Falls Holiday Village (formerly Maramba River Campsite), P O Box 60957, Livingstone, Zambia; tel: +260 3 32-4189, fax: +260 3 32-4266, is a pretty campsite situated on the Maramba River, about 5 km from the falls by road, shorter if walking through the bush. As well as campsites, they have permanent tents for hire and attractive, open tree-houses.

Jolly Boys, +260 3 32-1924, situated in the town and signposted off the main street, is a typical, not-too-clean, backpackers' hostel with dorm accommodation, camping, pool table, swimming pool and sauna. The phone usually doesn't work but you can just turn up anyway.

There are a number of beautiful thatched lodges set on the banks of the Zambezi, strung out upstream of Livingstone. Although each has its own character, all offer stunning views, good food and service and comfortable en suite accommodation. They all have swimming pools and are all highly recommended. There is no air conditioning and, although the sleeping areas are protected from mosquitoes, be prepared to encounter small many-legged visitors in your bathroom. In order of distance from town, they are:

Thorntree, P O Box 61009, Livingstone, Zambia; tel: +260 3 32-0823, fax: +260 3 32-0277, 32-0732, with comfortable en suite tents under thatch, is the closest. It also offers upmarket overland safaris.

Tongabezi, Private Bag 31, Livingstone, Zambia; tel: +260 3 32-3235, fax: +260 3 32-3224, aims at the very top end of the market and also runs a camp on Sindabezi Island.

Zambezi Tree Lodge Camp, operated by Chundukwa Adventure Trails, P O Box 61160, Livingstone, Zambia; tel: +260 3 32-4006, fax: +260 3 32-3234, offers accommodation in small, attractive chalets built from local materials and perched above the river on stilts.

Kubu Cabins, P O Box 60748, Livingstone, Zambia; tel: +260 3 32-4093, fax: +260 3 32-4091, 35 km upstream from Livingstone, offers comfortable en-suite reed and thatch cabins and a beautiful stone and thatch honeymoon suite. For more budget-conscious travellers, they have a pretty shady campsite.

Downstream from Livingstone, opposite rapid number 17, is the equally atmospheric Taita Falcon Lodge, PO Box 14656, Sinoville 0129, South Africa; tel: +267 12 57-2470, perched right on the edge of the gorge.

Maziba Bay Lodge, all booking through Pulse Africa, tel: +27 11 327-0468, fax: +27 11 327-0281, is a characterful lodge on the banks of the Zambezi near Sioma Falls. They have tented accommodation and a campsite.

THE KUNENE RIVER

Halfway between Ruacana and Epupa is the very rustic Kunene River Lodge which can only be reached by four-wheel-drive vehicle and offers camping, simple chalets and a festive bar. There is a campsite at Epupa Falls. On leaving Epupa towards Windhoek the closest accommodation is Ohakane Guest House at Opuwa, tel/fax: +264 6562 31.

THE RIVIERSONDEREND RIVER

You can camp at the Greyton municipal campground, which is where the trip starts, or you could try the Post House, tel: +27 28 254-9995, a pleasant, picturesque guesthouse in the town.

THE KOWIE RIVER

See Port Alfred accommodation in chapter 5 listings.

THE KAVANGO/OKAVANGO RIVER

There is a campsite at Popa Falls; book through the Director of Tourism, Private Bag 13267, Windhoek, Namibia; tel: +264 61 23-6975, fax: +264 61 22-4900.

See under "Operators" for Shakawe Fishing Lodge and Drotsky's Cabins.

THE TUGELA RIVER

The Sunwa trip meets at the Owl and Elephant, +27 363 4-1933, which is a charming bed-and-breakfast establishment just outside Weenen, so it would be a good place to spend a night if you plan to arrive a day early or leave a day late.

THE USUTU RIVER

If you are not staying at Mkhaya you could try Mlilwane, near Mbabane. It is not as expensive and offers a range of accommodation including camping, chalets, a youth hostel and traditional Swazi beehive huts. There is a swimming pool, shop and licensed restaurant. All booking is through Big Game Parks central reservations, see "Operators" section in this chapter.

Another option is the Bend Inn, P O Box 37, Big Bend, Swaziland; tel: +268 3-6111.

RETAIL OUTLETS AND MANUFACTURERS

Brian's Kayak Centre, Cape Town; tel: +27 21 511-9695.

Canoe Concepts, Johannesburg; tel: +27 11 486-1610.

Kayak Centre, Durban; tel: +27 31 765-7041.

Knysna Racing, Knysna; tel: +27 445 82-6220.

Pope's Canoe Centre, Pietermaritzburg; tel: +27 331 94-5729.

Replay Sports, Cape Town; tel: +27 21 25-1056 or +27 21 64-4222.

Roamer Rand, Johannesburg; tel: +27 11 822-1200.

Robbies Sports, Johannesburg; tel: +27 11 475-8156, Cape Town, tel: +27 21 461-2284.

Water Action Gear, Cape Town; tel: +27 21 61-1847.

Xtreme Equipment, tel: +27 21 363 4-1208.

CLUBS

Gauteng Canoe Union, tel: +27 11 646-9624.

KwaZulu-Natal Canoe Union, tel: +27 331 46-0985.

SA Canoe Federation, tel: +27 331 94-0509.

Western Province Canoe Union, tel: +27 21 551-1770.

TRAINING

See Adventure Runners under "Operators". They offer informal kayak training on their Black Eagle Trail.

SARA, P O Box 472, Magaliesberg 2805; tel: +27 142 77-1888 or +27 82 458-1442, fax: +27 142 77-1870, controls all guide training.

The Zambezi International White Water School, P O Box ZIWWS, Victoria Falls, Zimbabwe; tel: +263 13 3300, fax: +263 13 3299, offers white water training on the Zambezi.

CHAPTER 7

Take a hike

Hiking and kloofing

Hiking is one of the more well developed adventure activities in the region with many laid out trails, escorted hikes and designated wilderness areas, particularly in South Africa, Swaziland and Namibia. Designated Wilderness Areas in South Africa are not true wilderness areas, as a rule, but they are virtually pristine areas with no infrastructure other than footpaths. There are no trails in the wilderness areas and you must plan and navigate your own route. Botswana and Lesotho do not have the same level of infrastructure, but have miles of open or sparsely populated land through which you can hike independently. The most difficult aspect of hiking in southern Africa, especially South Africa, is figuring out who administers any particular hike. Not only are there hundreds of different authorities, they change jurisdiction and names frequently so it may take a few phone calls to get through to the right office to book a hike, but the information given here was correct at time of writing.

Other than kloofing and special trails for disabled people, only multi-day trails have been featured, but you can do a day walk almost anywhere where there is something worth seeing. Kloofing is immense fun and gives you a unique opportunity to get to know an area. It involves following a river through a mountain gorge (kloof) and necessitates some walking, long swims and leaping over waterfalls and into deep mountain pools.

The trails listed below have been divided up into different biomes, or environments, rather than political regions.

Getting started

You don't need any special skills to hike. It is best to start off by doing a few day-walks before attempting a multi-day hike but, if you are reasonably fit, you really shouldn't have any problems. It is a good idea to do your first hike with someone who has at least hiked before but, if you stick to the designated hiking trails, you are unlikely to get lost.

If you have no mountain experience and no knowledgeable friends with whom to do your first hike, your best bet would be to join a hiking club in your area. Failing that, you can contact the Mountain Club of South Africa or even commercial organisations such as the **Leading Edge** or **Orca Industries** in Cape Town or **Sanga Outdoor** in Johannesburg who can organise escorted hikes for groups.

The Mountain Development Training Trust (MDTT), which is contactable through the **Mountain Club of SA**, offers courses in mountain leadership for aspiring hiking leaders. They can be done by anyone and should be considered if you are planning to lead a hike, even if it is just with a few friends. You can call the **Hiking Federation** for information on hiking clubs in your area, or the area you plan to visit.

Equipment

Good equipment is absolutely essential. For day walks you can use almost any good walking or running shoes, but good quality hiking boots will be the most comfortable as they offer good arch and ankle support. You should carry a small day-pack containing water, sunscreen, warm and waterproof clothes and snacks. Wear a sunhat or peak. Unless you are following a very obvious trail, a map or guidebook will be necessary to prevent your getting lost.

Kloofing is usually only a one-day activity and your needs are much the same as above, except that you would almost certainly use a pair of running shoes rather than hiking boots. It is best to wear a swimming costume, light synthetic shorts and a T-shirt. Bear in mind that almost everything you carry will probably get wet, but you can try to keep non-waterproof items dry by storing them in plastic jars or wrapping them in plastic bags. If you are kloofing with a lilo, use a good quality, rugged model. The type children use in backyard swimming pools is not suitable. They soon end up either totally deflated or lose their inner compartments and thus become uncomfortably lop-sided and very unstable. If you are particularly susceptible to cold, you may like to kloof in a light wetsuit jacket but it may get rather hot between swims.

For multi-day hikes good quality boots, a well-fitting backpack, a sleeping bag with appropriate thermal qualities, water bottle and a sunhat are the basic essentials. You can get away with just this if you don't mind sleeping on the ground (or on a hike with huts) and eating cold food. Most people, though, would consider at least some of the following to be essential: hiking mattress, groundsheet, mug, plate, knife, fork and spoon, small camping stove and pot and a tent. As with all activities where you may be far from assistance, a small first aid kit is strongly recommended. If you are hiking in the mountains, a waterproof tent, a good sleeping bag rated to -5, preferably -10, warm clothes and a camping stove are essential.

Don't be tempted to save a few pennies by buying your hiking equipment from supermarkets. Not only will you miss out on the expert advice of qualified sales assistants, you will probably end up with unsuitable or inferior equipment.

Options for people with disabilities

The following is a short list of what is known to be accessible, including day walks near cities, although there are almost certainly trails in other areas. The **Disabled Adventurers Club**, based at the Sports Science Department of the University of Cape Town, and **Eco-access** are continually assessing new routes.

WESTERN CAPE

Kirstenbosch Botanical Gardens in the shadow of Table Mountain in Cape Town has a number of access features. There is a Braille trail and fragrance garden which is accessible to wheelchair users. It is always crowded with sighted, ambulatory people who seem to be irresistibly drawn to the fragrance garden — evidence that there is scope for many more. Toilets, walkways, picnic sites and viewpoints are accessible. On Sunday afternoons in summer a sunset concert is held on the lawns, which are easily accessible. Performances range from symphony concerts to marimba bands, and they are enormously popular so go early as it gets pretty crowded and it is tricky negotiating a wheelchair among the hordes of people. Take a picnic.

There is a Braille section in the Company Gardens at the top of Adderley Street in Cape Town.

In the Hottentots Holland Nature Reserve near Cape Town, the Palmiet Trail for the visually impaired is a 6 km circular trail. Parts of it can be done in a wheelchair without assistance and the whole trail could probably be completed with help. Contact **Cape Nature Conservation.**

The Karoo National Park has an interpretive fossil trail with Braille information and handrails which is also wheelchair accessible. Contact the **National Parks Board.**

The Postberg area of the West Coast National Park has spectacular flowers in spring. There are wheelchair-accessible toilets at the picnic sites. Contact the **National Parks Board.**

A group of adventurous wheelies, with keen assistants, have done three days of the Outeniqua Trail, near Knysna, see below. The facilities were not ideal but they managed and this is by no means an easy trail.

The Harkerville Trail near Knysna, see chapter 8, has a group centre in the forest which can be used as a base from which to do day hikes on forestry roads. It sleeps about 36 people and has outside showers and toilets which are not specially adapted but can be used with a little ingenuity. Contact the **Department of Water Affairs and Forestry**, Knysna. There is a wheelchair-accessible toilet at the Garden of Eden and the nearby circular walk through the indigenous forest is reasonably accessible.

GAUTENG

Riverclub walk along the Jukskei River has a wheelchair-friendly pathway; contact the **Sandton Municipality** for further information.

MPUMALANGA

The Blyderivierspoort Nature Reserve has, as well as a long hiking trail which is not really accessible, a number of areas which have been specially adapted. They have three chalets which are wheelchair accessible and a number of the viewpoints are accessible with a bit of help (just a pusher, really as the gradients are quite steep). The toilets and visitors' centre at Bourke's Luck Potholes are wheelchair accessible. The 180 m Lichen Trail is fully accessible with wide pathways, a tapping rail, tapes for blind people and pamphlets for the deaf. The lichens have very distinctive textures and may be felt. For bookings and enquiries contact the **Mpumalanga Parks Board.**

KWAZULU-NATAL

The Glenholme Nature Reserve in Kloof, behind the **SPCA**, has paved paths and an elevated walkway through a swamp forest. There is Braille information and the path is suitable for wheelchairs. The trail is 1 km long.

The Durban Botanic Gardens has elevated beds with over 200 tactile and fragrant plants. Labels are in print and Braille and a tape is available. The path is accessible to wheelchairs.

Coastal trails

Although the trails included here traverse a huge range of vegetation and climate types, in all of them the emphasis is on following the coastline and on scenery or life forms associated with the sea or shore.

KOSI BAY

This is a four-day guided, self-catered trail around the pristine lake system of Kosi Bay. Its major attractions are the scenery, ranging from long white beaches to dune and coastal forest, the wonderful snorkelling in the mouth (take your own gear) and the possibility of sighting turtles (in December/January when they lay their eggs or in April when the baby turtles hatch). Keen birders should look out for the palmnut vulture at the southern extreme of its range. The rather rare Kosi palm (*Raphia australis*), often mistaken for the true raffia palm (*Raphia farinifera*), is found here in abundance. The buoyant stalks of the leaves are used to make a raft with which you do a river crossing. Beware of hippos and malaria.

A major attraction of this hike is the opportunity to see the local people fishing with traditional traps, something which hasn't changed in hundreds of years.

The trail must be booked well in advance through central reservations, **KwaZulu-Natal Department of Nature Conservation**.

MZIKI TRAIL

This is a series of day walks from a base camp at Mount Tabor. The scenery is breathtaking, including long white beaches, coastal forest, the highest coastal dunes in South Africa, swamp forest, some grassland and Lake St Lucia, on which you may see crocodiles and hippos. Snorkelling in the tidal pools is excellent and you are likely to see a wide range of colourful tropical fish.

Booking is essential; contact central reservations, **Natal Parks Board**.

WHILE IN THE AREA

The popular diving resort of Sodwana Bay lies almost halfway between the Kosi Bay and Mziki trails (see chapter 5). The fishing is good at Sodwana and at St Lucia, just south of the Mziki Trail. Close by is the Hluhluwe-Umfolozi Game Reserve, where you can see a wide range of big game. The St Lucia and Umfolozi guided wilderness trails are described in chapter 15.

WILD COAST

This spectacular coastline has long been a favourite hiking destination. The facilities deteriorated badly at one time but are in the process of being upgraded. There are three different sections, of four, five or six days, which can be done on their own or linked up to form one very long trail. The coastal scenery is spectacular, with steep cliffs, waterfalls cascading into the sea, long white beaches and pretty tidal pools. Coastal grassland, coastal forest, dune forest and mangrove forests are the dominant vegetation types. There are people living all along the coast in traditional homesteads and, as a rule, they are friendly and willing to chat, barter or sell food such as freshly caught crayfish or oysters. You may need to examine your conscience a little before indulging, though, as the marine resources of this coast are under severe pressure. There is some excellent surfing along the coast.

Petty theft, and even violent crime, have occurred along this coast but you should be quite safe if you travel in a group of at least four people. If you leave your equipment unattended, though, it may be missing when you get back. Booking is through **Eastern Cape Tourism Board**.

STRANDLOPER TRAIL

This four- or five-day trail (the first day is an optional detour) can be done with or without a guide. The emphasis is on the different beach environments, the tidal pool ecology and the history of settlement of the area, ranging from the Strandlopers (coastal San) to the present day and including such unwilling settlers as shipwreck survivors. It is by no means a wilderness experience as the coast is quite developed. There are 13 river crossings, four of which are major rivers and are crossed by canoe. The distances are not great so you can take time out to go birdwatching up one of the rivers if you like. The overnight accommodation ranges from a converted pumphouse right on the high-water mark to a wooden cottage on the dunes. A highlight for those who don't like carrying vast supplies of food is that you can have lunch at a coastal hotel every day if you remember to bring sufficient cash. There is good surf and snorkelling.

Booking is through **Eastern Cape Nature Conservation**.

OTTER TRAIL

This five-day trail is one of the most popular in the region. It is named after the Cape clawless otter, which you may well see on the trail. It starts at the Storms River Mouth and ends in the small resort village of Nature's Valley. Most of the area is covered in coastal forest, which differs markedly from the coastal forest further north and from the indigenous forest inland. It is not very thick or high and is more scrubby than foresty, with remnant patches of fynbos in places. The scenery is spectacular with sheer cliffs dropping right to the sea in some places. There are a few small river crossings and one quite big one, the Bloukrans River, on day four. It is a good idea to consult a tide table to avoid arriving at high tide but, unless you are a non-swimmer, it is not really necessary to get up in the middle of the night to arrive at low tide. Mid tide, especially at neap tide, should be fine. The terrain is fairly rugged and you seem to be constantly going up or down hill. You can snorkel on the trail, but you may not remove anything at all from the sea.

Booking is essential and, as this trail is very popular, it is often booked up well in advance. You can try for cancellations, though. Booking is through the **National Parks Board**.

Cape mountain trails

These are in the winter rainfall areas and the mountains are mostly sandstone and shales. The dominant vegetation is mountain fynbos (proteas, ericas and restionaceae) with some montane forests in the kloofs. There is very little grass. It may snow in winter, summer is hot and dry and spring is exceptionally beautiful with a profusion of wild flowers. Right on Cape Town's doorstep is the Table Mountain Peninsula Mountain Chain on which there are numerous day walks; consult *Table Mountain Walks* by Colin Paterson-Jones.

CEDARBERG WILDERNESS AREA

This spectacular mountain region of 71 000 ha is crisscrossed by numerous paths and tracks. There are no laid out trails and no overnight accommodation. You simply state the area in which you wish to walk when obtaining your permit and then plan your own route. You sleep under the stars or take a tent. The scenery is spectacular with rugged rock formations, tinkling mountain streams, refreshing pools and interesting flora. The Clanwilliam cedar trees, (*Widdringtonia cedarbergensis*), after which the range is named, are often gnarled and windblown, etched against the skyline on rocky ridges. They are seriously endangered and are thought to have declined to a point where there are not enough of them to reproduce. Otherwise, the vegetation is mostly fynbos with large tracts of restionaceae in the moist low-lying areas and many species of flowers, including the endemic snow protea. The whole area is renowned for rock art and you can spend hours exploring likely overhangs, looking for paintings. Game likely to be seen includes the klipspringer, dassie (rock hyrax) baboons and grey rhebok. There are leopards in these mountains but you will be lucky to see spoor, never mind an actual leopard.

The number of permits is restricted so it may be necessary to book in advance, especially if you want to hike on a weekend. Booking is through the Citrusdal offices of **Cape Nature Conservation**.

WHILE IN THE AREA

The Western Province Parachute Club has its drop zone at Citrusdal (see chapter 12), so you could do a parachute jump or a tandem jump, and there are a number of laid out mountain bike trails (see chapter 8). The interesting town of Clanwilliam is nearby (see Doring River entry in chapter 6 for further information).

GROOT WINTERHOEK WILDERNESS AREA

This area covers just over 30 000 ha of mountain fynbos and has many tracks and paths. There are no laid out trails and you may plan your own route. There are no overnight huts but there is a camping site. This area of mountain fynbos is very similar to the Cedarberg but not quite as rugged. There are numerous streams, waterfalls and pretty rockpools. The flowers, especially in spring, are spectacular. Animals likely to be seen are much the same as for the Cedarberg.

Booking is through the **Cape Provincial Administration**, Porterville.

WHILE IN THE AREA

The farm Beaverlac, which has pleasant day walks, mountain biking, streams, waterfalls and pools, is close by (see chapter 8). The Dasklip Pass launch site for hang-gliders and paragliders is also not far (see chapter 9). If you are travelling from Cape Town, you might like to pop in to the West Coast Ostrich Farm to see and learn about these interesting indigenous birds. There is also a restaurant and curio shop. Phone (021) 972-1905 for directions or bookings.

HOTTENTOTS HOLLAND NETWORK OF TRAILS

A number of trails traverse the scenic 26 000 ha Hottentots Holland Nature Reserve. The area is spectacular in spring when the many species of indigenous flowers are at their best.

The three-day Boland Hiking Trail is probably the best known. It is a laid out trail with overnight accommodation. Also in the Hottentots Holland Reserve is the Palmiet Trail for the visually impaired. Bookings for these trails are through **Cape Nature Conservation**.

SWARTBERG TRAIL

This trail traverses the rugged Swartberg Mountains at the edge of this biome. The fascinating geological formations with huge folds and overfolds are easily visible because the environment is somewhat more arid and the vegetation relatively sparse. This range separates the Great Karoo from the Little Karoo and there are elements of Karoo vegetation on the lower slopes. There are a number of options, so you can choose to do the trail over anything from two to five days. Some sections are quite steep but the views are spectacular. Booking is through the Oudtshoorn offices of **Cape Nature Conservation**.

Montane grassland

Montane grassland is restricted to areas over 1 500 m above sea level and consists of huge tracts of short grasses and some mountain fynbos with montane forests in the kloofs. These areas are also known for the profusion of wild flowers which can be seen in the spring and summer.

DRAKENSBERG GRAND TRAVERSE

The Drakensberg, on the western side of KwaZulu-Natal, is designated a wilderness area so there are no laid out trails. The Grand Traverse, though, is well known as a major challenge for hardcore hikers, being 300 km long, high and subject to snow in winter or sudden violent thunderstorms in summer. This may not sound too daunting to people who have done some of the super-long trails in the USA, for example, but here there are absolutely no facilities. There are no villages to which you can duck out, and probably no other people on the trail.

It is best to start at the chain ladder at the Amphitheatre in the north and walk south. This way the sun and wind will be mostly at your back. You go over the 10 highest points in South Africa and the highest point in southern Africa (Thaba Ntlenyana) which is, strictly speaking, in Lesotho. You follow the border, which is also the watershed, most of the time. This trail can be done by masochists in 16 days (or even two weeks), but if you plan to enjoy yourself at all you will need at least three weeks.

The best time to do this trail is undoubtedly winter; summer is very dangerous as there are violent thunderstorms and spring and autumn are rainy and sleety, with icy, dangerous conditions. Winters are very cold and snow is common, but it is dry snow (which is less dangerous than the icy snows of spring and autumn) and there are few storms. (Incidentally, it can snow in these mountains even in midsummer.) You must not even consider doing this trail unless you are very fit and have all the appropriate equipment. Good boots, warm clothing, a warm hat, waterproofs, a tent, sleeping mat, a very good sleeping bag and a camping stove are all essential.

If this seems a bit demanding, you can choose to do only a short section of the traverse or any other section for only a day or more. Booking is through the **Natal Parks Board** and is essential. They have an excellent map which you should buy.

WHILE IN THE AREA

The Drakensberg is one of the most scenic areas in southern Africa. As well as hiking, you can do a horse trail through the Berg (see chapter 16) or just enjoy the scenery or try your hand at fly-fishing. See chapters 9 and 10 for information on gliding, hang-gliding and paragliding in the area.

WOLKBERG NETWORK OF TRAILS

This high, rather mysterious, mist-covered mountain region is where the Transvaal Drakensberg meets the Strydpoort Mountains. It is covered in grassland, sourveld and cycads with pockets of indigenous forest in the kloofs. There are a number of walks but no laid out trails. You can go out for days and just camp where you like. This trail is not for inexperienced hikers.

Booking is through **Nature Conservation and Environment**, Haenertsberg.

WHILE IN THE AREA

The cycad forest at Modjaji's village, near Tzaneen, is the largest cycad forest in the world, consisting of thousands of specimens of only one species, *Encephalartos transvenosus*, commonly known as the Modjaji cycad. It is the largest of the South African cycads, usually growing to between five and eight metres, sometimes reaching 13. The forest is under the strict protection of Modjaji, the Rain Queen, and has been thus protected by all her predecessors. She is the hereditary queen of the Lobedu and has the ability to make rain, a gift jealously guarded by her tribe. The forest was declared a national monument in 1936 (rather unnecessarily as Modjaji was doing a fine job of protecting it), and may be visited. It is administered by the **Department of Environmental Affairs and Tourism**, Pietersburg. See also Magoebaskloof Trails, under the section on indigenous forest trails. There are some wonderful caves in these mountains (see chapter 17).

MALOLOTJA NATURE RESERVE

This scenic nature reserve in the north-west of Swaziland offers some of the best hiking in the region. Rolling grasslands are relieved by small pockets of indigenous forest in the kloofs. Trilling streams, tumbling waterfalls and cool pools beckon on a hot day and there is an interesting variety of game. Zebra, wildebeest, eland, blesbok and other smaller antelope abound.

There are 200 km of hiking trail and you can choose to do a short day-walk or hike for up to seven days. There is a campsite in the reserve and comfortable self-catering wooden chalets. You can buy an inexpensive little guide to the trails from the park office or on booking. Booking is through the Senior Warden, **Malolotja Nature Reserve**.

WHILE IN THE AREA

The northern part of Swaziland is higher and cooler than the rest. You can visit Poponyane Lodge, which has nice day walks, a lovely swimming pool overlooking a waterfall and many species of birds. The Ngwenya Glass Factory, where you can see and buy a superb range of decorative and functional glassware all made from recycled glass, is nearby. It is open from 9 am to 4 pm. Other attractions include Lion's Cave, which is the oldest known mining operation in the world, dating from about 40 000 years ago.

CHIMANIMANI NATIONAL PARK

Set in the Eastern Highlands of Zimbabwe, on the Mozambique border, the Chimanimani Mountains are characterised by rolling grasslands, interspersed with mountain fynbos and montane forests in the river valleys. There are a number of streams, pools and waterfalls. There are numerous caves, so far proved to be the second deepest sandstone caves in the world but believed to be the deepest. Don't wander off into any cave you may come across; not only are they deep, but they have sheer precipices within them. There is a campsite at Base Camp and one hut a few hours' walk into the park. You should be entirely self-sufficient when hiking here. For information and booking contact the Warden, **Chimanimani National Park**.

WHILE IN THE AREA

Most people come here to hike. The Bridal Veil Falls is pretty and can be accessed from Chimanimani village by car. Further north, Bvumba and Nyanga offer more walks, horse riding through Nyanga and trout fishing. The Pungwe River is raftable between December and April (see chapter 6). Great Zimbabwe is less than a day's drive away, near Masvingo, and is well worth a visit. The structures at Great Zimbabwe are the biggest pre-colonial stone ruins in sub-Saharan Africa and show a distinct style of stonework which is found all over southern Zimbabwe and the northern parts of South Africa.

LESOTHO

Lesotho has no laid out trails but the whole country outside of the towns is worth hiking. You can do an escorted hike of a few hours or a few days from Malealea Lodge, and Sehlabathebe National Park (the only one in the country) on the eastern side also offers some nice day walks. With some advice from locals you should be able to hike out to see some rock paintings and even fossilised dinosaur footprints. This is one of those places you can just pack your backpack and walk across the whole country if you like. Take a map and make sure you are properly equipped to handle the extreme conditions. You must take a camping stove as there is no firewood in Lesotho. *A Backpacker's Guide to Lesotho* by Russel Souchet outlines a number of suggested routes (see Further Reading, at the end of this chapter).

WHILE IN THE AREA

Lesotho is best known for extensive horse trails (see chapter 16). There is also good trout fishing and lovely scenery.

Indigenous forest

There is very little indigenous forest left in southern Africa and, frankly, there never was that much to begin with. Although the forests were exploited for timber production early this century, the biggest threat is from uncontrolled fire and infestation by exotic trees. Most forested areas are interspersed with plantations of pine or gum but there are some areas where you can hike through reasonably extensive stands of indigenous trees.

MAGOEBASKLOOF TRAILS

The three-day Dokolewa and the two-day Debengeni Falls Trails are near Tzaneen in the Northern Province of South Africa. They are both set in extensive indigenous forest, making this one of the most beautiful trailing areas in southern Africa. The trail occasionally crosses pine and gum plantations. You can do them separately or combine them into a four-day trail. This area has an interesting history as these forests were the last refuge of Makgoba, chief of the Tlau clan of the Sotho nation. Evidence of older forestry practices exists in the form of old saw pits. There are many streams and pools, some virtually Olympic size.

Accommodation is in comfortable forestry huts with all the standard, but basic facilities.

Booking is through the Sabie office of **SAFCOL**.

WHILE IN THE AREA

There are horse trails on the other side of the Northern Province (see chapter 15), and the northern part of the Kruger National Park is close by. See also the Wolkberg network of trails, under the section on montane grassland trails.

AMATOLA TRAIL

This is an epic six-day trail covering 106 km through indigenous forest and plantations in the Amatola Mountains near King William's Town in the Eastern Cape. It is a linear trail but you can do one of a number of shorter circular options. These forests are a transitional zone between the forests of the southern Cape, e.g. Knysna, and the subtropical forests of KwaZulu-Natal. The trail is quite steep but it is worth it as the views are wonderful.

Booking is through the **Keiskamma Ecotourism Network**.

WHILE IN THE AREA

Do something totally different. Spend a few days as the guest of the community of the tiny hamlet of Hanover. This is not a romantic or scenic place, but an authentic, very poor, rural African village. The people are friendly and you will get the chance to experience how the majority of South Africans live. For details and bookings phone +27 4325 2556, or fax +27 433 2-5747.

HOGSBACK TRAIL

Not far from the Amatola Trail is the Hogsback Trail and the small, charming town of the same name. This is real Hobbit country. That is said of lots of places, but in this case it is true. When Tolkien lived in South Africa, he visited

Hogsback and was thus inspired to write *The Hobbit*. The trail is circular, done over two days, and goes through tangled natural forests and some pine plantations. There is an overnight hut which, at time of writing, was being upgraded.
Booking is essential and is through the Humansdorp office of **SAFCOL.**

WHILE IN THE AREA

Just soak up the peace and scenery. Get married in the tiny chapel of St Patrick on the Hill (you can only have four guests, though) or take a copy of *The Hobbit* and read it deep in the forest. After a long day's rambling turn up at one of the three quaint hotels and ask the barman for a Hogwash. If you have more than one, though, don't drive home.

OUTENIQUA TRAIL

This is a long trail — 107 km over seven days — near the Garden Route town of Knysna, but you can do shorter options. It meanders through indigenous Knysna forest, mountain fynbos and pine plantations. It also passes by the ghost town of Millwood, the scene of the Knysna gold rush of the last century. If you are feeling daring, you can venture into a disused gold mine. Keen birders can look out for the Knysna loerie and the Narina trogon.

WHILE IN THE AREA

There are a number of day walks, also through indigenous forest. You can visit the Big Tree which, as its name suggests, is the biggest yet discovered in the area. There are horse trails, surfing, mountain biking and diving (see chapters 5, 8, 14 and 16). The Storms River offers excellent kloofing.

Sections of this trail have been done by paraplegics but with considerable assistance. Do not for one moment think this means it is an easy hike: on the contrary, it is quite strenuous. (The Forestry Department was rather shocked to receive a complaint that the long drop toilet at the third day hut was not wheelchair-friendly.) This is a year-round rainfall area so you should bring waterproof clothing at all times and the river crossings may be hazardous if they are running high. There is a minuscule chance that you may see an elephant. If you do, consider yourself extremely lucky as there are very few left in the area.

Booking is through the **Department of Water Affairs and Forestry**.

Mpumalanga gold rush trails

This whole area is a hiker's paradise and many other trails, such as the Blyde River and the Fanie Botha trails, are close by. If you are particularly interested in the gold rush era of South African history, see also the Outeniqua Trail, above.

PROSPECTOR'S TRAIL

This is a combination of two trails, which can be combined to make a trail of between two and five days. It centres on the museum town of Pilgrim's Rest which was a major gold mining centre earlier this century. The last mine closed down in the 1970s and the whole town was turned into a living museum. The accommodation includes forestry houses, log cabins and one night spent in the stables across the road from the historical Royal Hotel in Pilgrim's Rest. The emphasis is on the geological processes which produce alluvial gold, the historical events which took place there and the technology of alluvial gold mining. You can even do a little panning for gold, if you like, but don't count on getting enough to buy a pizza. You walk through Robber's Pass, which was the site of the last mail coach robbery in South Africa. The scenery is beautiful, typical of Mpumalanga. Booking is through the Sabie office of **SAFCOL.**

KAAPSCHEHOOP

Three two-day trails can be done separately or can be combined into one five-day trail. The accommodation is particularly interesting; one night is in a train coach and another in the village. You pass through places with connections to the gold mining era; names like Starvation Creek conjure up fascinating images of the hardships the early fortune hunters endured.

Booking is through the Sabie office of **SAFCOL**.

Desert and semidesert trails

Much of southern Africa is very dry. If you have never spent time in this fascinating environment before, don't fall into the trap of believing that deserts are long stretches of nothing. Desert scenery is among the most spectacular in the world. It is almost as if you can see the very bones of the earth in the exposed geological strata. The hardy plants and animals that have adapted to this harsh environment are fascinating. The desert also has a way of testing your mind and soul that softer environments do not.

KLIPSPRINGER TRAIL

Covering only 40 km over three days, this trail is quite difficult because of the rough terrain, the dryness and the high temperatures. The trail is closed from mid-October to the end of March because of the heat. You must carry more than enough water; on the first and third days there is none between the huts. The attractions of this trail are the Orange River, a long sinuous oasis; Augrabies Gorge, the largest granite gorge in the world; and the interesting plants, the most notable of which is the kokerboom or quiver tree (*Aloe dichotoma*). This is a huge tree aloe, reaching between three to five metres, sometimes as much as seven. On older trees, the branches rot from the inside and fall to the ground. These make excellent quivers for arrows, as the indigenous San discovered hundreds of years ago, hence the common name. They bear beautiful bright yellow flowers in winter.

Animals which may be seen include, not surprisingly, the dainty klipspringer which is usually seen perched on a high rock, springbok, kudu, baboons, and dassies by the score. You are sure to notice the interesting blue-headed lizards (*Agama atra*) sunning themselves on the rocks. Birders will not be disappointed with regular sightings of African fish eagles, Goliath herons, kingfishers, cormorants and hamerkops along the river and many species of cisticolas, larks and chats in the veld.

Booking is through the **National Parks Board**.

WHILE IN THE AREA

Spend some time at the falls, try the half-day white water rafting trip above the falls, consider riding a camel across the veld for two or five days or embarking on the four-day canoe trip below the falls (see chapters 6 and 16). The Parks Board offers the Augrabies three-in-one and the Black Rhino excursion (see under the Orange River entry in chapter 6 for details).

GRAAFF REINET TRAILS

The Karoo biome is often called semidesert as it consists of very low scrubby plants, many of which are succulents, there is very little standing water and the rainfall is low. The area is heavily farmed, but not without significant stress to the land, the animals that graze it and the farmers who struggle to make a living off it. Over the last few years many farmers in the region have realised the potential of their "unfarmable" land and are laying out hiking trails, biking trails and horse trails and turning old (often very beautiful) buildings into cosy and quaint hiking accommodation. There are a number of trails in the Graaff Reinet area. Two of the more interesting are the Excelsior and Nardouw trails. They are both two-day trails but can be done together to form one three- or four-day trail with hutted accommodation. There is also a "wilderness" trail on Nardouw; there are markers but no established paths so you have to blaze your own trail. There are no overnight facilities on this trail but you may camp. Not too distant are the Tandjiesberg and Toorberg hiking trails.

Booking for all the above is through **Jacana Country Homes and Trails**.

WHILE IN THE AREA

Visit The Owl House in the nearby town of Nieu Bethesda. It is a simple small-town house which was transformed into a glittering work of art by its late owner, Helen Martins. She sculpted people, owls, camels and other fabulous creatures, all covered in ground glass and with huge glass eyes. The house is open to the public. Her tragic and fascinating life story was the subject of an award-winning play, *The Road to Mecca*, by Athol Fugard, one of South Africa's best-known playwrights. It was made into a film with the same title.

RICHTERSVELD NATIONAL PARK

This park, on the southern bank of the Orange River, offers stark, dramatic scenery with a seemingly endless procession of bare hills that march on to the horizon, fascinating geological formations and myriad unique and hardy plants. One of the most interesting is the halfmens (*Pachypodium namaquanum*), a large, spiny-stemmed succulent (see entry on the Orange River in chapter 6). The laid out trail is 45 km long, but you can do variations. You may do this trail on your own but, unless you are a very experienced hiker, it is safer to do it with a guide as there is no water in some areas and the terrain is very difficult. In order to get to the start of the trail, you have to travel 350 km in a four-wheel-drive vehicle.

The park is administered by the **National Parks Board** which also handles booking. **Richtersveld Challenge** offer guided trips.

WHILE IN THE AREA

There is a very popular canoe trip down the Orange River in this area and a four-wheel-drive trail through the Richtersveld (see chapter 6 for information on both).

FISH RIVER CANYON TRAIL

This is a tough one; 86 km over five days through this remote canyon in the Namib Desert in southern Namibia. There are no facilities. The temperatures are very high during the day and very low at night. The terrain consists of thick sand and steep rocky sections. It follows the Fish River, which does not actually flow (not in the open season, anyway) but may have water in pools. In dry years you may have to carry sufficient water for a few days. The scenery is absolutely stunning, the canyon is the second largest in the world and the colour changes at sunrise and sunset have to be seen. If you buy a permit, you may fish so take along your rod and you may catch supper in one of the pools. There is a comfortable campsite at Hobas, about 10 km from the start, and a very pleasant campsite with chalets at Ai Ais, which marks the end of the trail. Ai Ais also has hot springs and a bar with a rack for backpacks outside — it's usually the first stop at the end of the hike. A day in the indoor spa should sort out any sore muscles after the long hike.

This trail is closed from the beginning of October to the end of April because of the intense heat and the danger of flash floods. The trail is linear and you need to organise your own transport to the start but it is usually not too difficult to arrange a lift for one of your party with a passing tourist.

Advance booking is absolutely essential; you must also provide a medical certificate dated no more than 40 days prior to the commencement of the hike. Booking is through the **Director of Tourism**, Windhoek, where you also book for the two campsites.

WHILE IN THE AREA

Both the start and end of the trail are fairly isolated with nothing but the rest camps. You may see game such as mountain zebra and gemsbok. At Ai Ais there is a bar, restaurant, indoor spa, outdoor pool, interesting day walks and good birding. It is a great place to relax.

UGAB RIVER TRAIL

At the southern extreme of the harsh and inhospitable Skeleton Coast of Namibia, this trail follows the Ugab River for 50 km. It is a guided, self-catered trail and leaves on the second and fourth Tuesday of each month between April and October. Booking is through the **Director of Tourism**, Windhoek.

WHILE IN THE AREA

The day walk in the Uniab Delta is well worth doing; the contrast of this wetland with the surrounding desert is marked. Green reeds and waterbirds abound. This coast is very popular with anglers and the nearby campsite at Mile 108 is used almost exclusively by devotees of this pastime.

NAMIB-NAUKLUFT TRAIL

This tough, circular, self-guided 120 km hike in the Namib-Naukluft Park in southern Namibia is done over eight days but you can do a shorter trail over four days. Conveniently for the less fit, the steeper sections are in the last four days. This area is transitional between scrub savanna and true desert. The mountains hide deep kloofs, some with perennial springs which feed streams and deep pools and support small pockets of kloof forest. Game is plentiful but not that easy to see. Mountain zebra, kudu, gemsbok and klipspringer abound. Leopards are quite plentiful but you are unlikely to actually see one.

The trail is open from the beginning of March to the third Friday in October. All hikes must commence on the Tuesdays, Thursdays and Saturdays of the first three weeks of each month. Booking is essential and is through the **Director of Tourism**. You need to produce a medical certificate dated not more than 40 days prior to the commencement of the trail.

WHILE IN THE AREA

The Naukluft 4X4 overnight trail is a very tough test of vehicle and driver; booking is also through the Director of Tourism. You may drive off (in an ordinary two-wheel drive) into the Namib to see the moon landscape, a large flat area with eerie lunar rocks sticking up out of the shingly ground, or the Welwitschia Flats. This area boasts hundreds of specimens of this incredible plant, *Welwitschia mirabilis*. All that is visible are two huge, scruffy, tangled leaves and the top of a thick trunk. It is actually a huge tree but it has adapted to the intense heat and dryness by staying underground. It is the only member of the Welwitschia family and most of the medium-sized specimens have been dated to between 500 and 600 years old. The bigger ones may be about 2 000 years old. The male and female plants are separate and their "flowers" are midway between true flowers and cones, identifying this unique plant as being transitional between the gymnosperms (the cone-bearing plants such as cycads and pine trees) and angiosperms (the true flowering plants). Reit Safari (see chapter 16), runs a four-day horse trail in the nearby Namib Rand Nature Reserve and their Namib Desert Trail ends in Swakopmund, which is not too distant. See also chapter 11 for balloon trips and other attractions.

Kloofs

These are deep river gorges and, particularly in the Cape, have become a favourite venue for the relatively new sport of "kloofing". An essential part of kloofing is that you get wet and spend at least some of the time in the river. Most kloofs also involve a "point of no return" at some stage. This activity is restricted to summer as in winter hypothermia can set in quite quickly. Kloofing is great fun but it does have some inherent risks. If it is late in the season, the day is not particularly warm or the water is very cold, take a wetsuit.

SUICIDE GORGE

This is the classic Cape kloofing trail. It leaves from the forestry station at Grabouw and follows the Riviersonderend River for 18 km. It involves a number of jumps over waterfalls into deep pools. The highest compulsory jump is between 7 and 10 m (depending on how intrepid you are feeling at the time). You can choose to jump from about 15 m in some places.

Once in the pool, there is usually a swim of moderate length. The water is the colour of cola, this is typical of streams originating in areas of Table Mountain Sandstone.

It is not advisable to take flotation devices on this trail and non-swimmers are strongly advised to try something else. This trail involves a point of no return; once you have committed yourself you have to continue or take a long hike around. This trail is only open in summer and can be very cold towards the end of the season.

Booking is through **Cape Nature Conservation** who prefer it if at least one member of the party has done the trip before. **Day Trippers** offer escorted hikes down Suicide Gorge and Riviersonderend Gorge.

RIVIERSONDEREND GORGE

Lower down on the same river, this trip is shorter, about 12 km, and, if you like, easier. You can walk around all the jumps if they make you nervous, but if you feel like a bit of an adrenalin rush, you can do some very high jumps indeed which makes this a great choice for a party of people with varying fear threshholds. This trail is only open in summer and can be very cold towards the end of the season.

Booking is through **Cape Nature Conservation**, who prefer it if at least one member of the party has done the trip before. **Day Trippers** offer escorted hikes for those who prefer the assistance of a guide.

STEENBRAS RIVER (KAMIKAZE CANYON)

This is not strictly a kloofing trail but would be a good introduction to the concept. The trail starts near the mouth, on the R44 between Gordon's Bay and Pringle Bay (opposite the Sunbird Bed and Breakfast). It is a short walk to three deep pools and a spectacular waterfall. There are no compulsory jumps but there are many optional ones ranging from three metres to about 30 metres. Permits are essential and can be obtained from the **Cape Town City Council, Director of Parks and Forests**.

If you would like to try kloofing but are somewhat nervous, you may want to do this as an escorted trip. **Abseil Africa** offer guided walks; they will show you the best spots to jump and also offer an optional abseil down the 60 metre waterfall. This is a pleasant day's outing which includes lunch and refreshments.

WHILE IN THE AREA

See chapters 5, 6, 8, 9, 14 and 15 for the Palmiet River trip, nearby diving, Stellenbosch cycle trail, Betty's Bay paragliding, nearby surfing and Wine Valley Horse Trails. There are other day walks in the mountains and there is a picnic site at the start. The Enchanted River is downstream on the same river and the start, in the picturesque village of Greyton, is a short drive away (see chapter 6).

STORMS RIVER TUBE TRAIL

This is a one-day trip from the bridge on the old Cape Town road to the mouth of the Storms River in the Tsitsikamma National Park. It is not an easy trail. Most people take a tube along but a lilo would be just as good or even better as it is slightly more dirigible. You spend long periods in the water so a wetsuit is strongly recommended and, unless it is a particularly hot day, you will not be allowed to do the trail without one. Long shallow stretches are interspersed with deep pools and rapids. Don't go down the rapids on your tube unless you really know how to read a river and, having scouted it, know it to be safe. A tube is quite impossible to steer and you could end up in serious difficulty so rather walk around the rapids. The scenery is spectacular and there is a beautiful, deep canyon near the end. Take care at the end of the trip as, depending on river height and tide, the mouth can be dangerous. It is preferable to get out at the steps upstream of the bridge.

Booking is through the **State Forester**, Tsitsikamma. You can do an escorted trail with **Aloe Afrika Tours and Trails** or **Blackwater Tubing**.

WHILE IN THE AREA

The Tsitsikamma National Park is worth exploring on foot. There is good fishing, a snorkel trail, the Otter Trail starts here and there is good mountain biking not too far away (see chapter 8). See also chapters 5, 13 and 14 for further information about diving, surfing and bridge and bungi jumping along the Garden Route.

MAGALIESBERG

There are a number of interesting hikes in this lovely area and some nice kloofs. Most of the mountain is privately owned and access is through the **Mountain Club of SA**. You can enquire about the location of the kloofs when you get your permit.

SUIKERBOSCHFONTEIN

This is a two-day hiking trail near Carolina in Mpumalanga and is not strictly a kloofing trip. It would be a good introduction to the concept, though, as there is a lovely river with waterfalls and pools and you do follow the stream for a while. There are areas where you can jump in and swim along the pools, as you would on a real kloofing trip, but none of the jumps or swims is compulsory. There is comfortable accommodation in an old farmhouse and a hiking hut.

Booking is through **Jacana Country Homes and Trails**.

Listings

BOOKING AUTHORITIES AND OPERATORS

Abseil Africa, +27 21 25-4332, do the one-day Kamikaze Canyon trip on the Steenbras River.

Aloe Afrika Tours and Trails, +27 423 93-2313, offer guided trips down the Storms River.

Blackwater Tubing (Storms River Adventures), +27 42 541-1609, take escorted trips on the Storms River.

Cape Nature Conservation, Private Bag X1, Uniedal 7612, South Africa; tel: +27 21 886-5858, fax: +27 21 886-6575, take bookings for the Palmiet Trail for the visually impaired, the Hottentots Holland Trail, Suicide Gorge and Riviersonderend Gorge.

Cape Nature Conservation (Citrusdal), tel: +27 22 921-2289, fax: +27 22 921-3219, take bookings for the Cedarberg Wilderness Area.

Cape Nature Conservation (Oudtshoorn), tel: +27 443 29-1739, take bookings for the Swartberg Trail.

Cape Provincial Administration, P O Box 26, Porterville 6810, South Africa; tel: +27 2633 2900/7, fax +27 2633 2913, take bookings for the Groot Winterhoek Wilderness Area.

Cape Town City Council, Director of Parks and Forests, 12th Floor, Civic Centre, Cape Town 8000; tel: +27 21 400-3269, issue permits for the Steenbras River Trail.

Chimanimani National Park, Private Bag 2063, Chimanimani, Zimbabwe, take bookings for the trails in the park.

Day Trippers, +27 21 531-3274, take escorted trips down Suicide Gorge and Riviersonderend Gorge.

Department of Environmental Affairs and Tourism, P O Box 217, Pietersburg 0700, South Africa; tel: +27 152 295-3025, fax: +27 152 295-2165, take bookings for the Modjaji Cycad Forest.

Department of Water Affairs and Forestry, Private Bag X12, Knysna 6570, South Africa; tel: +27 445 82-5466, fax: +27 445 82-5461, take bookings for the Outeniqua Trail.

Disabled Adventurers, c/o Carol Schafer, Sports Science Institute, University of Cape Town, P O Box 2593, Clareinch 7740, South Africa; tel: +27 21 686-7330, ext 297, have a database of accessible adventures.

Eastern Cape Nature Conservation (East London), tel: +27 431 41-2212, take bookings for the Strandloper Trail.

Eastern Cape Tourism Board, P O Box 186, Bisho 5608, South Africa; tel: +27 401 95-2115, take bookings for the Wild Coast Trail.

Eco-Access, P O Box 1377, Roosevelt Park 2129, South Africa; tel: +27 11 673-4533, fax: +27 11 673-6297, have listings of venues which are accessible to people with varying types and degrees of disability.

Frasers Semongkong Lodge, P O Box 243, Ficksburg 9730, South Africa, tel: +27 5192 2730, can give directions to a number of hikes and day walks near their lodge in Lesotho.

The Hiking Federation, tel: +27 11 886-6524, has information on hiking clubs all over the region.

Jacana Country Homes and Trails, P O Box 95212, Waterkloof 0145, South Africa; tel: +27 12 346-3550/2, fax: +27 12 346 2499, takes bookings for the Suikerboschfontein Trail and the Graaff Reinet trails.

Keiskamma Ecotourism Network, 9 Chamberlain St, King William's Town 5600, South Africa; tel: +27 433 2-2571, administers the Amatola Trail.

KwaZulu-Natal Department of Nature Conservation, Private Bag X9024, Pietermaritzburg 3200, South Africa; tel: +27 331 94-6696, fax: +27 331 42-1948, take bookings for the Kosi Bay Trail.

The Leading Edge, tel: +27 21 797-3386, offer hiking training and will escort groups on hikes.

Malolotja Nature Reserve, P O Box 1797, Mbabane, Swaziland; tel: +268 4-3060, take bookings for the Malolotja trails in Swaziland.

Malealea Lodge, P O Box 119, Wepener 944, South Africa; tel/fax: +27 51 47-3200 or +27 51 448-3001, cell: +27 82 552-4215, e-mail: malealea@.dixie.co.za, can give directions to a number of hikes and day walks near their lodge in Lesotho, as well as offering guided hikes.

Mountain Club of SA, 97 Hatfield St, Gardens 8001, Cape Town; tel: +27 21 45-3412.

Mountain Club of SA, Transvaal section, P O Box 1641, Houghton 2041, South Africa; tel: +27 11 786-8367.

Mpumalanga Parks Board, P O Box 1990, Nelspruit 1200, South Africa, tel: +27 13 758-1035, fax: +27 13 759-4000, extension 4151, administer the Blyderivierspoort Nature Reserve and the short trail in the park for disabled people.

Natal Parks Board, P O Box 662, Pietermaritzburg 3200, South Africa; tel: +27 331 47-1981, fax: +27 331 47-1980, take bookings for the Mziki Trail and the Drakensberg Wilderness Area.

Nature Conservation and Environment, Private Bag X102, Haenertsberg 0730; tel: +27 15272 ask for 1303, take bookings for the Wolkberg network of trails.

National Parks Board, P O Box 7400, Roggebaai 8012, Cape Town; tel: +27 21 22-2810, fax: +27 21 24-6211, take bookings for the Otter Trail, the Klipspringer Trail and the Richtersveld Trail.

Orca Industries, tel: +27 21 61-9673, will do escorted hikes for groups.

Richtersveld Challenge, P O Box 142, Springbok 8240, South Africa; tel: +27 251 2-1905, fax: +27 251 8-1460, do escorted hikes on the Richtersveld Trail.

SAFCOL Head Office, (Ecotourism) tel: +27 12 804-1230, fax: +27 12 804-5103, can be contacted for information on all of their trails.

SAFCOL, Private Bag X537, Humansdorp 6300, South Africa; tel: +27 423 91-0393, fax: +27 423 5-2745, take bookings for the Hogsback Trail.

SAFCOL, Private Bag X503, Sabie 1260, South Africa; tel: +27 13 764-1015, take bookings for the Prospector's Trail, the Kaapschehoop Trail and the Magoebaskloof trails.

Sandton Municipality, tel: +27 11 803-9132/3, administer the walk along the Jukskei River.

Sanga Outdoor, tel: +27 11 339-3374, will do escorted hikes for groups.

Sani Top Mountaineers Chalet, tel: +27 33 701-1466 or +27 33 702-1069 (after hours), can give directions to a number of hikes and day walks near their lodge at the top of Sani Pass in Lesotho.

The State Forester, Tsitsikamma, Private Bag X530, Humansdorp 6300, South Africa; tel: +27 42 541-1557, fax: +27 42 541-1558, takes bookings for the Storms River Kloofing Trail.

The Trading Post Guest House, P O Box 64 Maseru, Lesotho; tel: +266 34-0203 (office hours) or +266 34-0267 (after hours), can give directions to a number of hikes and day walks near their lodge at Roma in Lesotho.

RETAIL OUTLETS

Cape Union Mart, tel: +27 21 457-611 (head office) sells and manufactures a wide range of hiking equipment. Cape Town branches are in Corporation St, Cape Town, the V&A Waterfront, Tyger Valley Centre, the Sun Gallery, Somerset West Mall, Cavendish Square, Claremont and the Blue Route Centre. In Johannesburg there are branches in Hyde Park Centre, Eastgate, Fourways Mall and Sandton City.

Replay Sports, 22a Long St, Cape Town, tel: +27 21 25-1056, buy, sell and rent new and second-hand camping and hiking equipment.

ACCOMMODATION

Most hiking trails have accommodation at the beginning and end of the trail. Those listed below are the exceptions.

Chimanimani

Base Camp is quite far from anywhere, so if you want to spend a day or two in Chimanimani town, try the Chimanimani Hotel or Heaven Lodge, a friendly backpackers' hostel which also offers camping.

Hogsback

Hogsback Holiday Cottages, P O Hogsback 5721; tel: +27 45 962-1045, and the Edge, P O Box 18, Hogsback 5721; tel: +27 45 962-1159, offer self-catering cottages for rent.

FURTHER READING

Hiking Trails of Southern Africa by W and S Olivier; Southern Book Publishers, Halfway House, 1995, describes 44 hikes in detail and lists others in the various regions.

The Complete Guide to Walks and Trails in Southern Africa by Jaynee Levy; Struik, Cape Town, 1993, gives a good outline of hundreds of walks and trails in the region.

A Backpacker's Guide to Lesotho by Russel Suchet; Russel Suchet, Himeville, South Africa 1994, outlines some suggested hiking trails in this mountainous country. It is obtainable from Sani Lodge or most backpackers' hostels.

Drakensberg Walks: 120 Graded Hikes and Trails in the Berg by David Bristow; Struik, Cape Town, 1988.

Garden Route Walks by Colin Paterson-Jones; Struik, Cape Town, 1992.

Table Mountain Walks by Colin Paterson-Jones; Struik, Cape Town, 1991.

Walks and Hikes by Andre de la Harpe and Leon Hugo; Queillerie, Cape Town, 1996.

CHAPTER 8

Free wheeling

Mountain biking, bikepacking and cycle tours

There are a number of ways of enjoying a cycling adventure. You could just do a gentle ride through some lovely scenery, join a supported multi-day trip, head off on a major excursion with all your worldly goods on your bike, or do some serious downhill mountain biking. There are a number of mountain biking events on offer throughout the year, including novice skills clinics, club social rides, ECO (Environmentally Concerned Offroaders) outrides, away weekends, social tours, night riding, the national and provincial championship race series (always in the first half of the year) and the classic mountain biking (MTB) events (always in the second half of the year). Although the leaders of the many races take them very seriously, most people join in just for the fun, exercise and camaraderie.

If you are keen on mountain biking you will be pleased to hear that there are a number of dedicated off-road cycling routes with more opening up at regular intervals. These are administered by various organisations but the biggest players are private landowners, the parks boards, local publicity associations and the forestry companies.

There are a few companies running escorted cycling trips in the region but the industry is in its infancy. You will find, therefore, that they do not have neatly laid out schedules with trips organised for the whole year as, for example, the river industry does. They will usually stick to a couple of tried and tested day routes and one or two longer trips throughout the year. Almost all will happily tailor-make a trip for a reasonably sized group, say a minimum of six cyclists. You can also find information on tours in local specialist bicycle shops.

Getting started

If you intend joining a supported cycle trail then you won't need much more experience than you gained cycling to school all those years ago. If, however, you fancy doing serious distances or heading off road, you should try to pick up some extra knowledge and skills. You can also join a short escorted trip; you will probably find it a lot easier than you thought, although many adults who take up mountain biking have to relearn the whole game.

For advice and training clinics, you can contact a local club, AST (Adventure Sports Trading) or AFTRAC (African MTB Training Racing Adventure Company). There are clubs in most big cities and some casual groups that ride together on weekends. Many of these advertise in specialist bike shops, cycling magazines or the local paper. Most also have informative newsletters, so try to get onto a mailing list.

Equipment

You need a bicycle, obviously, although you can hire one if you are just doing a trip to try out the sport or if you have travelled from afar. Think long and hard before you part with your hard-earned cash, though; bicycles are expensive. If you are going to spend 350 days a year cycling around town on tarred roads and two weeks on holiday, you may be better off buying a road bike. You can, of course, use a mountain bike quite happily on roads, especially if you get slick tyres.

Road bikes are usually lightly built, have thin wheels and are geared for speed. This means they will be easy to pedal fast on tarred roads but will need a little extra push up hills. They don't take kindly to being loaded up with panniers and the thin tyres make riding on uneven surfaces difficult. Mountain bikes, on the other hand, are generally stronger, although still reasonably light, and have much fatter wheels. They usually have knobbly tyres, although they can be fitted with slicks for tarred roads. Their gearing is designed to enable you to climb up very steep slopes so they are not particularly speedy on the flat, and the extra width of the tyre creates significant friction, also slowing you down. Hybrid, or touring bikes, are a compromise. The frame is somewhere between a mountain and a road bike, as are the wheels, and the gearing allows for faster general riding while still allowing for some climb. Obviously they are not as good on tar as a road bike, nor as good off road as a mountain bike, but they are great if you want to do moderate distances on tar and reasonably good gravel roads.

You will find, when shopping around, that you can spend an awful lot on a bike. Unless you are very wealthy, it is more sensible to buy a mid-range bike, e.g. one with a chrome-moly frame and reasonable components, and then upgrade it as your expertise and finances warrant. To put it bluntly, a beginner on a super hot-shot bike is still a beginner — albeit one with a lighter wallet. If you are buying a mountain bike, though, and can afford front shocks — go for it. They're worth the expense.

Women new to cycling often wonder why bicycle saddles are so uncomfortable. The answer is: they're designed for men! So when you buy a bike, insist on a gel-filled, "ladies style" saddle. You won't believe the difference.

You will need a water bottle which fits onto the frame, a pump, puncture kit and spare tube, and you will almost certainly want to carry other items on your bike, such as snacks and a camera. A moonbag is ideal for snacks, sunscreen and other small items, as are handlebar-mounted bags, but they can be damaged by long offroad stretches, especially if they are overloaded. If you want to really load up, though, you will need rear-mounted panniers. If you have a lot of luggage, you can fit front-mounted panniers as well but they tend to interfere with the steering and balance more than rear-mounted ones.

With regard to clothing, you can obviously cycle in anything but you will find padded cycling shorts virtually indispensable as they add greatly to your comfort. Jeans are the worst possible choice for long distances. Men's and women's cycling shorts are very different, so make sure you buy the appropriate style or you will find the padding in the wrong place. Gloves are useful, especially for long downhills, as cycling gloves are padded to take some of the pounding your hands receive. A cycling helmet is highly recommended and you will probably not be allowed on organised rides without one. If you are not going for specialised cycling footwear and pedals, you will find hiking boots fine for cycling. Although some people do complain of foot cramps when cycling in more flexible shoes such as running shoes, most people find them fine.

Women who have never ridden off road before will discover very quickly that a good sports bra is essential.

Options for people with disabilities

A team of handicapped riders from Logwood has entered the Argus Cycle Tour on funds generated by the Logwood Ranch Fat Tyre Weekend. Tandem riding is a good option for blind people, and you can even get tandem mountain bikes.

Regular events

The Grundig SA National Championship Series consists of four events which take place between April and June in order to choose a team to represent South Africa at the world championships in September. These events are not recommended for novices but there are usually related fun events such as dual slalom, observed trials and fun rides. For further information contact **SAMBA** (South African Mountain Bike Association) **AFTRAC** or **AST**.

Logwood Ranch Fat Tyre Fun Weekend, a fundraising event for Sunfield Homes for the Mentally Handicapped at Logwood Ranch, usually takes place in March. It is a full weekend of off-road riding, including a skills clinic and fun ride by AFTRAC on the Saturday and on the Sunday, a 60 km challenge and a 30 km social ride. For further information contact **AFTRAC** or **Logwood Ranch**.

The Natal Parks Board Conservation Trust Challenge, sponsored by Land Rover SA, is an 80 km test of endurance in the Giant's Castle Reserve in the central Drakensberg. Entries are limited to 200 riders, and each rider has to obtain R100 or more sponsorship (in addition to the entrance fee) to donate to the trust. The event will be used as a platform for the development of off-road cycling in the Drakensberg. For more information contact **AST** or **AFTRAC**.

The Karkloof Classic is organised by the **Karkloof Conservancy** near Howick in KwaZulu-Natal in May. It is an endurance challenge of 65 km with a fun ride of 30 km. For more information contact the organisers, **AST** or **AFTRAC**.

The Duiwelskloof Festival is an annual event in the Northern Province town of Tzaneen. Local cycling enthusiasts have organised a cross country lap race and a social ECO ride on a separate course on the Saturday. The highlight is the 19 km Debengeni Downhill on the Sunday, often followed by a swim in the Debengeni Falls. For more information contact **AST** or **AFTRAC**.

The Knysna Oyster Festival Fat Tyre Week is part of the Knysna Oyster Festival in July. This is a whole week of off-road heaven, starting with a one-day cross country tour on the first Saturday, a downhill competition the next day and a 24-hour team night race the next weekend. The weekdays in between can be spent sampling the beautiful MTB trails in the vicinity (or the oysters or the local beer). For more information contact **Knysna Cycle Works**, **AST** or **AFTRAC**.

The Koranna Two Mountains Challenge, see entry later in this chapter, is a tough, hilly single-track race of 60 km with a tricky 6 km downhill to the finish line. It is not for wimps. There is also a 30 km social ride. For more details contact **Marquard Cherry Trails**, **AST** or **AFTRAC**.

The RMBC (Rockhoppers MTB Club) 24 Hour Team Night Race takes place in September in the Readymix Quarry in Honeydew, Gauteng. This is a severe test of enthusiasm, as the action takes place all day and night. For more information contact **Rockhoppers MTB Club**, **AST** or **AFTRAC**.

The Citrusdal Fat Tyre Festival in September is an enormously popular event, possibly due in part to the amazing wild flowers which carpet the landscape in spring and the ever-present scent of orange blossom. For more information phone **Citrusdal Publicity Organisation**, **AST** or **AFTRAC**.

The Platberg Challenge is a 50 km race which climbs up from the small town of Harrismith to the Platberg Nature Reserve. It takes place at the same time as the Platberg Marathon, a running race. For more information contact **Harrismith Publicity Association**, **AST** or **AFTRAC**.

The Norwich Life Rhodes 84,5 km MTB Challenge, in October, is the most prestigious MTB event in South Africa. The course starts in the historic village of Rhodes in the Eastern Cape and climbs to an altitude of about 2 700 m. Even though the event takes place in summer it has been known to snow. The latter part of the course goes past South Africa's only ski resort, Tiffindel, on the Lesotho border. For further details contact **Rhodes MTB Club**, **AST** or **AFTRAC**.

The Hilton Classic is the oldest MTB race in southern Africa and is organised by the Hilton MTB Club. Tradition dictates that no competitor is allowed to see the 25 km course. There is also a dual eliminator downhill challenge on the same weekend. For more information contact **Hilton MTB Club**, **AST** or **AFTRAC**.

To Hell and Back is a two-day tour into the isolated valley called "Die Hel", one day in and one day out. This is limited to 100 riders only and all funds generated are paid into the Gamka Mountain Trust and utilised for the conservation of Die Hel. For further information contact **Paul Zink**, **AST** or **AFTRAC**.

The Pilgrim's Rest Classic is a great favourite with local riders, possibly because the cross country course goes through a 100-year-old pub. It is a lap course made difficult by the merciless sun (hence the detour through the pub). There is an ECO challenge the next day. The whole town of Pilgrim's Rest is a national monument (see the Prospector's Trail in chapter 7). For more information contact the **Pretoria MTB Club**, **AST** or **AFTRAC**.

Western Cape

This is a fairly bike-friendly place (as long as you stay off the roads, that is) and there are a number of specially laid out mountain bike trails.

CAPE POINT CYCLE TOUR

Downhill Bicycle Tours do an escorted cycling trip from the reserve gate to Cape Point and then back to Boulders Beach, where you may watch the penguins. Lunch is at the scenic restaurant at the point and is for your own account. **Bikeabout** also offers a trip through the reserve.

SILVERMINE SOUTH, FISH HOEK

This marked 5 km circular route in the Silvermine Nature Reserve is ideal for novices and family groups. There are interesting rock formations and flora, characteristic of the area. There is a charge for access at the gate on the Ou Kaapse Weg road. For further information contact **WPPA.**

WHILE IN THE AREA

Jaggers Walk is a gently curving paved path along the rockpools all around the south side of Fish Hoek Bay from which, in winter or spring, you may see southern right whales. The nearby towns of Simon's Town and Kalk Bay have interesting craft and antique shops and quaint restaurants. See chapters 5 and 14 for the excellent diving and surfing in the area.

TOKAI FOREST

This is a fun network of trails, offering a fairly long but reasonably easy climb on gravel roads to the top of the Constantiaberg and long downhills. It is administered by **SAFCOL** and you can buy the necessary permit at the gate behind the Tokai Manor House. **Bikeabout** does escorted day trips. You can also buy a permit for a year from the forestry office.

CONSTANTIA WINE ROUTE

Constantia was the original wine-growing region of the Cape. This is a gentle trip through the beautiful farmlands and vineyards. Wine tasting is on offer, but remember, you have to ride your bike afterwards. This trip is offered by **Downhill Bicycle Tours.**

TABLE MOUNTAIN DOUBLE DESCENT

This is an escorted day trip on two of the better jeep track and single track routes from Tafelberg Rd into the city. There is (of necessity) a short uphill slog between the descents, but it is on tar and not too strenuous. The trip is run by **Downhill Bicycle Tours**.

WHILE IN THE AREA

Investigate the local cuisine. Cape Manna, 34 Napier St, Bo Kaap, offers authentic Cape Malay curries, as does Biesmiellah and Africa Cafe in Lower Main Road, Observatory, was the first African restaurant in South Africa. Or take a picnic lunch to one of the beaches on the western side of the peninsula and watch the sunset. There is a whole lot more to do as well (see the Cape Town entries in chapters 5, 9, 15, 16, 17 and 18).

JONKERSHOEK NATURE RESERVE

This has been the scene of two national championships and has been proposed as the venue for Africa's first MTB world cup. It is very scenic, surrounded by towering mountains, and there are many challenging climbs and descents through commercial pine forests on forestry roads and jeep tracks. There are some mountain streams to cool off in, which are usually very welcome as it can get very hot in summer. You must buy a permit at the gate, or you can buy a permit for a year from the forestry office.

The reserve is administered by **SAFCOL**. Contact **WPPA** or **Village Cycles** for further information.

VILLAGE SPILLAGE WINE ROUTE BICYCLE TOURS

Although cycling and alcohol are a rather volatile mixture, there is a selection of tasting trips on offer through the wine-growing region of Stellenbosch. Remember, you're only supposed to taste the wine and then spit it out or you may have trouble staying upright. They will also organise picnics, lunches or dinners for a group of two or more.

WHILE IN THE AREA

There is a network of day walks in the Jonkershoek reserve and there are many wineries in Stellenbosch which you may also visit without a bicycle. You can even do the wine route on horseback (see chapter 16), or you may like to try a parachute jump (see chapter 12).

GRABOUW

There is a wide range of options here, ranging from easy to extremely challenging, with some mind-boggling downhills. Permits are essential and are available at the gate. You can buy a permit for a year at the forestry office. **Bikeabout** do one- or two-day escorted trips here on request.

WHILE IN THE AREA

See chapter 7 for information on Suicide Gorge and the Riviersonderend Gorge, which offer exhilarating kloofing in summer. You are within an hour's drive of Cape Town, so there is no lack of exciting options.

THE ENGEN DE HOOP MOUNTAIN BIKE TRAILS

De Hoop Nature Reserve is home to a huge diversity of flowering plants, has some spectacular coastal scenery and large herds of bontebok as well as eland, grey rhebok, zebras and many other smaller terrestrial mammals. The surrounding ocean is a marine reserve and in winter and spring is home to numerous migrating southern right whales. The cycle trails were laid out, and special accommodation built, with the assistance of Engen. The Cupidoskraal hut is used as an overnight base from which all trails are undertaken as day excursions. There are five separate trails in all and it is quite easy to do more than one per day. It is possible, in fact advisable, to combine one or two trips in one outing. Take swimming costumes and snorkelling gear as there are lovely tidal pools, especially at Stilgat and Noetzie. Cupidoskraal hut can accommodate 12 cyclists and has room for storing bicycles. To book, write to The Manager, **De Hoop Nature Reserve**; you will receive a detailed map of the trails when you book.

WHILE IN THE AREA

There are wonderful hikes in the reserve and the Breede River is not too far away (see chapter 6 for river trips below Swellendam). The nearby town of Bredasdorp has an interesting museum, concentrating on shipwrecks and artifacts salvaged from wrecks. The town of Caledon, also nearby, has hot springs and a wild flower garden which is, not surprisingly, at its best in spring.

GROOTVADERSBOSCH CONSERVANCY

Starting and finishing at Honeywood Farm, there are a number of trails across the 12 farms that make up this conservancy. There are a few portages over stiles and some steep uphills. Wonderful downhills with beautiful views of the Overberg and the evocative smell of Cape fynbos make all the hard pedalling worthwhile. There is a 6 km trail which you can book through the Grootvadersbosch Reserve. To do any of the longer trails you must buy a permit from **Honeywood Farm**. **Bikeabout** will do three-day escorted trails here on request. **Paul Zink** is a SATOUR-registered cycle guide with an extensive knowledge of this trail and the whole area around Swellendam.

WHILE IN THE AREA

After a long day's cycle head off to **Warmwaterberg**, near Barrydale, where you can soak your weary muscles in glorious hot spring water. There is a camping site and self-catering chalets.

HOMTINI CYCLE ROUTE

This is a superbly well marked out 19 km circular route. It begins and ends at the Krisjan se Nek picnic site, which offers shady parking and water. The trail consists of one steep 4 km climb, some pleasant single-track descents and some easy cycling through plantations. The view from the top of Portland Heights is spectacular and on a clear day you can see the Knysna Heads in the distance. The route crosses a number of streams where you can have a drink and a swim and also passes through extensive stretches of indigenous forest.

The trail is administered by the **Department of Water Affairs and Forestry**, and booking is not necessary but you must buy a permit and carry it with you at all times on the trail. You can buy permits at the boom at the entry to the Goudveld State Forest. In off-season entry is free and there is no one at the boom, but it is advisable to sign in.

PETRUS SE BRAND CYCLE ROUTE

This is a 25 km linear route between Diepwalle Forest Station and the Garden of Eden in the Knysna district. If you start at Diepwalle, you will have more downhill and less uphill than if you do the northbound route. You may do the trail in either direction and, although the route markers are designed for those riding south, they are visible from both sides. The trail goes through indigenous forest with ancient yellowwoods festooned with Old Man's Beard, crosses a few streams where you can swim and replenish your water bottle, and traverses an "island" of fynbos. The contrast between the bright sunny fynbos and the deep, dark, mysterious forest is quite marked. There are some relaxing level sections, a steepish climb or two and some nice single-track downhill runs. The last stretch before the Garden of Eden (about 6 km) is one of the most beautiful and entertaining sections of single-track you are ever likely to cycle.

The trail is administered by the **Department of Water Affairs and Forestry**, and booking is not necessary but you must buy a permit and carry it with you at all times on the trail. If you are starting from Diepwalle, you can buy your permit from the Diepwalle Forest Station (open 7.30 am to 1 pm, and 1.30 to 4 pm). If you are riding in the opposite direction, you can get your permit from the kiosk at the Garden of Eden.

HARKERVILLE CYCLE ROUTES

There are three cycle routes which weave in and out of the Harkerville hiking route. All three are circular and start and finish at the Garden of Eden on the N2. The Red Route is the longest and most scenically varied. The trail follows old tracks through the forest and, as a total contrast, traverses the high fynbos near the cliff line, affording wide open vistas of sea and fynbos. It is 22 km long. The Blue Route is the shortest, at 12 km, and traverses some indigenous forest and a mature glade of alien redwoods *(Sequoia sempervirens)* which may make visitors from North America feel at home. At 15 km the Green Route is a little longer, also traverses indigenous forest and offers a lovely view of the rugged coast from a spectacular viewpoint about midway along the trail.

The trails are administered by the **Department of Water Affairs and Forestry**, and booking is not necessary but you must buy a permit and carry it with you at all times on the trail. You can buy these at the Garden of Eden (open 8 am to 5 pm) or, in holiday periods, at Kranshoek Gate.

WHILE IN THE AREA

You could explore the coffee shops of Plett and Knysna, go to the angling museum in Knysna or visit Millwood, a reconstructed house from the gold rush era. There is also excellent diving off Plett and Knysna, horse trails are run by Equitrailing from just outside Plett and there are extensive hiking opportunities (see chapters 5, 7 and 16).

STORMS RIVER CYCLE ROUTE

This scenic 22 km circular route starts and ends at the police station in Storms River village (which should be a safe place to leave your car). It follows the old Storms River Pass through beautiful indigenous forest and pine and gum plantations. (This was the national road until the early 1960's.) The turning point is just above the Storms River Mouth, affording breathtaking views of the rugged coastline.

The trail is administered by the **Department of Water Affairs and Forestry**. You don't need to book and the trail is free. Please use the self-issue permit system at the gate and fill in your details in the register.

TSITSIKAMMA FOREST CIRCLES

This is a new development which, at the time of writing, was nearing completion. There are four or five trails which traverse plantation, indigenous forest and a working dairy farm.

A semi-circle of attractive, simple but comfortable self-catering chalets overlooks a beautiful pool in the Elands River. All trails lead from the cabins and non-cyclists may do day walks, including one down a steep coastal path to a small beach. The trails will be well marked and are self-guided. Contact **Tsitsikamma Forest Circles** for booking, or if you would like to do an escorted trip, contact **Outeniqua Biking Trails** in Knysna.

WHILE IN THE AREA

The Tsitsikamma National Park is well worth a visit. There are a number of short day walks in the forest and, if you are very quiet and lucky, you may see a Knysna loerie, one of the most beautiful birds of the region. There is a marked snorkel trail and a scuba trail at the mouth of the Storms River, in the national park. (There is no equipment for hire, though, and they do not fill cylinders.) The fishing is also very good.

OTHER GARDEN ROUTE CYCLE TRAILS

There are a number of other trails in this very popular area. For information on these contact the **Garden Route Regional Tourist Information Centre**.

BEAVERLAC

Bordering on the southern end of the Cedarberg, the Groot Winterhoek Mountains are every bit as spectacular, if lesser known. There are no dedicated trails, but there are some excellent jeep tracks on the farm **Beaverlac**, which welcomes mountain bikers. The farm is on top of the Dasklip Pass, between Piketberg and Porterville, off the N7. There is a shady campsite and a farmhouse which can be used by large groups. They also have small basic huts. Catering can be arranged in advance.

WHILE IN THE AREA

Beaverlac offers excellent day walks, good climbing and some lovely rock-pools and waterfalls for gentle relaxation. There is a paragliding and hang-gliding launch ramp on nearby Dasklip Pass (see chapter 9) and the Groot Winterhoek Reserve offers excellent hiking (see chapter 7).

CITRUSDAL/CEDARBERG

Citrusdal is set in a beautiful valley on the banks of the Olifants River. In spring, the scent of orange blossom is everywhere and wildflowers abound between the citrus groves and on the surrounding mountains. It is also the southernmost limit of the glorious Cedarberg Range, well known for its rugged terrain, splendid views, unique rock formations and crystal clear streams and pools. Landowners in the area, in conjunction with Tourist Information, have opened up a number of mountain biking trails and there is an annual mountain bike race in spring.

The trails range from easy scenic rides through the farmlands to fairly hectic downhill routes in the surrounding hills. There are no multi-day trails as yet and all trails are self-guided. There are 11 trails at present, but more may be developed in future. You can get a map with detailed directions from **Citrusdal Tourist Information.**

WHILE IN THE AREA

There are some lovely day walks, especially in spring and, a little further north, excellent hikes in the Cedarberg Wilderness Area (see chapter 7). The Western Province Sport Parachute Club has its drop zone on the banks of the Olifants River (see chapter 12). To relax those tired muscles after a hard day's cycling try out the Baths, a natural hot spring that surfaces at 43 °C.

SWARTBERG PASS

This is a spectacular, steep, gravel pass linking the Great and Little Karoos. Hairpin bends, sheer cliffs and mindblowing scenery make this an exhilarating ride, even though it is all on-road. **Joyrides**, based at Backpacker Oasis in Oudtshoorn, offer escorted trips, bicycle rentals or semi-escorted trips (they take you to the top and you make your own way back).

If you are feeling brave and tough, you can turn off and take the hectic downhill run to Die Hel. But remember — you have to cycle back up again!

ANYSBERG NATURE RESERVE

This is a veritable desert paradise with the landscape alternating between gently undulating terrain and rugged mountain gorges. As well as the scenery and interesting Karoo vegetation, there are rock paintings and ruins dating back to the late 18th century.

Booking is essential and is done through **Cape Nature Conservation**, Ladismith. Detailed directions will be given on booking.

HILLANDALE MOUNTAIN BIKE TRAILS

Based 50 km from Beaufort West and 40 km from Three Sisters, this trail covers a wide range of Karoo scenery and habitats. You cycle through mountains, valleys and extensive flat plains. The trail is not long, 45 km at most, and you can do it over a few days, staying in quaint hiking accommodation, or stay in the comfortable farmhouse on a fully catered basis and just cycle out every day.

Booking is through **Jacana Country Homes and Trails**.

DIE POSROETE

This trail is on the farm Louweseplaas in the district of Fraserburg, in the Great Karoo. Surrounded by the Nuweveldberge, it is an oasis of waterfalls and streams with numerous interesting fossils. One of the most exciting parts of the route is the Mail Coach Pass which is a radically steep downhill, definitely not for beginners. There is a letterbox at the bottom and, if you post your details in it, you will be sent a certificate.

For booking and information contact **Die Posroete**.

Eastern Cape

The very active mountain biking fraternity in this province is attempting to gain access to more and more routes, including inner-city sites.

VAN STADENS WILDFLOWER RESERVE

This is a pleasant, scenic outing for novices and family groups. There are some good gravel jeep tracks which provide access to lovely views and the many species of wildflowers and plants in this reserve 35 km west of Port Elizabeth. This could be a great day outing if combined with a picnic and a visit to the reserve's nursery, where you may buy indigenous plants. This trail is administered by the **Algoa Regional Services Council**. Booking is not essential.

BAAKENS RIVER MTB TRAIL

This trail, through the middle of Port Elizabeth, represents a triumph of land access negotiation. It is 23 km long and follows the Baakens River, which flows through approximately 500 ha of public open space, a green belt that effectively splits the city in two. As with any metropolitan trail, the markers may be vandalised and it is not wise to cycle alone.

For further information contact the **Baakens Trust** or **ECO MTB.**

LONGMORE FOREST

Access is restricted to Fat Trax MTB Club members, although members may bring guests. There are a number of jeep tracks through pine forest and ECO MTB have constructed a few short single-track sections through the plantations. One of the main attractions is the beautiful fern-fringed Emerald Pool, at the base of a pretty waterfall. It is not wise to ride alone here. For further information contact **ECO MTB.**

WHILE IN THE AREA

Port Elizabeth has lovely long beaches and the diving and surfing are both reasonable (see chapters 5 and 14). There is good hang-gliding near Maitlands River Mouth and Lady's Slipper, which is near Van Stadens (see chapter 9). For the more culturally minded Port Elizabeth has some lovely old buildings and monuments — so a walk through the city centre is quite entertaining.

KAP RIVER NATURE RESERVE

This small reserve on the East London side of Port Alfred offers a number of trails suitable for cycling. Locals suggest the following itinerary: after arrival, take a casual cycle down to the Fish River Mouth where you can overnight. The next day you can cycle 25 km to Roundhill where you can watch game from your bike (see if you can spot an oribi). You can choose one of a number of different routes back to Kap River the next day. Some options include the historic church building at Cuylerville or a scenic route along the Great Fish River, which takes in some Frontier War graves.

WHILE IN THE AREA

There is a short flat-water canoe trail on the Kowie River (see chapter 6), excellent surfing (see chapter 14), and good diving (see chapter 5), as well as long beach walks. If that sounds too energetic, there are good coffee shops, or you could enjoy a sundowner on the verandah of the Halyards Hotel.

BOKSPRUIT AND BIRKHALL FARMS

These two farms in the northern part of the Eastern Cape, on the Lesotho border, have a number of trails set out. This is a relatively unexplored area and the riding is quite tough with steep gradients and sometimes freezing and unpredictable weather. The arrangements are not formalised. Phone the contacts listed at the end of this chapter for information and directions.

KwaZulu-Natal

MIKE'S PASS MTB TRAIL

In the Cathedral Peak section of the Northern Drakensberg, this 32 km trail is one of the most scenically beautiful anywhere. It includes some steep climbs and a hair-raising 7 km downhill on the pass, which can be quite scary as there are likely to be cars on the road.

Contact **Natal Parks Board** for details and booking.

HOLKRANS TRAILS

This trail near Newcastle is on a private farm whose owners, Anna and Dirk van Niekerk, are dedicated to promoting the responsible enjoyment of its natural assets. The 96 km Panorama Trail can be done in one day by very fit riders or, as is more usual, over two days with an overnight stop. There is also a 17,5 km ride with luminous markers for night riding and a gentle 57 km on/off-road ride to Chelmsford Dam and back. There are excellent maps to all the trails. Clean dorm-style accommodation is available on the farm, which also offers typically South African hospitality in the form of a "bundu braai" for a group of 15 or more.

FERNCLIFFE NATURE RESERVE

The Ferncliffe area, near Pietermaritzburg, is a favourite for club, provincial and national championships because of the great single-track riding, but there are also some sedate forest roads. The gradients are not excessive and it is ideal for social riding. The Hatcheries Park next door is conveniently placed for tea and socialising afterwards.

Contact the **Pietermaritzburg Municipality** for information and permits or **SAMBA** for information.

WORLD'S VIEW/LYNNWOOD FOREST

This trail has some really steep gradients, mostly through gum and wattle plantations. The markers are a bit far apart and you can easily get lost if you don't use a map, which is available from the Pietermaritzburg Publicity Office. The most interesting part of the trail is an old, disused train tunnel which is long, curved and pitch dark. It is great fun to see how well you can keep your balance with no visual stimulus. Contact the **Pietermaritzburg Municipality** for permits.

FOREST CLIFF TRAIL

This area near Richmond is of great historical interest. The whole village of Byrne is a national monument and the farm cottage, which can accommodate 20 people, dates back to 1880. There are three trails which meander through plantations and beautiful indigenous forest.

For booking and enquiries contact **Forest Cliff Getaway Cottage**.

Gauteng

Gauteng has the most organised mountain biking community in the region. This is partly because there is a greater concentration of people, but also because road riding is very hazardous in this car-dominated society. If you take the trouble to look, though, there are some great mountain biking sites right near the city.

READYMIX QUARRY

This working quarry in Honeydew is home to the Rockhoppers MTB Club and access is restricted to members, each of whom may bring two guests. It is possible to do a 15 km circuit here, with lots of single-track riding through wattle forest. This is a great place to hone your bike-handling skills or train for competitions. Riding is permitted on weekends and public holidays only and the working part of the quarry is out of bounds.

Contact the **Rockhoppers MTB Club** if you would like to ride here.

BRAAMFONTEIN SPRUIT

This is Johannesburg's only continuous green belt of approximately 25 km, starting on Melville Koppies and ending near Leeukop Prison. It traverses the suburbs of Melville, Emmarentia, Parkhurst, Craighall, Riverclub, Bryanston and Rivonia. Two major roads must be crossed, Barry Hertzog and Jan Smuts, and these are best done on foot, pushing your bike. The whole ride is on single-track footpaths next to the spruit. Because of its accessibility, it is one of the most popular riding, walking and outdoor recreation venues in Gauteng. It has, unfortunately, been the site of "bike-jackings" and attacks on lone cyclists, so do this trail in a group. Be careful of dogs, some of which may not be on a leash, and be considerate to other users. It is not necessary to obtain a permit. The area is administered by the **Sandton Municipality**, from whom you can obtain maps, or look up the trail on any street map of Johannesburg.

PAMPOENSPRUIT/KLEIN JUKSKEI

Starting at the Randburg Waterfront, this is a pleasant ride through the suburbs of Ferndale, Bryanston, Jukskei Park, Chartwell and Farmall. It is not continuous but this is compensated for by some great single-track sections and some very pretty uninterrupted riding in the less developed areas of Chartwell and Farmall. This lends itself to exploration as it links up with other rides on the outskirts of the city. You can use a street map of Johannesburg as a guide. Beware of dogs and don't ride alone.

RIETFONTEIN TRAIL

This is a small but lovely area, containing as it does the only known bit of almost pristine highveld grassland in Johannesburg. It is constantly threatened by development, so cyclists should enjoy it while they can. It is bordered by the Jukskei River and the Rietfontein Tropical Diseases Hospital, which is 150 years old. There is a pleasant mix of single-track and dirt roads. You can access this area from the Dowerglen Shopping Centre, in which case you go under the freeway, or from the Tropical Diseases Hospital.

For further information contact **AFTRAC.**

NDABUSHE RESERVE

This small reserve just outside Tarlton, about 20 km from Randburg, is a safe and convenient getaway for hassled urbanites. You are almost guaranteed to see game while riding on the tracks and paths and there are pleasant views. Book through the reserve or through the **Kromdraai Conservancy**.

GROENKLOOF NATURE RESERVE

Just minutes away from downtown Pretoria lies this very interesting reserve, which is stocked with game and has some exciting, challenging mountain biking. Trails are marked but shared with hikers so please be considerate and give them right of way. The trails start in the **Fountains Valley Resort** where budget accommodation and picnic sites are available.

Mpumalanga

SALPETERSKRANS MOUNTAIN BIKE TRAILS

There are four trails all leaving from a base on the farm Draaikraal, at the foot of the Salpeterskrans Mountain, near the town of Lydenburg. The Steenkamps Mountain Trail ascends the Salpeterskrans, at 2 243 m the highest mountain in Mpumalanga. It is a circular trail of 45 km with spectacular scenery and plantlife. The main attraction of the Protea Loop, a 16 km trail, is the great variety of proteas which can be seen. The Klip River Trail crosses the river, ascends to the top of the plateau and, of course, descends. The Mapochs Cave Trail is probably the most interesting. It leads to a cave where the Ndebele chief Mapoch lived. You will see examples of the little-known stone buildings of this region. It is similar to that of Great Zimbabwe, albeit on a much smaller scale. The farm has two fully equipped huts.

Booking is through **Jacana Country Homes and Trails**.

DRIEKOP MOUNTAIN BIKE TRAILS

There are three colour-coded routes in the Driekop Forest. The yellow River route is 14,5 km long, the blue Drie Koppe route is 25 km and the orange Vaalhoek route is 42,5 km long. All three trails start from Church Street, near the First National Bank in Graskop. Markers are rather erratic due to vandalism and inadvertent damage by forestry workers. All riding is on forest roads and the longer routes are extended versions of the shorter ones. Permits are essential and are available from the **Graskop Publicity Bureau**.

CEYLON TRAIL

This trail starts and ends at the Castle Rock campsite or Merry Pebbles in Sabie. The mountain bike trail follows the Loerie Trail pretty closely, so if you lose the bike trail markers, try to find the Loerie ones.

The first section of the trail follows the Sabie River to the enchanting Bridal Veil Falls. Being flat, it is ideal for beginners or children. Just before the falls the trail turns left and climbs steadily up the Mount Moody Nek. At the time of writing, the markers were absent from this point on but you can see right down to the town and follow the powerlines to the railway line which runs past Castle Rock campsite.

Contact Leon at **Merry Pebbles Holiday Resort** for information on this and other trails in the area. He can organise guided rides.

LONG TOM STATE FOREST

This is a glorious 38 km mountain bike trail with beautiful views and picturesque sections of indigenous forest interspersed with pine plantations. Regrettably the markers are not well maintained and there are no reliable maps of the two trails. This is definitely not for beginners. There is a steep climb and an awesome 15 km downhill which has claimed more than its fair share of skin.

Contact Leon at **Merry Pebbles Holiday Resort** for information on this and other trails in the area. He can organise guided rides.

WHILE IN THE AREA

Mpumalanga is one of the premier tourist destinations in South Africa. The Kruger National Park is close by, there are excellent hiking trails (see chapter 7) and horse trails (see chapter 16), and trout fishing is very popular. The nearby Sudwala Caves are worth a visit (see chapter 17).

North-west Province

The only known cycling area in the North-west is the Dome conservancy, a large area that extends into the Free State.

DOME CONSERVANCY TRAILS

This area near Potchefstroom bears the scars of a catastrophic prehistoric event. The hills were formed when a huge meteor about 1 km in diameter collided with the Earth and formed the semi-circular area known as the Vredefort Dome. The geology of the region is fascinating and the variety of mineralisation incredible. There are five different trails, all on a mix of rocky single-track and farm roads. The National Mountain Bike Championship was held here in 1996. It is very thorny, so without tyre liners you will have a series of short rides between puncture repairs. Maps are available and will be sent to you on booking.

Northern Province

There is not much established riding in this province but it has great potential: it is just a matter of finding the sites and obtaining access.

THABAPASWA MOUNTAIN BIKE TRAILS

There are two cycling areas around the farm Groenkom, near Potgietersrus. The farm has about 40 km of trail covering hilly terrain with good views of interesting rock formations, a section through a game camp where you might see small game, and some easy tracks. There are water points but you still need to carry a good supply. There is a second trail network outside the farm. This is an easy ride on rural roads, visiting interesting small settlements as well as affording a view of the spectacular scenery. There are two base camps on the farm, both of which have beds, mattresses, showers, flush toilets and simple kitchens with gas stove and pots and pans. Booking is through **Jacana Country Homes and Trails**.

WHILE IN THE AREA

The trails are suitable for hiking. Horizon Horse Trails near Vaalwater offer multi-day horse trails or the opportunity to join in the farm as a working guest. Equus Horse Safaris, near Marken, offer luxury wilderness horseback safaris (see chapter 16).

Northern Cape

The Namaqualand Publicity Association has laid out a number of self-guided biking trails. They are worth doing any time but it is very hot in summer and the whole area is at its best in spring when iridescent carpets of many-hued flowers stretch to the horizon. Mountain biking is one of the best ways to appreciate this spectacular display.

THE KAMIESBERG AREA

There are four routes in this attractive area to the east of the small town of Kamieskroon. Vissersplaat and Leliefontein A are short circular routes that can be attempted by almost anyone. Nourivier is a relatively easy 29 km circular route and the Leliefontein B route is a bit more challenging, especially if you choose to do the whole 49 km circular route rather than use a second vehicle and do only the 30 km linear option. Be careful of the sun and take plenty of water. A permit, which you can buy from the **Springbok Regional Information Office**, is essential. You will receive a detailed map and directions when you buy your permit.

GOEGAP NATURE RESERVE

This small reserve near the town of Springbok is renowned mostly for its varied plantlife but there is some small game, most notably small migratory herds of springbok, gemsbok and Hartmann's mountain zebra. There are two mountain bike trails, one 14 km long and the other 20 km long. They are both varied with some steepish climbs, fast downhills, rock and some sand tracks. Be careful of the sun and take plenty of water. It is not necessary to book, but you pay extra for your bicycle when you enter the reserve. Write to the Reserve Manager to book accommodation in the reserve.

WHILE IN THE AREA

You can do a horse trail through the Goegap Nature Reserve if you bring your own horse. The Namaqualand 4x4 Route starts from the picturesque mission village of Pella and continues for about 650 km to the mouth of the Orange River at Alexander Bay. The main attraction of this route is the incredible variety of succulent plants, many of which are endemic. Booking is through the Regional Information Office in Springbok. The whole area is interesting and well worth exploring. There are some charming and historically interesting settlements. There is good surfing, crayfishing in season, a horse trail and sea kayak trails on the nearby west coast (see chapters 14 and 16). The Orange River canoe or rafting trip starts from Noordoewer, which is not too far north, and in spring, the Doring River may be running (see chapter 6).

Free State

The eastern Free State area around Marquard, Ficksburg, Clocolan and Clarens is a beautiful mountainous region bordering Lesotho. There are numerous hiking trails, horse trails, interesting historical sites and cosy bed-and-breakfasts. The Cherry Trail Guide was put together as a marketing tool for the whole region. The Koranna Two Mountains MTB race, one of the toughest in the region, is run in October.

BOKPOORT MOUNTAIN BIKE TRAIL

The farm Bokpoort is set against the magnificent sandstone cliffs of the eastern

Free State, near Clarens. There are three very different trails. The 56 km Rooiberg Trail is suitable for fit and reasonably experienced cyclists. It ascends to a height of 2 000 m above sea level and descends on a long, 5 km downhill. It then follows the Caledon River and eventually returns to the farm via a tarred road. The Game Trail is suitable for beginners. It is a 5 km trail on an adjoining game farm. The nearby village of Clarens is a pleasant ride away, and it has many art galleries and craft shops to visit. Accommodation on the farm is either in a hikers' hostel or in chalets. You can choose a catered or self-catered stay.

WHILE IN THE AREA

The farm also offers hiking and horse trails (see chapter 16). The nearby Golden Gate Nature Reserve is well known for its spectacular red sandstone cliffs and rolling grassland.

RIETFONTEIN CONSERVANCY RIDES

There are a number of trails in the Rietfontein Conservancy Area near Marquard. The Rietfontein Ride consists of five circular trails ranging in distance from 10 to 66 km. Of these, the Cherry Challenge is for experienced riders only but the others are quite pleasant and scenic. The Wolwerand Ride has three trails, one of 25 km and one of 45 km and a hectic 6 km single-track cross-country course known as the Bergies Bash. All the trails are colour-coded and clearly marked. Tyre liners are essential in this area otherwise the devil thorns will shred your tubes. Accommodation for the trails is in quaint cottages, either on the farms or in the village, depending on the trail you choose. In all cases there are beds with mattresses, ablution facilities with hot water, cooking facilities and lighting, either electric or paraffin.

You can book directly through the **Cherry Trail** offices or through **Jacana Country Homes and Trails**.

KORANNABERG CONSERVANCY MOUNTAIN BIKE TRAILS NETWORK

There are seven trails in this area, including the Koranna Two Mountains Ride, a real challenge and the venue of the annual competition of the same name. This 60 km trail, largely designed by cows, is the very essence of mountain biking. There are two wicked climbs which are compensated for by the scenery from the top and some hectic downhill single-track cow trails which rollercoaster on forever. The final 7 km descent, is known as "Suicide Hill" and has been likened to riding on marbles. It twists and turns like a dragon chasing its tail and spirals down the mountain at an insane angle.

At the other end of the spectrum, the Flora Rides are a number of easy circular rides which are suitable for beginners or family groups. All the trails are colour-coded and clearly marked. Comfortable accommodation, with hot water ablutions and fully equipped kitchens, is available.

You can book directly through the **Cherry Trail** offices or through **Jacana Country Homes and Trails**.

Lesotho

If you really want to get away from the rat race, pack your bike and head off into the hills, this is the place to do it. Lesotho is a bikepacking heaven. There are miles of gravel roads — some good, some fair and some atrocious. All pass through exquisite mountain scenery, fascinating villages with friendly inhabitants and often cross or follow the course of gurgling mountain streams. You could spend a few days or a few weeks exploring this fascinating country. Your best bet would be to get a map (the AA map is the most recent, and even that is already outdated) and plan your route with the help of knowledgeable locals. The **Trading Post** at Roma, **Malealea Lodge**, **Sani Top Mountaineers Chalet** or **Sani Tours** are good places to ask for advice.

Do be prepared for any eventuality. Pack a tent, a very warm sleeping bag, warm clothes, a camping stove (there is virtually no wood in Lesotho) and enough food and fuel to keep you going for a few days if you get stuck. Many of the areas you will cycle through are very remote and they are in the high mountains. If you get misted or snowed in, just stay put. (Take a good book.)

WHILE IN THE AREA

Lesotho is a wonderful destination for horse trails, hiking trails and four-wheel-drive excursions. The trout fishing is good and in winter there may be skiing at Oxbow or Sani Top.

SANI PASS

The pass itself is between the South African and Lesotho border posts, so this is not strictly Lesotho but it is more commonly associated with Lesotho than with South Africa.

This is one of the classic four-wheel-drive routes in southern Africa and is becoming just as popular with mountain bikers. It is 8 km of steep gravel road with twisty hairpin bends and a height gain of 972 m.

The main attraction, of course, is the downhill. It is a very challenging run with sharp curves and steep drops — not the place to practise your downhill turns for the first time. Traffic is also a hazard. Sani Pass is the only southern route into Lesotho and it carries a considerable amount of freight and passenger traffic. This is by no means foolproof but there is, as a rule, less traffic in the middle of the day than in the morning or evening. In summer there may be mist or thunderstorms and in winter some of the corners are permanently iced up. On a nice sunny day, though, it is a fun ride.

If you want to do the downhill but not the uphill (or vice versa if you have masochistic tendencies) you can do one way with **Sani Tours**, who are based at the bottom of the pass. Purists, of course, would cycle both ways. Although the pass itself is the major attraction, it is worth spending some time at the top admiring the spectacular view before coming down. The Sani Top Mountaineer's Chalet is an unpretentious, comfortable and friendly establishment with incredible views and, they claim, the highest pub in southern Africa. There is some good cycling at the top; you could explore and find other tracks or just ride around the village. Or, of course, you can head off across Lesotho.

WHILE IN THE AREA

In winter there may be skiing at Sani Top; you can rent skis from the mountaineer's chalet. (Not the latest models, though.) The hiking is interesting and you can rent ponies from villagers at the top (the proprietors of the chalet will organise this for you). There is also much to do at the bottom of the pass. There are some wonderful hikes in the parks of the Drakensberg (see chapter 7), or you could do a horse trail through the park (see chapter 16).

Swaziland

This small country is fun to cycle around if you stay on the back roads. The road between Manzini and Mbabane should be avoided as it is particularly dangerous for cyclists, being very narrow and carrying a huge amount of traffic (mostly trucks and dilapidated buses).

MKHAYA

For a real big game adventure, try an escorted cycling trail through Mkhaya Game Reserve. Since it is rather flat it is not particularly challenging cycling terrain. The emphasis, though, is on the game which you are likely to see. Cycling close to elephants, white and black rhino and buffalo is just as much of an adrenalin rush, if not more, as the steepest downhill route. You may bring your own cycle or rent one from the reserve.

Booking is through the Central Reservations Office of the **Big Game Parks of Swaziland** and is essential.

MLILWANE

Mlilwane is also run by the Big Game Parks of Swaziland and also offers escorted mountain bike rides. The game is not quite as spectacular as that at Mkhaya, consisting mostly of antelope such as impala, nyala and blesbok and giraffe and zebra. The terrain is much more interesting, though, with some steep gravel tracks and perilous rocky sections, if you choose to do them.

If you want to hire bikes from Mlilwane, you will need to book this in advance as they are usually kept at Mkhaya. You will be charged a nominal fee at the gate if you bring your own bike in. Booking is through **Big Game Parks of Swaziland**.

WHILE IN THE AREA

There are a number of other ways of watching game in both Mkhaya and Mlilwane (see chapter 15), or you could paddle the Great Usutu River (see chapter 6). Swaziland is a tourist's dream come true, with interesting villages, pretty mountain passes and quaint craft shops and restaurants.

Listings

OPERATORS, CLUBS, BOOKING AUTHORITIES AND RETAIL OUTLETS

AFTRAC (African MTB Training, Racing, Adventure Company), e- mail: aftrac@global.co.za P O Box 1059, Olivedale 2158, South Africa; tel/fax: +27 11 794-1713, are an excellent source of information on all aspects of mountain biking.

Algoa Regional Services Council, P O Box 318, Port Elizabeth 6000, South Africa; tel: +27 41 95-5649, administer the Van Stadens Wildflower Reserve Trail.

AST (Adventure Sports Trading); tel: +27 41 54-7159, are a useful contact for obtaining information about most trails in the region.

Baakens Trust, P O Box 888, Port Elizabeth 6000, South Africa; tel: +27 41 32-4150.

Beach Break Surf and Cycle; tel: +27 41 55-4303, sell and rent mountain bikes.

Beaverlac, tel: +27 2623 2945, is a lovely mountain resort with many jeep tracks on which you can cycle.

Big Game Parks of Swaziland, Central Reservations, P O Box 234, Mbabane, Swaziland; tel: +268 4-4541, fax: 4-0957. Weekends and after hours, tel: +268 6-1591/2/3 or 6-1037, fax: 6-1594, take bookings for Mlilwane and Mkhaya.

Bikeabout, 8 Pineway, Pinelands 7405, South Africa; tel: +27 21 531-3274, will do escorted trips in the Cape Town area on request.

Bokspruit and Birkhall Farms, P O Box 15, Rhodes 9787, South Africa; contact Dave Walker, tel: +27 4542 ask for 9203, or Carien Vosloo, tel: +27 4542 ask for 994, or Pieter Steyn, tel: +27 4542 ask for 158 (bus) or 454 (h), for information on the trails.

Cape Nature Conservation, Private Bag X216, Ladismith 6885, South Africa; tel: +27 23 551-1922, administers the Anysberg Nature Reserve.

Casual Adventures, Suite 3, Postnet X65, Halfway House 1685, South Africa; tel: +27 11 314-2844, will do escorted trips in the Gauteng and Mpumalanga areas on request.

Citrusdal Publicity Association, Private Bag X11, Citrusdal, 7340; tel +27 22 921-3210.

Coimbra, 4th Ave, Newton Park, Port Elizabeth, tel: 27 41 35- 2066, fax +27 41 35-2023, is a full service cycle shop.

De Hoop Nature Reserve, Private Bag X16, Bredasdorp 7280; tel: +27 28 542-1126.

Department of Water Affairs and Forestry, Knysna, tel: +27 445 82-5466, fax: +27 445 82-5461, administer the Harkerville, Homtini and Petrus se Brand cycle routes.

Dome Conservancy, P O Box 21138, Noordbrug 2522, South Africa; tel: +27 148 294-8572, fax: +27 148 297-7976.

Downhill Bicycle Tours, 133a Bree St, Cape Town 8000, tel: +27 21 23-2527, fax +27 21 23-7149, cell: +27 82 459-2422, do the Table Mountain Double Descent, Constantia Wine Route and Cape Point trips.

ECO MTB, e-mail: TAYLR-GJ @ pelican.vista.ac.za, tel: +27 41 55-9661, for information about the Baakens River MTB Trail and others in Port Elizabeth.

Forest Cliff Getaway Cottage, P O Box 738, Richmond 3780, South Africa; tel: +27 3322 3370.

Fountains Valley Resort, tel: +27 12 44-7131, take bookings for the Groenkloof Trail.

Garden Route Regional Tourist Information Centre, P O Box 1514, George 6530; tel: +27 441 73-6314, fax: +27 441 74-6840, can give information about further trails in the Garden Route area.

Goegap Nature Reserve, Private Bag X1, Springbok 8240, South Africa; tel: +27 251 2-1880, fax: +27 251 8-1286.

Graskop Publicity Association, P O Box 171, Graskop 1270, South Africa; tel: +27 13 767-1321.

Grootvadersbosch Nature Reserve, tel: +27 2934 22412, sell permits for the short trail in the reserve.

Harrismith Publicity Association, P O Box 43, Harrismith 9880, South Africa; tel: +27 5861 2-3523, fax: +27 5861 3-0923, for information about the Platberg MTB Race.

Hilton MTB Club, P O Box 1345, New Germany 3620, South Africa; tel: +27 331 43-4687, for information about the Hilton Classic MTB Race.

Holkrans Trails, P O Box 2734, Newcastle 2940, South Africa; tel: +27 34 351-1600 for bookings and directions.

Honeywood Farm, tel: +27 2934 21823, fax: +27 2934 21939, administer the longer trails in the Grootvadersbosch Conservancy.

Jacana Country Homes and Trails, P O Box 95212, Waterkloof 0145; tel: +27 12 346-3550/1/2, fax: 346-2499, acts as central booking agent for the Marquard Cherry Trail, Hillandale Mountain Bike Trails, Salpeterskrans Mountain Bike Trail and the Thabaphaswa Mountain Bike Trails.

Joyrides, P O Box 203, Oudtshoorn, tel: +27 443 29-1163, offer escorted or unescorted trips over the Swartberg Pass.

Kap River Nature Reserve, P O Box 10, Port Alfred 6170, South Africa; tel: +27 464 25-0631.

Karkloof Conservancy, tel: +27 332 30-4602, organise the Karkloof Classic.

Knysna Cycle Works, tel: +27 445 82-5153, for information about trails in the area and the

Oyster Festival MTB Race.

Kromdraai Conservancy, P O Box 393, Paardekraal 1752, South Africa; tel: +27 11 957-0241, fax: +27 11 957-0344, for information on and bookings for Ndabushe.

Logwood Ranch, tel: +27 11 659-0586/0480, organise the Logwood Ranch Fat Tyre Fun Weekend.

Malealea Lodge, P O Box 119 Wepener 9944, South Africa; tel: +27 51 447-3200, cell phone: +27 82 552-4215, fax: +27 51 447-5114, e-mail: malealea @ pixie.co.za., can give directions for the many hiking or biking trails near their lodges.

Marquard Cherry Trail, P O Box 140, Marquard 9610, Free State; tel: +27 51 991-0126. They take bookings for five different mountain bike trails in the eastern Free State. They organise the Cherry Trail Challenge and the Koranna Two Mountains MTB Race.

Merry Pebbles Holiday Resort, tel: +27 13 764-2266, is at the start of the Long Tom and Ceylon Trails.

Ndabushe Reserve tel: +27 11 956-6338, fax: +27 11 956-6341.

Outeniqua Biking Trails, P O Box 592, Plettenberg Bay 6600; tel: +27 4457 7644, +27 445 82-5153, fax: +27 4457 7648, offer escorted day or multi-day trips in the Knysna, Outeniqua and Tsitsikamma forests.

Pietermaritzburg Municipality, Conservation Section, P O Box 31, Pietermaritzburg 3200, South Africa; tel: +27 331 42-1322, administer the Ferncliffe Nature Reserve.

Die Posroete, P O Box 21, Fraserburg 6960, South Africa, tel: +27 2072 ask for 1813 or +27 2072 ask for 1111.

Pretoria MTB Club, 213 Harvard Ave, Clubview East, Pretoria 0157, South Africa; tel: +27 12 654-6212 or +27 82 568-0070, organise the Pilgrim's Rest Classic.

Replay Sports, 22a Long Street, Cape Town; tel: +27 21 25- 1026, buy, sell and rent second hand bicycles.

Rhodes MTB Club, P O Box 1397, Johannesburg 2000, South Africa; organise the Norwich Life Rhodes 84,5 km MTB Challenge. Contact Sam Hallett, tel: +27 11 615-7131 (bus), +27 11 648-3573 (h) or fax: +27 11 615-7517.

Rockhoppers MTB Club, Daan van Niekerk; tel: +27 11 787-1757, control access to the Readymix Quarry and organise the RMBC 24-hour team night race.

SAFCOL (South African Forestry Company Limited), P O Box 428, Pretoria 0001; tel: +27 12 804-1230, fax: +27 12 804-5103.

SAFCOL, Grabouw; tel: +27 21 859-2606.

SAFCOL, Jonkershoek; tel: +27 21 886-5715. This is also the district head office. You can enquire about an annual permit to cover all the Cape SAFCOL areas.

SAFCOL, Tokai; tel: +27 21 727471.

SAMBA (South African Mountain Bike Association), P O Box 1227, Pinetown 3600, South Africa; organise The Grundig SA National Championship Series and are a good contact for general information on mountain biking.

Sandton Municipality, P O Box 78001, Sandton 2146, South Africa; tel: +27 11 803-9132/3, fax: +27 11 803-2066, administer the Braamfontein Spruit and Sandspruit trails.

Sani Top Mountaineers Chalet; tel: +27 33 701-1466, +27 33 702-1069 (a/h); can give you information about Sani Pass and the route from there into Lesotho.

Sani Tours; tel: +27 33 702-1615, can give you information about Sani Pass and the route from there into Lesotho.

Springbok Regional Information Office, P O Box 5, Springbok 8240; tel: +27 251 2-1543, fax: +27 251 2-1421, sells permits for the Kamiesberg Cycle Trails. If you can't contact them or they are closed, you can get permits from the Kamieskroon Hotel; tel: +27 257 614, fax: +27 257 675.

The State Forester, Tsitsikamma, Private Bag X530, Humansdorp 6300; tel: +27 42 541-1557, fax: +27 42 541-1558, administers the Storms River Cycle Trail.

Summerland Cycle Shop, P O Box 6504, Nelspruit 1200, South Africa; tel: +27 13 755-1147, can give you information about cycling routes in Mpumalanga.

The Trading Post Guest House, P O Box 64, Maseru, Lesotho; tel: +266 34-0202 (o/h), 34-0267 (a/h), can give you information on off-road routes in Lesotho.

Tsitsikamma Forest Circles, P O Box 20, Witelsbos 6304; tel: +27 42 750-3952, fax: +27 42 750-3816, cell: +27 83 261-4826 or +27 83 261-6637, e-mail: nigell@sprintlink.co.za.

Village Cycles, P O Box 2277, Stellenbosch 7599, South Africa; tel: +27 21 883 8593, e-mail: village@aztec.co.za

Village Spillage, tel: +27 82 658-3883 (speak to Andre) runs a cycling wine route in Stellenbosch.

WPPA (Western Province Pedal Power Association), tel: +27 21 689-8420 can give you information about trails in the Jonkershoek Nature Reserve.

Zink, Paul; +27 291 4-3012, can organise escorted trips in the Western Cape and can offer information on the trails near Swellendam.

ACCOMMODATION

Most of the cycle trails are on farms or reserves with accommodation. The accommodation listed below is for those which are not.

Citrusdal

The Baths has a hot spring as well as comfortable, stylish self-catering accommodation and shady camping. Tel: +27 22 921-3609 or write to The Baths, P O Box 133, Citrusdal 7340, South Africa.

The Cedarberg Lodge is a comfortable two-star country hotel, tel: +27 22 921-2221, fax: +27 22 921-2704, or write to The Cedarberg Lodge, P O Box 37, Citrusdal 7340.

Warmwatersberg

As well as lovely hot springs, there are chalets and camping. There is also a steep, rocky, 6 km day walk which you may cycle. Tel: +27 28 572-1609.

Sani Pass

There are two backpackers hostels near the bottom of the pass. They are Sani Lodge, tel: +27 33 702-0330, and Ha Makhakhe's, tel: +27 33 702-0340. They are very reasonably priced, casual and fun. The Sani Pass Hotel, tel: +27 33 702-1320, also near the bottom of the pass is a very comfortable establishment. At the top of the pass, Sani Top Chalets, tel: +27 33 701-1466 is described in the text.

Knysna

See Accommodation in chapter 5.

Plettenberg Bay

See Accommodation in chapter 5.

Namaqualand

You can stay at the Kamieskroon Hotel; tel: +27 25-7614, fax: +27 25-7675 or on the farm Pedro's Kloof, tel: +27 257 666. There is also accommodation in the Goegap Nature Reserve Private Bag X1, Springbok 8240; tel: +27 251 2-1880, fax: +27 251 8-1286.

FURTHER READING

Life Cycle is the official newsletter of the WPPA and is available from newsagents in South Africa.

Mountain Biking in South Africa — the Best Places under the Sun, Herman and Suzy Mills, Bicycle Books, Active Travel Series, San Francisco, 1997.

A Guide to Mountain Bike Trails, Western Cape, Paul Leger, Red Mole Publications, Cape Town, 1997.

CHAPTER 9

The ecstasy of flight

Hang-gliding and paragliding

"Why fly? For once you have tasted flight you will walk the Earth with your eyes turned skyward; for there you have been and there you long to return." Leonardo da Vinci, designing flying machines in the 16th century, only dreamed of flying but, with the mind of an engineer and the soul of an artist, he could taste the magic.

In the late 20th century flight is no big deal, but there is, of course, a world of difference between being a passenger sipping plastic coffee in a jumbo jet and gliding through the air with only the windrush of your movement or the flapping of your canopy disturbing the silence. This is true flight — and it is addictive.

Both paraglider and hang-glider pilots usually take off from a hill, slope or mountain, using the speed of their initial few steps to give them some lift as the ground falls away under them. They will then stay aloft, using one of two techniques. They will either find thermals, which will enable them to rise, or they will fly near the edge of a mountain or hill, catching the oncoming wind as it lifts to clear the ridge. This is known as ridge soaring and, once you have mastered the art, you can spend hours flying backwards and forwards along the front of the ridge.

The temptations of the huge thermals that build up over the hot (and unfortunately completely flat) interior are hard to resist, though. Experienced pilots fly these areas by doing a winch launch and often set off for long-distance cross-country flights. The **South African Hang- and Paragliding Association (SAHPA)** was formed to regulate safety and training standards, and all clubs are affiliated to the association.

What's the difference?

Hang-gliding and paragliding are very similar in principle. As a rule, it is just you and your glider. A hang-glider has a rigid structure, usually of aluminium, with nylon fabric stretched tightly across it, forming a wing. A paraglider is designed along the lines of a ram air parachute, in essence an inflatable wing. The movement of air through the canopy inflates it and gives it its aerodynamic shape. You hang underneath it in a harness attached by a number of lines. The whole thing is soft and packs up into a bag which can easily be carried around. Its portability is its main advantage over the somewhat more efficient hang-glider.

Not satisfied with utilising only the power of the wind, gravity and thermals, some pilots have started paramotoring. With a standard paraglider and a motorised fan tied to your back, you can turn yourself into an "aeroplane". This has the advantage of enabling you to fly where there are no convenient launch sites but it is, of course, noisy.

Getting started

Southern Africa is a paradise for hang-gliding and paragliding enthusiasts, with schools scattered all over the region. It's essential to join a club or enrol on a course if you want to learn to fly properly and safely.

There are schools or clubs in most South African cities where you can do a weekend introductory course. This usually covers some of the theory of flight, how the glider is constructed, how you steer it and how you stall it for landing. You then learn, in the case of paragliding, how to inflate your canopy. You do this on a flat area, such as a sports field. Once you have mastered the theory and the few simple practical skills, you will be given the opportunity to fly from a low sand-dune or grassy hill. If you enjoyed that, you should do a basic course. This consists of a lot more theory and many more flights in different conditions and from different heights. Once you have obtained your basic certification you may fly on your own in areas you are familiar with.

If you just want to give it a try to see if you like it, you can do a tandem flight with an instructor or licensed tandem pilot which enables you to experience the exhilaration of a long, reasonably high-altitude flight.

Equipment

If you are just doing a weekend introductory course or a tandem flight you need no specialised equipment. Wear comfortable clothes and sensible shoes. Lightweight hiking boots are the best as you can walk in them and they offer some ankle support on landing. If you don't have any, running shoes or any comfortable shoes will do. The schools will provide all the other equipment as part of the introductory course.

Once you decide to do a basic hang-gliding or paragliding course, you will probably want to buy your own glider and all the expensive accessories that go with it. Do some research before splashing out a lot of money, though.

Most students would find a basic or intermediate glider suitable for their needs. These are not particularly fast or flashy but they are forgiving — a very important consideration when learning. Bear in mind that both hang-gliders and paragliders are rated for different weights of pilot, so ensure you buy the right size. Ask your instructor for advice, especially if you find a bargain in the smalls in the local paper. Gliders only have a limited life, so make sure you don't buy one right at the end of its allotted time. The actual fabric of the glider can become porous through age, abrasion and exposure to the sun. Your instructor will know how to check for this so do take his or her advice.

Options for people with disabilities

Many of the launch sites are quite difficult to get to and most have no facilities whatsoever. In order to fly a paraglider or hang-glider, you need to be able to launch (which usually means being able to run), have the use of your arms, have reasonable eyesight and be able to land on your feet. However, most people with disabilities will be able to do a tandem flight with an instructor. This would be no problem at all for blind people. In the case of paraplegics, or others who cannot use their legs, it is important to choose an instructor who is quite a bit taller than you. Although I don't know of any in southern Africa, there are people overseas who fly paragliders or hang-gliders in their wheelchairs. You would need to learn the skills tandem, though, and only go solo with your wheelchair once you really know what you are doing.

Regular events

The following are reasonably regular competitions but the venues, and even time of year, may change. Contact **SAHPA** for further details.

PARAGLIDING

The Gauteng Provincial Championships are usually held in Barberton in winter, the KwaZulu-Natal Championships are held in Bulwer in spring, the Free State Championships in Botshabelo in autumn and the National Championships at Dasklip in summer.

HANG-GLIDING

The Free State Open is held in Botshabelo in autumn, the Gauteng Open in Barberton in winter and the KwaZulu-Natal Open in Bulwer in spring. These times may change without notice.

Western Cape

There are more than 40 excellent paragliding and hang-gliding sites, some of the more popular of which are described below. For information on these and other sites contact one of the local clubs, **Parapente Cape**, **Fun to Fly Cape** or **Cape Skyriders**.

LION'S HEAD

This is an exhilarating flight over the Atlantic seaboard suburbs of Cape Town. It is great on summer evenings when you can literally fly off into the sunset and, with luck and skill, land on the beach in front of the very popular sundowner spot La Med. It is also a popular site for tandem flights. Contact **Parapente**, **Cape Skyriders** or **Fun to Fly**, **Cape**.

For more information on this site, contact the Glen Paragliding Club.

SIGNAL HILL

This site, right next to Lion's Head, is very popular with hang-glider pilots. It is a bit tricky for paragliders, though, as the landing site at Mouille Point Sports Ground is quite far away and there is nothing before that except a very built-up area with busy roads.

Contact Albatross Hang-Gliding Club for information.

TABLE MOUNTAIN

This must be one of the world's classic flights. It is high and steep and the views are mind-blowing. It is an advanced site and should not be attempted without the advice, and preferably company, of an experienced local. Contact Cape Albatross Hang-Gliding Club or Glen Paragliding Club for information.

WHILE IN THE AREA

You could do a lot worse than to watch the sunset from La Med or, if you don't fancy the beer-swilling company, one of the many western seaboard beaches. Relax, chill out and just watch the horizon tilt up to meet, and eventually engulf, the sun.

DASKLIP PASS

This launch has a very short metal launch-ramp and a steep take-off. The scenery is spectacular, if a little monotonous, with endless wheatfields rolling away beneath you. It is suitable for experienced and intermediate pilots and has been the site of numerous successful competitions. Contact Cape Albatross Hang Gliding Club for further information.

WHILE IN THE AREA

There is great hiking in the Groot Winterhoek Mountains (see chapter 7), and the nearby farm Beaverlac (see chapter 8) has a pleasant camping site, lovely mountain streams, pools and waterfalls. You may do day walks or short mountain bike trails on the farm.

BETTY'S BAY DUNE

This dune is generally considered to be the beginners' slope of Cape Town paragliding schools. It is an even, snow-white dune of about 100 m but students usually launch from halfway, or even a quarter of the way, down. Flying here is hard work as you have to walk back up the dune after your flight. Experienced pilots do sometimes fly here but you can't get a long flight.

MAP OF AFRICA

This is a favourite launch site near the popular Garden Route resort town of Wilderness. It is suitable for intermediate pilots; the take-off is on a grassy slope, you have to negotiate some trees and make sure you don't land on the national road or the railway line.

The landing is on a long, glorious beach. In winter or spring you may see whales or dolphins from the air.

For more information about this popular site contact **Cloud Base** or Sky Wings Hang Gliding and Paragliding Club.

WILDERNESS

There is a wooden launch-ramp next to the parking lot of the Wilderness Holiday Inn. It is suitable for newly certified pilots. You can get a nice little ridge soar against the dunes, there's a great view of the beach and you have a soft landing anywhere on the long beach. There is no charge but you must sign in at the hotel. You can drive to the launch site, and the walk back from the beach takes about 20 minutes.

For more information contact **Cloud Base** or Sky Wings.

BRENTON-ON-SEA

This is a pleasant flight from a grassy hill about 80 m high onto the beach. It is suitable for beginners and is often used for training. There is a walk of 500 m to the launch and from the landing.

For more information contact **Cloud Base** or Sky Wings.

KLEINKRANZ

This is an easily accessible low dune of about 50 m which is usually used for training. When the conditions are right, though, you can take off here and fly Paradise Ridge, which is about 10 km of ridge-soaring there and 10 km back. Not bad considering the take-off is on a 50 m dune!

For more information contact **Cloud Base** or Sky Wings.

UPLANDS

This is about 15 km inland from Plettenberg Bay. It offers lovely easy thermal soaring and fantastic views of Plett and Knysna. It is flyable all year but is best in summer.

For more information contact **Cloud Base** or Sky Wings.

PIESANG VALLEY RIDGE

This site offers four or five different take-offs, all of which will fly over the scenic Piesang River. Best flown in an east to south-west wind, it is flyable all year but is most consistent in summer.

For more information contact **Cloud Base** or Sky Wings.

WHILE IN THE AREA

If you are travelling up from Cape Town, stop at the spectacular Gouritz River Bridge, where you can do a bridge jump or bungi jump (see chapter 13). There is good diving off Knysna (see chapter 5), excellent hikes along the coast and in the forests (see chapter 7), fun mountain bike trails (see chapter 8), reasonable surf (see chapter 14), and a really good hourly or daily horse trail (see chapter 16).

Eastern Cape

There are a number of good sites in this huge province, but they are quite far apart. For information about local flying contact **Fun to Fly**, or **Hawkwind**.

RONDEBOSCH MOUNTAIN AND RIDGE

Close to Humansdorp and Jeffrey's Bay on the N2, Rondebosch Mountain works only on a south wind while Rondebosch Ridge will work on anything from south-west to south-east. The thermals here can be impressive in summer (as fast as 8 m/sec) and some reasonable cross-country flights have been flown, the longest to date being 48 km. Contact **Hawkwind** or **Fun to Fly** for details and information on the unique site rules.

WHILE IN THE AREA

The nearby town of Jeffrey's Bay is the surfing mecca of South Africa (see chapter 14). The beach is also great for just lazing on and it is blessed with an astonishing variety of washed up shells, which you may collect (in reasonable quantities).

LADY'S SLIPPER

About 25 km west of Port Elizabeth, this launch is off an 8 km ridge which you can soar along, flying over the Van Stadens Pass which cuts through it. It works best when the south wind is changing to south-east. The back of the mountain works on a north wind, when you will be guaranteed the most amazing convergence lift. This area is a sensitive reserve with beautiful indigenous flowers. Contact **Hawkwind** or **Fun to Fly**, who have keys to get through the gate to the launch site.

WHILE IN THE AREA

There are some fun mountain biking tracks in the reserve (see chapter 8), and it is worth visiting just for the flowers, especially in spring.

MAITLAND RIVER MOUTH

This site is very popular with local pilots who boast about the "hawkwind", a wind with a magic lift. The site is flyable in anything from a south-southwest to a south-southeast. Take-off and landing is from a tarred road or a grassy hill on private property. To organise flights here contact **Hawkwind** or **Fun to Fly**.

GRAAFF REINET

The semidesert plains of the Karoo send up incredible thermals and Eastern Cape pilots flock to the small town of Graaff Reinet to take advantage of them. You take off over the Valley of Desolation, a fitting name, and can then fly distances of up to 90 km, over the flat, stark, rocky Karoo, often enlivened by the presence of dust devils. If you ever want to see your back-up vehicle again, take a radio. This site can be flown in anything from a south to a north-east wind. Contact **Fun to Fly** for further information.

WHILE IN THE AREA

There are some interesting hikes in the area (see chapter 7), and the Owl House in Nieu Bethesda, also described in chapter 7, is worth a visit.

QUEENSTOWN

Although it is not quite as popular as Graaff Reinet, the conditions at Queenstown are similar. The take-off and landing are both very rocky and thorn trees abound, so wear good boots. You can fly this site in almost any wind. The main site is a cliff launch and unwary pilots have been surprised by sneaky dust devils on take-off before, so be careful. If landing in the reserve watch out for the rhinos: they may be frightened by a multi-coloured visitation from the sky.

For further information, contact **Piet Neethling** or **Fun to Fly**.

KwaZulu-Natal

Although the most spectacular flying is concentrated in the Drakensberg, there are a number of launch sites close to Durban and Pietermaritzburg and some good flying areas around Vryheid and Newcastle. For information about these and other KwaZulu-Natal sites, contact Durban Paragliding Club, Pietermaritzburg Hang Gliding Club or **Wild Sky**.

BULWER

Bulwer, in the southern Drakensberg, has very dependable hang- and paragliding most of the year and has often been the site of competitions. Like most of the region it is very scenic. You can drive to the take-off, which is about 300 m above landing, but novices can use a lower take-off if they are prepared to walk to it. Landing is on the outskirts of town, making for easy pick-ups. For further information, contact **Wild Sky Paragliding**.

ARTHUR'S SEAT

This scenic site in the central Drakensberg is very popular with intermediate and advanced pilots. Take-off to landing is about 500 m and both are easily accessible. The **Kelvin Grove Campsite** at the bottom is a great place to stay while flying here and can give you directions to the launch. Or you could get information from **Isibongo Lodge** or **Wild Sky Paragliding**.

THE HOEK

Oliviers Hoek Pass, in the northern Drakensberg, is a popular site with experienced pilots and students alike. The take-off is close to Drifters Inn and is about 150 to 200 m above landing. Both launch and landing site are easily accessible by car. You can do a resident paragliding course at **Isibongo Lodge** and do your flights from here or Arthur's Seat, also a spectacular flight. They will also give you information about the site, and the staff at **Drifters Inn** can direct you to the site.

Mpumalanga, Gauteng and Northern Province

Because of the huge concentration of pilots in the Gauteng area, this province and those near it have a number of good flying sites.

MPUMALANGA

Many pilots drive here from Johannesburg as it is a journey of only a few hours. The spectacular scenery and the mountainous relief make this a very popular flying destination. In winter, especially, the flying conditions are suitable for long-distance cross-country flights.

For more information about local conditions and directions to the many launch sites, contact Bambi Paragliding Club, **Para Sport**, **SA Paragliding**, **Paraventure** or **Paragliding Afrika**.

GAUTENG

There are not too many paragliding or hang-gliding sites close to the city. Krugersdorp and Walkerville have low launches, about 100 m, but the best-known site is the Hartebeespoort Dam. It is only 330 m high and there is a cableway. It is a very popular site, more due to its proximity to Johannesburg than anything else. There is a ceiling at 700 m above take-off as controlled air space starts there, so you will not be allowed to fly this site without an altimeter (at least). Surprisingly, a number of good cross-country flights have been made under this ceiling. For further information contact First Paragliding Club SA, **Thermal Riders**, **Paragliding Afrika** or **Sky Scrapers**.

NORTHERN PROVINCE

Some local pilots have done a few pioneering flights near Pietersburg but there is still much to be discovered in this vast and rather wild province.

North-west Province and Northern Cape

The area around the border of these two provinces is paragliding heaven; flat and with immense thermals, especially in summer. Many long cross-country flights, all winch launches, have been done from here. Flights of over 300 km are possible but you must be very careful to avoid the controlled air space of Johannesburg International Airport, Bloemfontein and Kimberley. The favourite launch sites are Vryburg in the North-west Province and Kuruman, just over the border in the Northern Cape. Flights are mostly from the local airfields. If you want to take advantage of the launching infrastructure, you will need to contact **SAHPA**.

Free State

The area east of Bloemfontein has some good hang-gliding and paragliding sites. Botshabelo and Thaba Nchu offer good launch sites and quite long distance cross-country flights have been made from here. There is also some good cross-country flying over the Dealesville area, where all launches are by winch. You have to be careful to avoid the Bloemfontein controlled air space. For further information contact **Fly Extreme**.

Lesotho

There are a number of good launch spots in this mountainous country but they are mostly advanced sites. For further information and details on how to find the sites, contact **Tristan Behr** in Maseru who will give you more information and, if it is convenient for him, may fly with you. Frankly, though, if you want to fly here you must be able to do your own flight plans and look after yourself.

BUSHMAN'S PASS

Bushman's Pass is a great site for experienced hang-glider pilots and very experienced paraglider pilots. The wind is very dependable as anything from north to south-west is funnelled through the pass. The top to landing height is about 380 m but top landing is recommended otherwise you'll need a four-wheel-drive to get back to the road. There are powerlines to be avoided and the site must be flown in the early morning as the winds become very strong and turbulent later in the day.

THABA BOSIU

Thaba Bosiu, near the historic birthplace of the Basotho nation, is suitable for very experienced hang- and paraglider pilots. The area just below take-off is very rocky and the top to landing height is about 170 m. The take-off is westerly and the wind direction is mostly north-west.

WHILE IN THE AREA

It was at Thaba Bosiu that Moshoeshoe gathered displaced people from all over southern Africa during the terrifying and devastating Mfecane, the period of bloody warfare that ravaged the subcontinent in the 19th century. Thaba Bosiu is a perfect natural fortress and Moshoeshoe, by offering a refuge to all comers, laid the foundation for a kingdom which has lasted to this day. There is an information kiosk on the road where you can make enquiries before exploring this interesting historical site. The summit of the fortress is usually covered in wild flowers and the views in all directions are spectacular.

MATSIENG

Matsieng is suitable for intermediate pilots. You need a four-wheel-drive to get there but there is a nice take-off on a smooth, grassy, north-west facing slope. Top to landing is about 200 m.

MASITE

Masite is a nice spot, suitable for intermediate pilots. The take-off is on a gentle north-facing slope and the top to landing height is about 150 m. It is best in a north wind, but can be flown in a north-west.

WHILE IN THE AREA

Morija, the site of Lesotho's only museum, is not far from here. As well as dinosaur bones and casts of dinosaur footprints, there is a lot of interesting historical material.

KATSE DAM

There is a spectacular launch site near Katse Dam, offering a wonderful flight for very experienced pilots; you fly into a long, narrow valley and the top to landing height is 1 100 m, with a distance of 2,5 km. The wind can be very strong, so this site is only flyable in the early morning and late afternoon.

Namibia

In this vast country flying sites are few and far between but they are worth travelling for as phenomenal thermals build up over the immense expanse of desert.

THE DUNES NEAR SWAKOPMUND

These are among the highest sand-dunes in the world and are excellent sites for beginner or intermediate pilots to log reasonably high flights on a relatively easy slope. It is hard work climbing the dunes but worth it for the view of endless red dunes and the Atlantic coast.

BITTERWASSER

Although it is better known as a gliding venue, paragliders have recently started flying this site using winch launches and have made some spectacular cross-country flights. There is accommodation on the farm. For further information, contact **Chris Lotter** or **Fun Ventures**. Also see chapter 10 for further details of this spectacular flying venue.

Swaziland

Some locals have done a few flights in Mlilwane Game Reserve. If you are an experienced pilot, you can ask Darron Raw at **Mlilwane**, and he will point you in the right direction. There are potentially many more sites in this hilly country and they are currently being explored. Start your enquiries with **Fun Ventures**, who can tell you who is flying there.

Listings

Telephone numbers of clubs are usually those of the current chair or secretary, so they are not dependable. It is best to contact SAHPA, who can give you the latest number. You could also write to the clubs, care of SAHPA.

SCHOOLS, OPERATORS AND GENERAL CONTACTS

Behr, Tristan tel: +266 32-3665, or tel/fax: +266 31-0537, is a keen hang-glider pilot living in Maseru and will happily give information on the sites he flies.

Cape Skyriders, tel: +27 21 52-3964, is a hang-gliding school in Cape Town.

Cloud Base Paragliding, tel: +27 441 877-1414, run paragliding courses, do tandem flying seven days a week and offer friendly budget bed-and-breakfast accommodation.

Drifter's Inn, tel: +27 36 438-6130, can tell you how to get to The Hoek.

Free Flight, tel: +27 11 837-5395, is a hang-gliding school in Gauteng.

Fun to Fly, Cape, tel: +27 21 557-9735, is a paragliding school in Cape Town.

Fun to Fly, tel: +27 423 96-1911, is a paragliding school operating from Jeffrey's Bay.

Fun Ventures, tel: +27 11 609-1678, fax: +27 11 452-1654, operate paragliding tours.

Hawkwind Hang Gliding School, tel: +27 41 53-4358, operates in Port Elizabeth.

Isibongo Lodge, tel: +27 36 438-6707, offers resident paragliding courses in the Drakensberg, KwaZulu-Natal.

Kelvin Grove Campsite, tel: +27 36 488-1652, is conveniently situated near the base of Arthur's Seat in the Drakensberg.

Lotter, Chris; tel: +264 61 24-6310, operates paragliding tours in and to Namibia.

Lowveld Paragliding School, tel: +27 1375 4-2133, operates in Nelspruit.

Mlilwane is one of the Big Game Parks of Swaziland and can be contacted through their Central Booking Office, P O Box 234, Mbabane, Swaziland; tel: +268 44541, 6-1591/2/3 or 6-1037, fax: +268 4-0957/6-1594.

Neethling, Piet; tel: +27 451 8-2891, can tell you how to get to the Queenstown launch sites.

Para Sport, tel: +27 137 51-2883, is a paragliding school operating in Mpumalanga.

Paragliding Afrika, tel: +27 11 646-9714, fax: +27 11 486-2112 is a paragliding school in Johannesburg that operates in the Volksrust/Wakkerstroom area of Mpumalanga.

Parapente Cape, tel: +27 21 705-5801, is a paragliding school in Cape Town.

Paraventure, tel: +27 11 485-3293, is a paragliding school operating in Mpumalanga.

SAHPA (the South African Hang and Paragliding Association), P O Box 1993, Halfway House 1685, South Africa; tel/fax: +27 11 805-5429, can give you names of schools or clubs in your area.

SA Paragliding, tel: +27 137 50-1663, is a paragliding school operating in Mpumalanga.

Sky Scrapers, tel: +27 11 447-1793, is a paragliding school in Gauteng.

Thermal Riders, tel: +27 12 47-2952, or +27 82 892-3664, is a hang-gliding school in Gauteng.

Wild Sky Paragliding, tel: +27 336 32-0224, run courses and fly around the Bulwer area in the southern Drakensberg.

EQUIPMENT MANUFACTURERS AND IMPORTERS

Fun Wings, tel: +27 11 609-1678, retail local and imported paragliding equipment.

Parapente, tel: +27 21 705-5801, manufactures paragliders locally.

Peregrine Para Sports, tel: +27 11 706-3795, import a whole range of paragliding equipment.

CHAPTER 10

On the wings of a dream

Gliding

Southern Africa is a superb gliding venue, and a number of world records have been set in two spectacular sites: Bitterwasser in Namibia and Gariep Dam in the Free State Province of South Africa. Many pilots come to the region for the summer to enjoy the wonderful conditions and set records: either world records or just their personal best.

Getting started

In South Africa, glider pilot training is rather informal. Contact your nearest club, turn up on a morning when they are flying and put your name on the list for an introductory flight. You will be briefed on ground handling and emergency procedure and then fly in a dual-control glider with an instructor who will let you try using the controls and will explain the principles as you go along. If you enjoy the experience you will need to join a club, undergo a medical examination and continue your training.

This is usually a rather haphazard affair in terms of time management, but not in terms of safety. In South Africa glider instructors are not paid to teach; they do it for the love of the sport, and the fees you pay are for the use of the glider and tow plane and to keep the club financially liquid. So you can't book for a particular time, turn up for your lesson and leave afterwards. You need to spend the whole day at the airfield in order to do one or two flights. You will also find that the more running around you do to help other pilots, the more flying time you will get. This is just the way it works at present.

Because each student is different (for example, some may be experienced pilots with thousands of hours in motorised aircraft, and others may never have flown at all), the theory is not taught in formal lectures. Your instructor will tell you what you need to know as you progress and can put the theory into practice.

Once you have proved yourself competent, you will be allowed to fly solo and then, after performing a number of different tasks such as a flight of five hours, a flight of 50 km, a height of 1 000 m above the ground and spot landings, you will obtain your silver C certificate and your glider pilot's licence.

If you can't afford the time it will take to get this far, there are two ways to circumvent this lengthy process. You can join one of the week-long training camps run by the clubs from time to time, or go to Bitterwasser in Namibia where professional instructors are available in the gliding season (November to January). These are usually European pilots who come to Namibia for the wonderful conditions and finance their flying by doing flight instruction.

You will probably still need to put in many hours to obtain your licence and, unless you buy your own glider, will have to spend ages at the airstrip waiting for a chance to use a club glider. For this sport you need either a lot of time or a lot of money!

Equipment

A glider is a sophisticated aircraft, usually built from very light space-age materials such as a composite of glassfibre, carbon fibre and Kevlar. Although they are designed by pragmatists who are concerned almost solely with performance, they are beautifully proportioned, a bit like an albatross, with long thin wings and a smooth streamlined body.

Once in the air a glider can float like a hawk, gracefully circling ever higher and higher on a thermal until it veers off and starts to fly cross country, losing altitude until it finds another thermal to "refuel". The problem, of course, is getting the bird — as these beautiful craft are often quite aptly called — into the air. This is done in one of two ways, either by a tow plane or by winch. All gliding equipment (such as the glider radio) and all safety equipment (such as parachutes) is supplied by the club.

If you are about to do an introductory flight you won't need any special equipment or clothing, but do bring a peaked cap and sunglasses as it can be very bright in the glider. Also bring a cardigan or jacket that opens up completely so you can just pull it over your arms and chest without unstrapping your safety harness if it gets cold. (And it sometimes gets very cold indeed if you go high enough.) For the ground waiting time, bring sunscreen, a deck chair and a picnic lunch. It is a good idea to bring a book as well, but the chances are you will spend so much time chatting about gliding that you won't even look at it.

Options for people with disabilities

You need to be able to use both hands and both feet to fly a standard glider and must, obviously, have reasonable eyesight. You also need sufficiently good hearing to communicate on the radio. Although it has not been done in southern Africa, there are wheelchair-bound people in other parts of the world who fly modified hand-controlled gliders.

Regular events

The Magalies Gliding Club holds a Wave Camp at Bulwer in the southern Drakensberg in KwaZulu-Natal for two weeks around the end of July or beginning of August.

Towards the end of December or beginning of January, gliders from all over the world converge on the area around the Gariep Dam in the Free State for the Records Camp, where everyone tries to better their own (and others') records.

Regional championships are held in the various provinces in October and the national championships are held towards the end of December at Jan Kempdorp north of Kimberley.

Western Cape

The Western Cape Gliding Club is based at Worcester, about 100 km from Cape Town. Although the thermals are not as dependable as those inland, there is excellent ridge soaring all through the year and strong wave in north-westerly winds (usually in winter). The scenery is far prettier than inland; you fly over vineyards and spectacular Cape fold mountains. The club offers both aero-tow and winch launches and also has one motor-glider.

WHILE IN THE AREA

Non-flying companions may choose to visit the nearby village of MacGregor. (See chapter 5 under Breede River for details, and also for the Breede River Wine Route and other attractions in the area.)

Eastern Cape

The Eastern Province Gliding Club has its base in Uitenhage, just inland from Port Elizabeth. Contact the **Soaring Society of South Africa** for more information.

KwaZulu-Natal

There are two gliding clubs in this province, the Howick/Pietermaritzburg Gliding Club and the Estcourt Gliding Club, but the most spectacular flying is at the Drakensberg in late winter. For further information about the local clubs, contact the **Soaring Society of South Africa**.

THE WAVE CAMP

Towards the end of July, the Magalies Gliding Club bring their gliders down to Bulwer for two weeks of wild and wonderful wave-riding. The south-west wind blows over Lesotho and as it reaches KwaZulu-Natal it falls over the side of the Drakensberg, hits the ground and rises up in a huge wave. It can be a little hair-raising getting into the wave but once in it you can ride this smooth, powerful updraft for the length of the escarpment. The scenery is spectacular and there is a good chance of snow on the high Berg. This is well worth travelling down for. Contact the Magalies Gliding Club or the **Soaring Society of South Africa** for more information.

WHILE IN THE AREA

The Drakensberg is famed for its wonderful hiking (see chapter 7), there may be ice climbing (see chapter 18), and horse trails can be arranged (see chapter 16).

Gauteng and Free State

There are a number of gliding clubs in these provinces as the gliding can be superb, especially in summer when huge thermals build up. In these conditions you can do long cross-country flights, and many pilots from all over the region (and all over the world) congregate around the Gariep Dam area in late December to do their best. For more information about this event, contact the **Soaring Society of South Africa**. In winter the flying is still excellent as good thermals build up in the clear, sunny weather experienced in this season and there is less risk of thunderstorms. As the terrain is rather flat, the scenery is not as pretty as at the coast.

The Magaliesberg Gliding Club is by far the biggest in the region and operates from Orient Airfield, which is conveniently situated about an hour's drive from Johannesburg. The club has four twin-seaters and two single-seaters for hire and there are over 100 private gliders permanently at the airfield. Launches are by aero-tow. Visiting flyers are welcome to camp in the grounds or stay at one of the many nearby guesthouses.

Botswana

Since it is large, flat and hot, gliding conditions are excellent over the Kalahari, but the only club in Botswana is the **Kalahari Wings Gliding Club**, which is based at the Orapa Diamond Mine near Serowe. This is a closed mining town and, although guests are welcome, it takes a lot of paperwork to arrange a visit. You need to write to the chair of the club who will organise security clearance and, if you like, accommodation in their guest cottage.

The club has four gliders, one trainer and three single-seaters, and is planning to purchase another single-seater soon. All launches are by winch. There is a fully equipped clubhouse.

WHILE IN THE AREA

The Khama Rhino Sanctuary, where you may see black and white rhino and other game, is very close by. Not too far away by Botswana standards are the Makgadikgadi Pans and the Okavango Delta (see chapters 15 and 16).

Namibia

This desert country produces awesome thermals. Bitterwasser, near Mariental, is one of the best gliding venues in the world; five world records have been set here and numerous diamonds flown. The thermals are exceptional and there is a natural airfield in the form of a salt pan. Bitterwasser can also be used as a springboard for long cross-country flights to other parts of the country. In the main soaring season, November to January, you can train here under the auspices of well-qualified European instructors who follow the swallows south for the excellent summer flying. If you have broken a record or flown your first 1 000 km flight you may plant a palm tree; there is already a long avenue of palms leading to the farm.

For further information contact the **Soaring Society of Namibia**.

WHILE IN THE AREA

At Bitterwasser there is accommodation in the form of comfortable chalets, a swimming pool and a full bar and restaurant. There are mountain biking and hiking trails, horse riding is available and game drives can also be arranged, so non-gliding companions should be well occupied. A tennis court is planned. Also see chapter 7 for the Fish River Hiking Trail and chapter 6 for the Orange River Canoe Trail, both which are not too distant by Namibian standards.

Listings

To contact one of the South African gliding clubs, phone the Soaring Society and find out who the present committee members are.

Kalahari Wings Gliding Club, write to the Chairman, c/o Private Bag 1, Orapa, Botswana; tel: +267 27-0201 and ask for the chairman of the gliding club. This is the main switchboard of the mine, so it could be an expensive call.

Soaring Society of Namibia, Private Bag 13003, Windhoek, Namibia; tel: +264 6672 3830 or tel/fax: +264 61 24-9664.

Soaring Society of South Africa, P O Box 1993, Halfway House 1685, South Africa; tel: +27 11 805-0366/8/9.

CHAPTER 11

Get carried away

Passenger flights in unusual craft

For a totally different perspective of southern Africa, take a bird's-eye view. A number of regular balloon and microlight trips are offered in various parts of the region. The following are some of the more interesting. I have not included flights in ordinary light planes but you can charter one almost anywhere.

All passenger flights are subject to the same rules governing major airlines. Balloons, helicopters and light planes are the only aircraft that are licensed to take paying passengers, but trips in microlights or ultralights are offered, for example, at Victoria Falls. These are not passenger flights per se. When doing these flights, you are treated as a first-time student and are given an introductory flight lesson with an instructor. (The instruction content is, in fact, minimal but the trips are marketed this way for legal reasons.)

Balloon trips anywhere in Africa are conducted at sunrise because this is when the air is most stable. Later in the day, thermals and winds can make ballooning rather tricky. This means getting up very early indeed, but in most parts of southern Africa dawn is a very pleasant time of day.

Recommended clothing

Because balloon flights start early in the morning you will need a really warm jacket, especially if you are transported in an open vehicle. You will need to be able to strip down, though, so dress in easily removable layers. Comfortable shoes are a good idea and a hat is almost essential. For once, it's not to keep the sun off — the burners are just above your head and, although it is perfectly safe, it is quite hot when they are given a burst of flame. A nice sturdy hat should protect you from this minor discomfort. It might get bright after the sun rises, so take sunglasses.

On a microlight trip ensure that you don't wear anything loose such as a hat or scarf. The position in which you sit on a microlight is not elegant so skirts are not practical at all — rather wear jeans or shorts.

Opportunities for people with disabilities

Airtrack Balloon Adventures have flown wheelchair users in the past, but you do need to give them advance notice. They will either take the whole wheelchair on board or build in a raised padded seat with armrests. This can be done only in absolutely ideal flying conditions when a soft landing can be guaranteed, because if the landing is a bit hard, passengers need to brace themselves and land with bent legs to avoid injury. People with disabilities must be accompanied by someone who is prepared to take responsibility for them, as the pilot will be preoccupied with flying. There should be no problem with any of the other craft, as you are strapped into a seat. You will probably just need someone to help you into and out of the aircraft.

Gauteng

There is good flying within a very short drive of the main urban areas.

MAGALIESBERG BALLOON TOUR

This is a gentle float over the farmlands of the Magaliesberg. Depending on the wind, you may go over the Hartebeespoort Dam, the mountains, or a nearby game farm. The whole trip is very lighthearted and you are guaranteed to have fun. Flights last about an hour.

You are given coffee/tea and biscuits on arrival and you can watch the inflation of the balloon. Champagne and/or orange juice are served in flight or on landing and you enjoy a sumptuous sit-down brunch on return to the launch site. There are flush toilets near the launch site.

You can make your own way there (about an hour's drive from Johannesburg), or you can be picked up from a number of participating guesthouses (details from the operator). Alternatively, you can be picked up from any city hotel.

The flight is operated by **Bill Harrop's Original Balloon Safaris**, and booking is essential.

CROCODILE RIVER VALLEY

This flight leaves from the grounds of the Glenburn Lodge in the Swartkops Mountain Gorge on the edge of the Magaliesberg, about half an hour's drive from Johannesburg. Tea and coffee is served on arrival and you may watch the inflation of the balloon. The flight lasts about an hour and is over the lion and rhino park, where you are very likely to see a large variety of game, including the two species after which the park is named. You end the trip with an English breakfast at the lodge.

This trip is run by **Airtrack Balloon Adventures**, and booking is essential.

WHILE IN THE AREA

After your flight, you might like to visit the lion and rhino park from ground level, see the Wonder Cave, or even Sterkfontein Cave (see chapter 17), ride a horse or visit a trout farm. Information on all the above, except Sterkfontein, is available from the **Kromdraai Conservancy**.

North-west Province

Tourism in this province is based mainly on game-viewing. Consequently, the flights in this area actually take place within a game reserve or national park.

PILANESBERG

The Pilanesberg National Park covers an area of 50 000 ha in the North-west Province. Much of the park is on a huge extinct volcanic crater which is only really discernible from the air. You can be collected from any of the hotels or lodges in the Pilanesberg/Sun City area and are transported to the launch in open game-viewing vehicles, allowing you a quick half-hour game drive. By the time you get out of the vehicle the balloon should be fully inflated as the launch is right in the reserve, and it is not advisable to hang around aimlessly. Animals you are likely to see, either on the flight or the game drive, include black and white rhino, elephant, buffalo, cheetah, zebra and many species of antelope. Brown hyena and leopard also occur in the park. The flight is mostly at a low level, allowing you a good view of the game, but you do go up high enough for a short while to get a good view of the crater. The trip lasts about an hour and champagne is served on landing. You then enjoy another game drive on your return to Bakubung Lodge where you are served a full English breakfast before being transferred back to your hotel or lodge.

The trip is run by **Airtrack Balloon Adventures**, and booking is essential.

WHILE IN THE AREA

Phone the Safari Desk at Sun City, +27 1465 2-1561, to book a game drive at Pilanesberg, go surfing in the Valley of the Waves, visit the Palace of the Lost City, or throw away your hard-earned cash at the casino at Sun City.

MADIKWE

At time of writing, **Bill Harrop's Original Balloon Safaris** had just started game-viewing flights over this 75 000 ha reserve right on the Botswana border. Animals known to occur in the reserve include rhino, lion, elephant, wild dog, cheetah, wildebeest and many species of antelope. While not flying you may enjoy a game drive or escorted walk.

Mpumalanga

This popular and very scenic province is spectacular from the air. The standard balloon trip here varies and may take off from any one of a number of different venues, depending on weather or pre-arranged passenger preferences. You are served tea or coffee on arrival and you may watch the balloons being inflated. Your flight lasts about an hour and is over the pine plantations, forests, streams, waterfalls and hills. After the flight you have breakfast at a nearby lodge. If you wish, you can arrange in advance to fly over the Blyde River Canyon, Pilgrim's Rest or a private game reserve. You can arrange to be collected from any hotel in the Hazyview, White River or Nelspruit area. You then meet at the launch site, which is usually in or near the grounds of one of the many charming lodges or guesthouses in the area.

This trip is run by **Airtrack Balloon Adventures**, and booking is essential.

WHILE IN THE AREA

Mpumalanga is particularly well known for game. Besides the Kruger National Park there are 71 conservation areas in this small, but spectacular, province. Beautiful scenery, including steep mountain passes and pretty waterfalls, and myriad hiking trails (see chapter 7), are just some of the other attractions.

Namibia

The first (and so far only) balloon trip in Namibia is run over the Namib in the region of the Namib-Naukluft Park. As usual the trip starts at dawn, allowing you a view of the gentle desert sunrise. There is a chance of seeing a variety of game, the most likely being gemsbok and springbok. Breakfast is served after the flight.

The trip is run by **Namib Sky Adventures**, and booking is essential.

WHILE IN THE AREA

You can camp at Sesriem campsite, near the Sesriem Canyon, which always holds water and is a great place to escape the midday heat. A drive of about 63 km takes you to the parking lot near Sossusvlei. A further 4 km, negotiable only by four-wheel drive, will take you to Sossusvlei, where you can climb the highest sand-dunes in the world and, if there is water in the vlei, see thousands of flamingoes. You are almost certain to see springbok and gemsbok. If you do not have a four-wheel-drive vehicle, you can walk a few hundred metres to a series of very high dunes and climb those instead. You can rent a four-wheel-drive vehicle for the day; enquire at park reception.

Zambezi Valley

"Scenes so lovely must have been gazed upon by angels in their flight." David Livingstone said it all. Victoria Falls from the air is an unforgettable sight.

BATOKA SKY MICROLIGHTING

This is a 15-minute flight over the falls from just upstream on the Zambian side. A half-hour flight includes game-viewing in the adjacent Mosi-oa-Tunya National Park, or you could just do a half-hour game-viewing flight. It is in a trike-style microlight with an open cockpit and you sit behind the pilot. Your field of vision is as wide as the flexibility of your neck and you fly open to the sky; it is an exhilarating feeling. This craft is a "pusher", which means the engine is behind you. This has one major disadvantage: if you drop anything it will go into the propeller and almost certainly cause a crash. For this reason, you are asked to empty your pockets of everything before take-off and not to wear hats or other loose articles of clothing. This means you can't take a camera along, but there is a wing-mounted 35 mm camera into which you may put your own film and the pilot will operate the shutter when you signal to him. It has a wide-angle lens and the microlight (and occupants) are visible in each photo. You wear a helmet with a headset so you can communicate with the pilot at all times.

The flight is operated by **Batoka Sky** on the Zambian side. You can book direct, through your hotel or through any one of the booking agents in the area.

BUSHBIRDS FLYING SAFARIS

This flight over the falls starts from the Zimbabwean side. It is in an ultralight, with a plexiglass windshield and a front-mounted propeller so you may take your own camera or video camera. Because of the windshield, you can even change film or lenses while in the air. For your own peace of mind, ensure that your camera has a strap. The flight starts at the Victoria Falls international airport, which is quite a distance from the falls on the main Bulawayo road. You sit next to the pilot and can communicate through a headset. There are two identical planes, so you can arrange to fly at the same time as a companion and photograph each other in the air.

Your flight to the falls is over some Brachystegia woodland and then along the gorge. If you start early enough in the day, you may see the rafting. You then fly over the falls and return to the airport. You can choose to do a 50-minute flight and include a game flight over the Zambezi National Park.

The flight is operated by **Bushbirds Flying Safaris**. Booking is through **Safari par Excellence**, your hotel or any one of the booking agents in the area.

OTHER FLIGHTS AT VICTORIA FALLS

If the above sounds a bit too adventurous you can fly over the falls in somewhat more conventional craft. You can choose between a seaplane, which leaves from upstream, or a helicopter which leaves from near the Elephant Hills Hotel on the Zimbabwean side. Booking is through **Shearwater**, your hotel or any one of the booking agents in the area.

WHILE IN THE AREA

See chapters 6, 9, 12, 13 and 16 for information on river rafting and canoeing, skydiving, bungi jumping or horseback safaris.

Listings

OPERATORS AND BOOKING AGENTS

Airtrack Balloon Adventures, P O Box 630, Muldersdrift 1747, South Africa; tel: +27 11 957-2322/3, 957-2350, fax: +27 11 957-2465, do balloon trips in Mpumalanga, the Crocodile River Valley and the Pilanesberg Game Reserve.

Batoka Sky, P O Box 60305, Livingstone, Zambia; tel: +260 3 32-3672, fax: +260 3 32-4289, do microlight flights over the Victoria Falls.

Bill Harrop's Original Balloon Safari, P O Box 67, Randburg 2125; tel: +27 11 705-3201, fax: +27 11 705-3203, do balloon trips in the Magaliesberg and over Madikwe Game Reserve.

Bushbird Safaris do ultralight flights over Victoria Falls. Bookings are through Safari Par Excellence, P O Box 108, Victoria Falls, Zimbabwe; tel: +263 13 4424/2051/3/4, fax: +263 13 4510. Zambia: tel: +260 3 32-3349/32-1432, fax: +260 3 32-3542. Johannesburg: P O Box 1395, Randburg 2125; tel: +27 11 888-3500, fax: +27 11 888-4942.

Kromdraai Conservancy, tel: +27 11 957-0034, 957-0241.

Namib Sky Adventure Safaris, P O Box 197, Maltahöhe, Namibia; tel +264 6632, ask for 5703, do balloon trips over the Namib.

Shearwater, P O Box 125 Victoria Falls; tel: +263 13 4471, fax: +263 13 4341, Harare; tel:

+263 4 75-7831/6, fax: +263 4 75-7836. Johannesburg: P O Box 76270, Wendywood 2144, South Africa; tel: +27 11 804-6537, fax: +27 11 804-6539, take bookings for the helicopter and seaplane trips at Victoria Falls.

ACCOMMODATION

Victoria Falls/Livingstone

See the listings at the end of chapter 6.

Mpumalanga

Liaise with Airtrack Balloon Adventures as the launch site may change.

Gauteng

The most convenient place to stay for the Airtrack Balloon Adventures trip is the Glenburn Lodge, P O Box 492, Muldersdrift 1747, South Africa; tel: +27 11 957-2691, fax: +27 11 957-2697.

Bill Harrop's Original Balloon Safaris will happily book you into one of a number of delightful lodges (see above for address), or accommodate you in their spacious home on a B&B or DB&B basis.

Pilanesberg

The Palace of the Lost City and Sun City, Sun International Reservations, P O Box 784487, Sandton 2146, South Africa; tel: +27 11 780-7800, fax: +27 11 780-7457, are both rather glitzy, luxurious casino resort hotels.

Pilanesberg National Park, tel: +27 11 465-5423, has varied accommodation including camping, tented camps, self-catering chalets and private self-catering camps. There is a restaurant and swimming pool.

Kwa Maritane and Bakubung are both luxurious RCI-affiliated timeshare safari lodges. Booking address for both is P O Box 1091, Rivonia 2128, South Africa; tel: +27 11 806-4100.

Namibia

Namib Sky Adventures are based at the Namib Rand Game Ranch and will organise accommodation there for you if you arrange it in advance.

There is a campsite at Sesriem in the Namib-Naukluft Park, booking through the Director of Tourism, P O Box 13346, Windhoek, Namibia; tel: +264 61 284-2111, fax: +264 61 22-1930.

The Sossusvlei Karos Lodge, P O Box 6900, Windhoek, Namibia; tel: +264 61 24-8338, is a very comfortable, upmarket establishment near the Sesriem campsite.

CHAPTER 12

The ultimate high

Skydiving

Skydiving has absolutely nothing to do with parachutes. They are just a necessary encumbrance to ensure that you survive the skydive. What counts is the short but sweet time when you are "flying" free, albeit downwards. Once you reach terminal velocity, you can turn in the air the way a surfer turns in the sea. You can't go up, but you can track sideways and speed up or slow down your rate of descent. Once you are stable and can control your flight, you can link up with other skydivers and make formations in the sky; an art form second to none for sheer creativity and exhilaration.

Getting started

Initial training is usually a one-day or weekend activity. You meet your instructor and fellow students, usually at the drop zone (DZ), and commence with theory training. Once you have mastered some of the complexities of how parachutes work, how to steer them and how to land them, you do some practical exercises. You will practice exiting the plane, simulating pulling your ripcord and landings. And then you will do your first jump. In years gone by there was no choice. You did a static line jump from about 2 500 ft (aviation has not metricated: that's about 800 m). There are now two other options. If you are serious about wanting to skydive you can do an accelerated free-fall (AFF) course. You exit from about 10 000 ft (about 3 000 m) with two instructors who hold on to you and stabilise you, ensuring that you get into the right position. They stay with you until you have deployed your canopy and then track away to deploy their own. If you just want to give it a try, do a tandem jump. As you would expect, you are quite firmly attached to the instructor, who controls the whole jump. Once he or she has deployed the canopy you may steer the parachute until the landing.

Equipment

While you are learning, the club will supply all the equipment you need, such as a parachute, helmet and jumpsuit. You just need to wear comfortable clothes such as shorts or leggings and a T-shirt. You should wear comfortable shoes, such as running shoes. Hiking boots are fine as long as they don't have little hooks for lacing up.

Options for people with disabilities

If you have limited or no use of your legs you could do a tandem parachute jump. Obviously this would be absolutely no problem at all for people with impaired eyesight or hearing.

Regular events

There is usually a boogie over Easter and Christmas. The venues change from year to year so contact the **Aero Club of SA** for information.

Regional and national championships usually take place in summer and the venues vary.

Western Cape

WESTERN PROVINCE SPORT PARACHUTE CLUB

The DZ is at Citrusdal, about an hour's drive from Cape Town on the N7. It is very pretty with views of the surrounding mountains and the orange groves. The club flies a Cessna.

WHILE IN THE AREA

Non-skydiving companions can go for day walks, do one of the mountain bike trails (see chapter 8), or hang around by the pretty river at the bottom of the DZ. The hot springs known as the Baths are just a few kilometres down the road (see chapter 8).

CAPE PARACHUTE CLUB

The DZ is in Stellenbosch, in the heart of the Cape winelands. The views are stunning with the Hottentots Holland Mountains and the whole of False Bay unfolding beneath you. The club flies a Cessna.

WHILE IN THE AREA

The obvious thing to do here is a wine-tasting trip, which could take up a whole day. In summer the diving nearby is very good (see chapter 5). See chapter 16 for horseback wine tasting trips and chapter 8 for cycling wine tasting trips.

KwaZulu-Natal

The main club in this province is the Pietermaritzburg Parachute Club but there are two smaller clubs, Vryheid Parachute Club and Drakensberg Parachute Club in Ladysmith. They all operate Cessnas.

Gauteng/Mpumalanga/Northern Province

There are a number of clubs in this area, most of which are less than two hour's drive from Johannesburg. Pretoria Skydiving Club at Wonderboom is the biggest and flies two Pilatus Porters so you can do up to 20-way formations. Companions not wanting to skydive may like to do a hike or gentle one-day horse trail in the nearby Windybrow Reserve, see chapter 16.

Leopard Rock Skydiving Club is right next to Sun City so you can go and throw your hard-earned cash away at the casino after a day's skydiving, go inland surfing in the Valley of the Waves at the Lost City or enjoy a gentle balloon flight over the Pilanesberg National Park (see chapter 11). There are clubs in Carletonville, Klerksdorp, Mmabatho and Witbank.

Free State/Northern Cape

There are two drop zones in this area, at Bloemfontein and Kimberley. Both clubs fly Cessnas.

Namibia

There are skydiving clubs in Windhoek, Tsumeb and Swakopmund. The Windhoek club flies a Cessna Caravan, which takes about 13 skydivers.

Botswana

There is a skydiving club in Botswana but it doesn't have its own plane. The Leopard Rock Skydiving Club flies its plane up once a month and the local skydivers go wild. For information contact Leopard Rock.

Victoria Falls

Victoria Falls is a great place to skydive as the scenery is quite spectacular (also see chapter 11). If you are a qualified skydiver, bring your certification and logbook or, if you would like to learn, do a first jump course with Zambezi Vultures or a tandem jump with Tandemmania. They operate from the Victoria Falls Airport. Bookings for both are through **Safari par Excellence**.

Listings

CLUBS AND OPERATORS

The committee members of clubs change regularly so contact the Aero Club of SA for the latest contact numbers.

Aero Club of South Africa, P O Box 1993, Halfway House 1685, South Africa; tel: +27 11 805-0366, fax: +27 11 805-2765.

Safari par Excellence, P O Box 108, Victoria Falls, Zimbabwe; tel: +263 13 4424/2051/3/4, fax: +263 13 4510. Zambia: tel: +260 3 32-3349/32-1432, fax: +260 3 32-3542. Johannesburg: P O Box 1395, Randburg 2125; tel: +27 11 888-3500, fax: +27 11 888-4942, take bookings for Zambezi Vultures and Tandemmania.

MANUFACTURERS AND RETAIL OUTLETS

Parachute Industries of Southern Africa, P O Box 391447, Bramley 2018, South Africa; tel: +27 11 444-2640, fax: +27 11 444-4116, designs and manufactures all parachute equipment.

Icarus Airwear, tel: +27 11 805-2812, fax: +27 11 805-2317, manufactures skydiving accessories and retails all skydiving equipment.

CHAPTER 13

Go jump off a bridge

Bridge and bungi jumping

There's not much to this rather adrenalin-intensive activity. It's as easy as falling off a bridge. But there's nothing easy about taking that first step up onto the railing and looking down into the void . . .

Bungi jumping is the practice of throwing yourself head-first off a bridge with an elastic band tied to your feet. It is a big elastic band, it is well tied, and you do wear a back-up safety harness, but you still jump off a bridge with an elastic band tied to your feet. The sport evolved from the Pacific Island practice of jumping from specially constructed bamboo platforms with vines tied around one's feet in order to ensure a good yam crop. The islanders were a little more daring than modern bungi jumpers, though. They would calculate very carefully so that their heads would just touch the ground before they bounced back. Professional bungi jump operators calculate that their clients will bounce quite a few metres above the ground. Experienced bungi jumpers do water jumps at Victoria Falls, though; they work things out so that their heads dip in the water before they are bounced back.

In South Africa, bridge jumping was devised on a windy day by frustrated BASE jumpers (people who jump off bridges with parachutes). Compared to this practice, bridge jumping is extremely safe and positively dull.

Equipment and clothing

All equipment is supplied by the operators and is checked and replaced regularly. The bungis are made according to a secret recipe and the ropes for bridge jumping are climbing ropes that are specifically designed to stop a fall. Harnesses are standard climbing harnesses. Clothing is optional.

Options for people with disabilities

At least one paraplegic has done a bridge jump at the Gouritz River. Bungi jumping, though, would be foolishly risky for paraplegics and people who have very limited use of their legs as it places a considerable stress on your joints.

The Gouritz River Bridge

The Gouritz River Bridge, near Albertinia on the N2 (between Cape Town and Port Elizabeth) comes alive on weekends, public holidays and during the December holiday season. It is just perfect: on a major road, high (about 75 m) and, best of all, it has a structurally ideal, accessible and unused bridge. The old bridge is where all the action takes place: there's plenty of parking, toilets and, in season, mobile snack stalls.

BRIDGE JUMP

This can be done in only a very few places in the world and the two Gouritz River bridges are just the right height and distance apart. Standing on the old bridge, you kit up in a climbing harness and attach yourself to three climbing ropes (two working and one back-up) which are attached to the new bridge across the void. You climb onto a custom-built platform, level with the top of the protective railing and wait. And then you hear "54321 bridge jump!" and you're off. You freefall for about 40 to 45 m and are then pulled into a huge arc, accelerating all the time. You reach the end of your swing and pendulum backwards and forwards a few times before you are lowered to the ground and then you face the steep walk back out of the gorge.

This jump is operated by **Wild Thing Adventures** who are there every weekend, public holidays and the whole holiday season, weather permitting. It is not necessary to book — just turn up on the day. They have a camp near the bridge, where you can arrange to stay if you want to make a weekend of it.

HELL SWING

This is also done with climbing ropes but, instead of being attached to the new bridge, the ropes are attached to the opposite underside of the bridge from which you jump. You jump off, fall, get pulled into a backward swing, getting a close look at the bridge girders and then settle into a gentle wide swing. You are lowered to the ground and walk up out of the gorge.

This jump is operated by **The Edge**, who may or may not be there on weekends and holidays. It is not necessary to book — just turn up on the day.

BUNGI JUMP

You are weighed, allotted the right thickness and length of bungi cord and tied in. The cord is tied very securely around your feet and you have a backup harness around your waist. You then climb up onto the platform and wait for the count. You dive head-first off the bridge, the bungi stretches to its limit and you are then bounced back up. You bounce around a few times and are then lowered to the bottom.

This jump is operated by **Kiwi Extreme** who are there every day, weather permitting. It is not necessary to book — just turn up on the day.

Bloukrans River Bridge

If and when this comes on line it will be the highest commercial bungi jump in the world — usurping the position previously held by Vic Falls. The bridge is 216 m high but the jump is only about 160 m. You jump from the arch support of the bridge — not from the road — and getting there and back is an experience in itself. After the jump you are winched back up to the bridge.

This jump is operated by **Kiwi Extreme** who are on the bridge every day.

WHILE IN THE AREA

There is good surfing at Stilbaai and Mossel Bay (see chapter 14). The diving at Mossel Bay can be good and, if you are prepared to venture further afield, it is often great at Knysna (see chapter 5). The Gouritz River marks the beginning of the Garden Route which has loads of adventure activities. See chapters 7, 8, 14 and 16 for further information.

Victoria Falls Bridge

When the Bloukrans jump comes on line, this will no longer be the highest commercial bungi jump in the world — but at 104 m it is still pretty high. The procedure is much the same as described above, except that, regardless of which country you are staying in, you need your passport to get onto the bridge; tell the immigration official that you are just going onto the bridge and get a gate pass. After the jump, you are winched back up to the bridge.

As well as the huge adrenalin rush due to the height of the jump, the view is incredible. If you are only ever going to do one bungi jump in your life it should be this one. If you like, you can do the "Gruesome twosome"; you bungi off the bridge, are lowered into a waiting raft and then do the best one-day white water rafting trip in the world. No self-respecting adrenalin junkie would miss out on this opportunity.

The jumping is operated by **Africa Extreme** but you can book through all the adventure companies in Victoria Falls or through your hotel.

WHILE IN THE AREA

Victoria Falls is the adventure capital of Africa. See chapters 6, 11, 12 and 16 for information on river rafting and canoeing, skydiving, microlighting and ultralighting or horseback safaris.

Listings

OPERATORS AND BOOKING AGENTS

Africa Extreme, P O Box 125, Victoria Falls, Zimbabwe; tel: +260 3 32-4156, do the bungi jumping off the Victoria Falls Bridge. You can book directly or through any of the booking agents in Victoria Falls or Livingstone: see listings at the end of chapter 6.

The Edge do the Hell Swing off the Gouritz River Bridge from time to time. Their presence on the bridge is not quite as predictable as Kiwi Extreme or Wild Thing.

Kiwi Extreme, tel: +27 444 97-7161 or +27 444 7448, offer bungi jumping off the Gouritz River Bridge and the Bloukrans River Bridge.

Wild Thing Adventures, tel: +27 21 461-1653, offer bridge jumping off the Gouritz River Bridge.

CHAPTER 14

Catch a wave

Surfing and sea kayaking

Of the countries covered in this book, only South Africa and Namibia have coastlines — and both have some excellent surf.

Mozambique does have some good surfing, especially at Ponta do Ouro, Tofinho and Tofo, but it is not within the scope of this book. It is certainly worth taking a board if you are travelling to Mozambique; there are probably numerous unknown breaks. Be very wary about exploring the Mozambican countryside, though. It is foolish to travel on any but well-used roads as there are many landmines lying around.

There are many excellent spots in South Africa, and some in Namibia, ranging from big, hollow waves to nice little beach breaks. Some of the best waves are conveniently close to cities but some are way off the beaten track. The following is just a rough guide for the visiting surfer or for beginners who aren't sure where to try out. Further information can be obtained from surf shops, local surfers or from *Surfing in Southern Africa* (see reference under Further Information at the end of this chapter).

If you are not keen on trying to find surf spots yourself, contact one of the surf safari companies in the listings or enquire at surf shops. This is not a major industry in South Africa, so they will probably be happy to tailor-make a trip for a reasonably sized group.

Getting started

In the past, surfing was something you just tried out and learned by trial and error. Although most people still use this time-honoured method, it is now a lot easier for the aspiring surfer. A number of dedicated surfing training operations have started up around the country. Some of the better known are **Pro Surf Coaching** and **Ocean Sports Centre** in Durban, **Bay Surf School** in Port Elizabeth and **Screeming Blue** in East London. In Cape Town there is a free surfing clinic for beginners at Muizenberg Beach from 8.30 am to 9.30 am on Sunday mornings, winter and summer, rain or shine. In summer it's worth coming early as they sometimes start around 8.00 am. You can just turn up but if you want more information contact **Charlie Moir.**

Equipment

Surfing is one of those glorious sports you can do with absolutely no equipment whatsoever — apart from a swimming costume, and that isn't really necessary, it's just considered polite. In fact, body surfing is probably the purest form of the sport. In order to catch faster waves, ride for longer or do interesting manoeuvres, though, you will need some artificial assistance. The simplest are fins and webbed gloves, which enable you to body surf more efficiently. A hand "gun" gives you a little more control while still essentially body surfing. And then you move on to boards.

The art of designing and building surfboards has become very sophisticated. They range from fairly simple general-purpose boards to ones designed specifically for a particular wave. If you are sufficiently advanced to consider those, though, you won't be reading this for advice. Your safest bet is to choose a board similar to those that most people of your size and weight seem to be using in your area.

Body boards are often, but not necessarily, made of softer material than real surfboards and are much shorter. You wear fins while using them and, once you have caught a wave, stay down on the board. This is the type of thing most children do on holiday but it is not kids' stuff. Once you have mastered the art you can ride awesome waves and do some radical manoeuvres, such as full 360s or barrel rolls. These boards are still the board of choice for people who just like to "play in the waves" though, and have the added advantage that the softer boards cause less damage if you wipe out.

If the idea of standing up on a board seems somewhat daunting, but you don't fancy lying on your tummy either, try a kneeboard. The advantage of kneeboards is that you can use fins to paddle out and catch waves, which is very important if you are still working on your upper body strength.

Some people surf sitting down, of course. There are a number of "boats" which are commonly used for surfing. The most common is the paddleski — specifically designed for fun surfing. They are stable, easy to manoeuvre and roll and are constructed like a surfboard from fibreglass with no interior spaces. Surf-skis are very different. These are mostly used by lifesavers to get out through the waves quickly. They are very long, thin craft, also with no interior spaces. They are pretty unstable and require considerable skill to paddle, especially to surf. Many river kayakers play in the surf with their white-water kayaks with a great deal of success and specially designed sea kayaks are also great for surfing. The disadvantage of kayaks is that, due to the considerable space within them, you have to return to the beach to empty the water out of your boat if you fall out and don't get your roll right.

In the Cape you will not be able to surf without a wetsuit, and even along the coast of KwaZulu-Natal you will be a lot more comfortable and be able to stay in the water longer if you wear one. In the warmer water you can get by with a 3 mm shortie, or you might find a suit with detachable sleeves useful. As you move closer to the Cape, you will need a more substantial suit.

The most practical all-round suit for South African conditions is a 3 mm spider suit, which you can use from KwaZulu-Natal to the Cape. If you are planning to do a lot of Cape surfing, though, consider a West Coast, Blizzard or similar suit. These are just trade names for a 3 mm spider suit with a 5 mm single nylon chest section — ideal in chilly water. In the Cape, you may even like to wear a hoodie as, as you can well imagine, pushing under an 8 °C wave can be very painful. Depending on your cold tolerance you might also like to wear gloves and booties. You may think this will make you look like a wimp, but don't worry. In Cape Town, no-one will laugh at you!

Organised surfing trips

Not many of these are available in southern Africa. Tekweni Backpackers Hostel in Durban sometimes organise budget "surfaris". Coastal Kayak Trails, in the Western Cape, will organise a whole day or weekend of kayak surfing if there is sufficient demand, otherwise they do flatter scenic trips.

KwaZulu-Natal

The main attraction of this coast, which extends from the Mozambique border to Port Edward, is the warm water. You can surf here without a wetsuit although, obviously, you can stay in much longer with a light shortie. There are some world-class breaks and many fun spots for beginners.

NORTH COAST

This glorious subtropical coast, also known as the Dolphin Coast, is a very popular holiday destination with many resorts strung out along the beaches. There are, nevertheless, many small unspoilt beaches left to be explored. This is not the greatest surfing destination, though, and probably your best bet for a wave would be Ballito. The best spot for beginners is the inside of Ballito, well away from the rocks.

Conditions are best in light north-westerly winds in the early morning. In summer it is practically unsurfable after about 11 am. The water is usually fairly warm, at about 24 °C.

WHILE IN THE AREA

There is reasonable diving off this coast and excellent diving a bit further north in Maputaland (see chapter 5). A visit to the Sharks Board in Umhlanga Rocks is a must for anyone remotely interested in these magnificent creatures. The nearby Umhlanga Lagoon and Umhlanga Bush nature reserves offer lovely day walks and very good birdwatching. The excellent Natal Parks Board reserve Hluhluwe-Umfolozi is nearby (see Chapter 15 for more information).

DURBAN AREA

This is surf city. There are a number of excellent spots with big hollow waves, many of them clustered around the main tourist beaches. Most are protected by shark nets. Names like Bay of Plenty, Dairy Beach and Cave Rock (New Pier) will be familiar to anyone who follows local surfing competitions. The best spots for beginners are the inside of Bay of Plenty or wherever it's not too crowded. The conditions are most dependable from early to mid-winter and surfing is almost always better in the early morning.

WHILE IN THE AREA

This is a major tourist destination and you can go for rickshaw rides on the beachfront, play on the amusement park rides, visit the snake park, bird garden, aquarium or even watch captive dolphins jumping through hoops for their dinner. There are also a number of interesting restaurants and clubs and live music venues.

SOUTH COAST

There are some good spots scattered along this coast, but the better ones are not protected by shark nets and this is an area where sharks have been known to attack swimmers and surfers.

Try Greenpoint, between Umkomaas and Scottburgh, and the Spot, just south of Hibberdene. You will also find surfable, but not necessarily wonderful, waves at Amanzimtoti, Umkomaas, Park Rynie and Margate. The best spot for beginners is the beach break at Scottburgh.

The best conditions are in winter with light south-west winds, and the water is usually a glorious 24 °C. There is usually hardly any surf at all in summer as it is blown out by the north-east winds, and the weather is fairly hot and clammy as well. This is also peak holiday season, so the beaches are very crowded and you couldn't get to the water if you tried.

WHILE IN THE AREA

Plenty of restaurants, night life and general tourist facilities abound in this area. You can play tennis, golf or bowls, or sample some of the best diving on the coast (see chapter 5).

Eastern Cape

This coast is colder than the KwaZulu-Natal coast and is very exposed to the open ocean, so there are sometimes huge swells, not all of which are surfable. There are, however, some superb spots along this very varied and scenically beautiful coastline.

WILD COAST

Surfing trips to the Wild Coast are a rite of passage for South African surfers. Traipsing around looking for the perfect wave, braving the numerous (and apparently quite aggressive) sharks that frequent this coast and generally roughing it in this gloriously wild and isolated part of South Africa is all part of the experience. There are a few better-known spots, of which Ntlonyane, just north of the Haven, is the most consistent.

Finding your own secret spot is what surfing the Wild Coast is all about, though, and if you don't have the sense of adventure to do so, this area is not for you. Just as a little tease ... there are two known spots on this coast that are better than Supertubes, but you'll have to find them for yourself.

Beginners really should try somewhere else or, if you have been dragged here by a macho companion, stick to smaller beach breaks and make sure the macho surfs with you.

It is best to travel in a fairly large group here as there have been cases of theft, muggings and worse.

WHILE IN THE AREA

The scenery is stunning, the fishing great and the spearfishing equally good. Diving for crayfish or oysters is also a possibility, but you can buy seafood very cheaply from the locals. There are a number of excellent hikes along the coast but, again, do them as part of a fairly large party (see chapter 7 for more information).

EAST LONDON

This pleasantly sleepy resort city is well known locally for its excellent surf. Nahoon Reef, off the mouth of the Nahoon River, is probably one of the most consistent big-wave spots along the entire coast. It is, consequently, often crowded and has been the site of a number of shark attacks on surfers. Other spots worth trying include Gonubie, which sometimes has a nice right and left point break but is often crowded. You can also try the beach breaks at Orient Beach or Eastern Beach. The popular resorts of Yellow Sand, Glengariff and Glen Muir are worth trying as they have some fairly good spots. The best spots for beginners are the Corner and the inside of Nahoon Reef.

WHILE IN THE AREA

The East London Museum is well worth a visit. As well as exhibiting the first coelacanth to be scientifically identified, it also has the only known dodo egg in the world. The diving is good (see chapter 5), there are pleasant day walks around the town and most urban facilities can be found. The Strandloper Hiking Trail (see chapter 7) is a must for beach lovers. For an authentic cultural experience, visit the tiny village of Hanover for a day or two. See entry under Amatola Trail in chapter 7 for more details.

PORT ALFRED

Port Alfred, affectionately known to the locals as "Kowie", has a good right break with a very convenient rip current for paddling out, off the eastern pier at the mouth of the Kowie River. This is a favourite spot with students from Rhodes University, about 100 km inland. Other sites in the general area which are worth investigating include Kleinemunde, which has a pretty sloppy beach break, and Mpekweni, near the Fish River Sun Casino, which should work on a southerly swell. Beginners can try their luck at either of these or the beach break at Port Alfred. Your best chances of getting decent surf are with a light north-west to south-west wind and a big south swell.

WHILE IN THE AREA

This area is a very popular holiday destination. There is a half-, one- or two-day canoe trail on the Kowie River (see chapter 6), and the diving can be excellent (see chapter 5). Wildlife enthusiasts can visit Shamwari Game Reserve or the Addo National Park, not too far away in the direction of Port Elizabeth (see chapter 15). There are sufficient pleasant pubs, restaurants and coffee shops to keep your spirits up. The Fish River Sun can supply all the glitz and glamour you could wish for and an opportunity to fritter away your hard-earned cash at the casino. If you're feeling peckish, drive up to the oyster farm at Hamburg and "pick your own".

PORT ELIZABETH

Surfing is very popular in this medium-sized industrial cum tourist city, so most of the waves are pretty crowded when they are working, but they lack the power of those further up or down the coast. If you are there for other reasons, though, you may well get in some good surfing. Conveniently, the sites close to town, such as King's Beach, Summerstrand and Millers are good spots for beginners to try their luck. Windsurfers can try Hobie Beach, which has great sailing but unexceptional wave-jumping.

Surfing is best on this coast when there is a light north-west to south-west wind on a big south swell.

ST FRANCIS AND JEFFREY'S BAY

When it's working Supertubes at Jeffrey's (J-Bay) is legendary — reputed to be the fastest and best-formed wave on the South African coast. Cape St Francis also has an exceptional right point break (Bruce's Beauties) on the rare occasion that it works. It is worth hanging around for, though. There are many other breaks and a whole surf culture to keep you occupied when these aren't working. Beginners can try the beach break at Seal Point or Jeffrey's Bay.

This once-beautiful spot is a prime example of how a place can be too perfect for its own good. The endless summer is over for J-Bay, as housing developments crowd out the view of the beach and hundreds of surfers in search of "peace and the perfect wave" crowd out the breaks. The surfing is still great, but many locals prefer to head off to quieter, less well known spots. You'll notice they're not listed in this book — keep looking!

A big south swell and light north-west to south-west winds bring out the best that this coast has to offer.

GARDEN ROUTE COAST (MOSSEL BAY TO TSITSIKAMMA)

The best spots are Herold's Bay, Victoria Bay, Swartriet and Mossel Bay. There is a seal colony on an island in Mossel Bay and, consequently, a number of white sharks. They are usually quite happy to restrict their diet to seals but surfers should nevertheless keep a lookout for them.

Victoria Bay, about 10 km east of George, is a beautiful little bay with a great right point break. Although very popular all year round, surfing is restricted during the peak holiday season (December and January) to accommodate the hordes of tourists. Wilderness is an accessible beach break which is great for beginners, as is Sedgefield.

WHILE IN THE AREA

There is good diving off Knysna, Plett and Mossel Bay (see chapter 5). Mossel Bay, the place where Bartholomeu Dias first landed in what is now South Africa, has a plethora of interesting museums and national monuments for the culturally minded. Knysna is a delightful town with a huge lagoon on which you can paddle, sail or rent a houseboat and nearby forests with interesting ghost towns and museums. There are numerous hiking trails along the coast or in the forests in this area, some interesting cycle trails and horse trails (see chapters 7, 8 and 16). Not too far inland is the Calitzdorp hot spring, a great place to rest those tired muscles after a few days of surfing.

Western Cape

This area includes the Southern Cape Coast, the glorious area around Cape Town and the wild, cold, but wonderful, West Coast.

SOUTHERN CAPE COAST (HANGKLIP TO MOSSEL BAY)

Arniston, Struisbaai, Stilbaai, Jongensfontein and Gouritzmond all offer rocky right point breaks for advanced surfers. Beginners can try the beach break at Arniston or the east side of the river at Stilbaai. This coast also works best on a big south swell and light north-west to south-west winds.

WHILE IN THE AREA

The Gouritz River Bridge, not far from Stilbaai, is an obligatory stop for adrenalin junkies. You can throw yourself off the bridge in three different ways and almost certainly survive (see chapter 13). The southernmost point of Africa, Cape Agulhas, is near the town of Struisbaai and, although there is no surf there, it's worth a visit — at this point there is nothing but the heaving sea between you and Antarctica. All the above-mentioned surf spots also offer excellent spearfishing. For a bit of culture — visit the historic mission village of Elim.

FALSE BAY

Kalk Bay Reef, within sight of sundowner-quaffing patrons of the very popular Brass Bell restaurant, is probably the best break in the bay. It is a very hollow left reef break which works best in winter, when the wind is west to north-west, but also works in big swells in summer. Koeëlbaai, on the east side of the bay, has a big hollow beach break and works well on calm summer mornings or in berg wind conditions (this is a hot wind blowing down from the mountains). Glencairn is very popular with windsurfers.

Fish Hoek is one of the best spots for beginners although Muizenberg, which usually has a long, shallow wave, seems to be where most Capetonians learn to surf. It can be tough paddling out there though, as there is often a constant line of foamies and it is a long way to the back break.

The water temperature is usually between 14 and 16 °C but can go as low as 12 or as high as 18 °C. A big south swell and light north-west winds, which usually occur in winter, produce the best surf on the western side of the bay. On the eastern side berg or south-east winds will give the most joy.

The great thing about Cape Town is that when the western side of False Bay isn't working there is a good chance that the eastern side of the bay or the western seaboard of the peninsula may be, and they are all within an hour's drive of the city.

WHILE IN THE AREA

The western side of False Bay is quite charming. Interesting suburbs and villages are squeezed between the mountain and the sea. You will find fun coffee shops and restaurants, atmospheric pubs, funky shops and a fascinating mix of people living in the area. Gnarled fishing folk rub shoulders with trendy yuppies, rastas, surfers and artists. The mountain is close by and there are some lovely walks and interesting caves to visit (see chapter 17 for more information).

The eastern side of False Bay offers some good diving (see chapter 5), and is close to a couple of good paragliding launch sites. The Stellenbosch winelands are also close by and should keep non-surfing companions well entertained (see chapter 16 for the winelands horse trail).

CAPE TOWN WESTERN SEABOARD

Long Beach, Outer Kom and Crayfish Factory are all big wave spots clustered around the very scenic Scarborough/Kommetjie area. Further up, Llandudno and Glen Beach offer powerful, hollow beach breaks which are often crowded.

This coast is wave-jumping heaven and serious boardsailors should try Misty Cliffs and Crayfish Factory. Big Bay at Bloubergstrand is often windy in the afternoons and is a favourite windsurfing spot that also offers some reasonable wave jumping.

Beginners should try Hout Bay, which is very sheltered and has a soft, slow beach break. The beach break to the south end of Llandudno can sometimes be very small, but perfectly formed, offering beginners an exciting ride.

The water is cold, often hovering around 12 °C and sometimes even less. The Atlantic Ocean stretches out from here to South America in the west and Antarctica in the south, so there can be a very big groundswell, especially in winter. The good news is that the coast is quite indented and good surf can usually be found somewhere.

WHILE IN THE AREA

Cape Town offers such a variety of activities that it is pointless trying to list them here. See the relevant chapters for climbing, diving, paragliding, caving or horse riding. Watch the press for the dates of the Summer of Love concerts, which usually happen near Scarborough — a perfect way to end a good day of summer surfing.

WEST COAST

The favourite surf destinations on this coast include Eland's Bay, Lambert's Bay, Cape Columbine and Yzerfontein, which have a number of point breaks that work in big swells and south winds.

St Helena Bay is often used by Coastal Kayak Trails for kayak surfing. Langebaan is a popular windsurfing spot as, in summer, the wind comes up almost every afternoon with surprising regularity. You can sometimes do reasonable wave jumping in front of Club Mykonos.

Beginners should be able to find a reasonable beach break in most of the bays, such as Yzerfontein, Britannia Bay or St Helena Bay.

The water is invariably cold, around 12 °C. Much of the coast is rough and rocky with not very well formed waves. The bays tend to have nice sandy beaches and you can usually find some kind of a beach break. In general, the best time to surf this coast is in summer or autumn when the winds are offshore.

WHILE IN THE AREA

There is a horse trail near Eland's Bay (see chapter 16), interesting birdlife in the Verloren Vlei and rock paintings in the shallow cave at Baboon Point. In spring the wild flowers are spectacular. Langebaan is a well-developed holiday resort with a national park, excellent birdwatching, spectacular flowers in spring and a significant tourist infrastructure. Lambert's Bay has an interesting fishing harbour and the crayfishing is excellent. (Open season is from 15 November to 31 May; get a permit and obey size and bag limits or you could have an expensive lunch.)

Namibia

There are some well-known spots on this coast but there are bound to be more just waiting to be discovered. Much of the coastline is, unfortunately, totally inaccessible, being in the *Sperregebiet*, the restricted area controlled by the diamond mines.

SWAKOPMUND/WALVIS BAY

There are some great, easily accessible breaks here. A nice right reef off Walvis, Mussels, works in huge swells and Guns, a nearby left point/reef break, works in a 2 m to 3 m swell.

CAPE CROSS

This is a truly isolated spot but there is a spectacular long left break which works well in big winter swells. When conditions are right it can break continually for hundreds of metres. When surfing here you must avoid harassing, disturbing, frightening or in any way causing stress to the resident seals. (There are thousands of them.) Enter the water to one side of the colony and then paddle to the reef. To surf here you will have to camp and bring all your own food and water.

Listings

SURF OPERATORS AND RETAIL OUTLETS

Bay Surf School; tel:+27 82 570-3277, offer surf training in Port Elizabeth.

Beach Break, 111 Russel St, Port Elizabeth, South Africa; tel: +27 41 55-4384.

Billabong Surf Shop, Magna Tubes Trio Centre, 44 Da Gama Rd, Jeffrey's Bay, South Africa; tel: +27 423 96-1797.

Coastal Kayak Trails, +27 21 551 8739, offer kayak trails in the sea and kayak surfing trips, mostly in the Cape Town area, but also some further afield.

Lifestyle Surf Shop, 21 York Rd, Muizenberg, South Africa; tel: +27 21 788-8218.

Moir, Charlie, for free surfing clinic; tel: +27 21 701-2727.

Natural Energy, Sanlam Centre, Beach Road, Strand; tel: +27 24 53-1151, are on the east side of False Bay.

Ocean Sports Centre, P O Box 11471, Marine Parade 4056, South Africa; tel: +27 31 368-5318, offer advanced and beginners surf training.

Pro Surf Coaching, c/o Palace Hotel, P O Box 10539, Marine Parade 4056, South Africa; tel: +27 31 368-5488, do advanced and beginners surf training.

Replay Sports, 22a Long Street, Cape Town, South Africa; tel: +27 21 25-1056, buy, sell and rent second-hand boards, wetsuits and other sports gear.

Screeming Blue, cnr. Esplanade and Quanza Rds, Beachfront, East London, South Africa; tel: +27 431 43-9835.

Second Hand Surf Shop, 267 Point Road, Durban, South Africa; Tel: +27 31 32-1875, buy and sell surf gear. If you are visiting, you can buy a board and/or wetsuit from them and, if it is in good condition, they will buy it back from you for up to 70% of your purchase price.

Surf Lifesaving Association of South Africa (SLASA), 35 Livingstone Rd, Durban 4001, South Africa; tel: +27 31 37-0448, controls training of surf lifesavers.

Surf Obsession, 42 Brickhill Rd, Durban, South Africa; tel: +27 31 368-1070.

Tekweni Surfaris, tel: +27 31 303-1433, offer surf safaris in the KwaZulu-Natal region.

FURTHER INFORMATION

Surf reports for the KwaZulu-Natal area are on East Coast Radio, at 6.45 am and 3.30 pm, for the Eastern Cape on Radio Algoa at 7 am (Monday to Friday) and 6.50 am on Saturdays and for the Cape Town area on Radio KFM at 7.45 am.

Much of the information here was obtained from *Surfing in Southern Africa* by Mark Jury, Struik, 1989, Cape Town, courtesy of the author. Unfortunately it is out of print, but try to beg, borrow or steal a copy as it is a great publication and will give you all the information you need.

For more technologically advanced surfers, the Internet weather forecast and swell maps should enable you to plan your surfing well. The address is: http://os2.iafrica.com/weather

CHAPTER 15

On the wild side

Safaris with a difference

Southern Africa is one of the premier safari destinations in the world and seeing game is probably the single most common reason foreign visitors choose to visit the region. Until recently, a game-viewing safari in southern Africa would consist of sitting in a vehicle and driving, or being driven around, looking at animals. This is still the case at many game destinations but, as this chapter will show, there are many other ways of seeing game nowadays.

Undoubtedly, part of the attraction of a game-viewing trip is the opportunity to see the "big five", but smaller game can be just as rewarding if you take the time to watch and learn. Even watching dung beetles can give you an insight into the bush that you may not get from seeing a never-ending procession of rhinos and lions. It is not so much seeing the animals; it is taking the time to understand the relationships between them and between the animals, plants, soil, atmosphere and people that is rewarding. Depending on your attitude, you could return from a safari with a species list full of tick marks or a mind and spirit refreshed, renewed and invigorated with a sense of wonder at the complexity and beauty of the universe.

Equipment and clothing

When on a safari, even a vehicle-based one, try to wear clothes that blend in with the bush. Khaki, dull green and light brown are the best, and patterns of these colours are even better. White, red, orange, yellow and blue are the worst colours as they stand out very clearly in the bush and may frighten the animals. If khaki or green really doesn't match your eyes, you can wear very muted, faded shades of other colours, even pink or purple, as long as they are not too light. It is most important that you are comfortable, especially on a walking safari. Wear long or short pants that are reasonably loose and don't chafe anywhere. Shorts are cool but longs protect your legs from burrs and thorns. Loose cotton shirts are the best, and T-shirts are not ideal as they allow your neck to get sunburned. A broad-brimmed hat is essential. Socks should be good walking socks and shoes should be comfortable: hiking boots are the best. Failing these, running shoes or anything in which you feel particularly comfortable will do. Always take a waterproof jacket and something warm. Take at least two pairs of socks for each day on a walking safari, as you may want to change them if they become infested with prickly vegetation.

Options for people with disabilities

Kruger National Park has at least one accessible hut and cottage at a number of camps, contact the **National Parks Board** or **Eco-Access** for further information. At Berg-en-Dal Camp, one of the accessible camps, there is a 600 m tactile trail with a gravel path which is wheelchair-accessible with a bit of help.

Emfuleni Lodge, near Klaserie and the Kruger National Park, has accessible rooms and a swimming pool. You can do vehicle-based safaris into the park from here. The Cheetah Project at Hoedspruit is wheelchair-accessible. The Elephant Expedition at Xudum in the Okavango Delta would be a wonderful experience for blind people as you can touch and communicate with the elephants.

Ndabushe Wildlife Sanctuary, very close to Johannesburg, has a number of antelope such as bushbuck, impala and springbok. They have sand roads which are wheelchair-navigable with help. They have wheelchair-friendly toilets and are planning an accessible chalet.

Wilderness Wheels Africa have a land cruiser with a lift for wheelchairs, accessible tents, toilets and showers, and operate four-day safaris to the Kruger Park, ten-day safaris to Botswana and Zimbabwe as well as tailor-made safaris.

Western Cape

The Western Cape is not traditionally a safari destination and the reserves here don't have much big game. There are, however, a number of beautifully wild and rugged reserves and national parks, most of which have a good selection of medium-sized and small game.

CAPE OF GOOD HOPE NATURE RESERVE

The Cape of Good Hope Nature Reserve, near Cape Town, is primarily a floral reserve with an immense diversity of plant types for its small area. You may see game there if you stay in one place quietly and wait, or do one of the short day-walks. Bontebok, Cape mountain zebra, grysbok, grey rhebok, eland (which is the largest antelope) baboons and ostrich may be seen.

WHILE IN THE AREA

To round out your wildlife experience of the area go to Boulders Beach, between the reserve and Simon's Town, and watch the jackass penguins. You can even snorkel in the sea here, in the hope of seeing one under water. (Penguins swim quite strangely; they use their little wings and seem to "fly" under water.) In winter and spring, you can pick a spot anywhere along the coast and have a good chance of seeing southern right whales. The diving in False Bay is excellent in winter (see chapter 5).

Do take some time to study the incredible plantlife, much of which is endemic to this area. Another attraction is the beautiful rugged coastline and Cape Point which is said by the locals to divide the Atlantic Ocean from the Indian Ocean, even though Cape Agulhas is officially the dividing point.

See chapter 8 for details of escorted cycling trips through this reserve.

DE HOOP NATURE RESERVE

The De Hoop Nature Reserve, about 150 km from Cape Town on the N2, is also not a "big five" venue but you will see many interesting smaller animals such as antelope, baboons and other small game there. There are a number of day walks and mountain bike trails (see chapter 8).

BONTEBOK NATIONAL PARK

The Bontebok National Park, near Swellendam, is one of the success stories of conservation in South Africa. Proclaimed in 1931 to protect the last 22 surviving bontebok, it is now home to a successful breeding herd and regularly captures bontebok to be translocated to other reserves around the country. It is a good place to see bontebok (obviously), red hartebeest, Cape mountain zebra, grey rhebok, steenbok, grysbok and duiker. There are two short walking trails. Booking is through the **National Parks Board**.

WHILE IN THE AREA

The Breede River rafting trip starts and ends not too far from both these reserves (see chapter 6). Cape Agulhas, the most southerly point of Africa where the two oceans officially meet, is not far from De Hoop. It is a wild and rugged place, a fitting end to a wild and rugged continent.

Eastern Cape

This area was virtually denuded of game to make way for cattle farms but, due to the difficult farming conditions, much of it is slowly being returned to natural bush. The Addo Elephant National Park, near Port Elizabeth, is one of the best-known parks in the area. It was proclaimed in 1931 to protect the remaining 11 elephants in the area and is yet another of the success stories of conservation in South Africa. Besides elephant, there are a few black rhino and many species of smaller game. All booking and enquiries must be done through the **National Parks Board**. The Sam Knott, Andries Vosloo and Double Drift reserves near Grahamstown have been consolidated and together make up one of the largest conservation areas in the Eastern Cape, known as the Great Fish River Complex, where you may see black rhino, buffalo, kudu and many other smaller species. Booking is through **Eastern Cape Tourism Board**.

SHAMWARI WALKING SAFARI

Between Port Elizabeth and Grahamstown is the quite newly proclaimed private game reserve of Shamwari. It is very upmarket and most of the guests limit their activities to game drives. You can, however, choose to do a walking safari, under the guidance of an armed ranger, and approach large game such as elephants and black and white rhino. Accommodation options include two luxurious lodges or, for the more budget conscious, two self-catering cottages which are quite affordable for groups of up to six people. The main selling point of this reserve, as compared with most other private game parks in southern Africa, is its position in a malaria-free area.

MOUNTAIN ZEBRA HIKING TRAIL

This is included in this chapter instead of the chapter on hiking because it offers a unique opportunity to approach the rather rare Cape mountain zebra in the wild, on foot. Besides zebra you are likely to see mountain reedbuck, eland, kudu, springbok, blesbok, black wildebeest and red hartebeest.

The trail is usually done over three days and is not too strenuous. Accommodation is in comfortable, but very basic, huts. Booking is through the **National Parks Board**.

WHILE IN THE AREA

Olive Schreiner's home in Cradock has been converted into a museum. She was one of South Africa's greatest writers and is particularly remembered for her novel *The Story of an African Farm*, which would have been considered a feminist work if the word had existed in her day. The **Olive Schreiner Grave Trail** is a short day-walk to her grave on a farm outside the town. The work of the artist Helen Martins, another interesting, strong and independent woman, may be seen at the Owl House in Nieu Bethesda.

KwaZulu-Natal

The national parks of KwaZulu-Natal conserve a very diverse range of biomes, from the high montane grasslands of the Drakensberg to the dune forests of the Greater St Lucia National Park. They also include the mixed woodland of Hluhluwe-Umfolozi, the kind of environment many people consider to be "the real Africa". There may be an opportunity to do a short game walk or drive through the Tugela Conservancy while doing a river trip on the Buffalo or Tugela rivers (see chapter 6). See also Qwibi Horse Trails in chapter 16 for information on the Ophate Game Reserve, through which they operate.

UMFOLOZI WILDERNESS TRAIL

Umfolozi is one of South Africa's oldest reserves, having been proclaimed, along with the nearby Hluhluwe, in 1897. (They have since been joined by the proclamation of a corridor between them.) It is most famous for its role in bringing the white rhino back from the brink of extinction and also for running the first wilderness trail in southern Africa in 1957. It proved so successful and popular that it is still running. It is a three-day walking safari deep into the wilderness area of the park. You are accompanied by an experienced, armed game ranger who will explain the complexities of your surroundings, as well as identify animals and birds. Accommodation is in tented bush camps. You carry only a day-pack as the rest of your gear is taken to the camp on pack donkeys (which do not accompany you). Prices are inclusive of meals but special diets are not catered for. The trails operate from the beginning of March to the end of September, although weekend trails are run all year round.

The trails are run by the **Natal Parks Board** and all booking is through their central booking office.

ST LUCIA WILDERNESS TRAIL

This four-night, three-day trail starts at Bhangazi Base Camp on the banks of Lake Bhangazi in the Greater St Lucia Wetland Park, from where you walk out into the wilderness area in the company of an armed and knowledgeable ranger. You are likely to see animals such as red duiker, black rhino, reedbuck, hippos and crocodiles. You may paddle for a stretch on the lake if you like, and if you take your own gear you may go for a snorkel in one of the many rockpools filled with myriad colourful tropical fish. Birdwatching is excellent here.

The trail is run from the beginning of April to the end of September. Booking is essential and is through the **Natal Parks Board**.

PHINDA

This very upmarket lodge encompasses a number of different biomes, ranging from seasonally inundated wetlands to bushveld. A stay at this lodge can be combined with scuba diving at Sodwana (see chapter 5), turtle-watching trips (see entry on Kosi Bay in chapter 7), and big-game fishing. Game drives and walks are standard, the accommodation is very luxurious and the service always attentive. Game likely to be seen includes elephant, white rhino, lion, cheetah and many species of antelope. Phinda is run by **Conservation Corporation Africa**, who handle all bookings.

Mpumalanga/Northern Province

This is the safari centre of South Africa. Besides the Kruger National Park, which extends into both these provinces, there are many private game parks in the area. You can visit Kruger independently, as long as you are driving a closed vehicle, or you can stay at one of the many private game lodges and, for a price, be pampered in primitive luxury and watch game under the supervision of a knowledgeable ranger.

KRUGER WILDERNESS TRAILS

The Kruger National Park is the biggest and best-known park in South Africa. Covering an area of almost 20 000 km^2, it incorporates a number of different biomes, each home to a different assemblage of animals. You may have heard of the tarred roads and the rest camps that look like suburban centres, but don't let this deter you. These exist but they comprise a very, very small part of the park.

There are seven separate wilderness trails, each limited to groups of up to eight people, aged between 12 and 60. The trails run from Wednesday to Saturday or Sunday to Wednesday. You meet at 3.30 pm on Wednesday or Sunday at the relevant rest camp, where you are briefed before being transferred to your wilderness camp. This will consist of four very basic huts, with bedding, towels and soap, and communal ablutions consisting of flush toilets and showers. You spend the next two days walking, returning to the wilderness camp every night, and, on the morning of the third day, are transferred back to the rest camp. The trips are fully catered but special diets are not accommodated.

The Bushman Trail, as well as offering the opportunity of seeing big game, takes you past a number of archaeological sites, including rock paintings. It is in the far south-east corner of the park and the scenery is dominated by dramatic granite hills.

The Metsimetsi Trail is an excellent trail to do in the dry winter months as it follows the Nwaswitsontso River for a while. This is one of the few dependable water sources in winter and therefore attracts a lot of game, especially elephants.

The Napi Trail traverses an area rich in white rhino and other big game. All of the big five have been seen in this area, although not necessarily on the same trail. You may be lucky though.

The Nyalaland Trail is in the northern part of the park in truly subtropical bush; fever trees and baobabs are typical, birds are plentiful and game abounds.

The Olifants Trail starts from a camp on the banks of the Olifants River. The scenery is spectacular, ranging from riverine bush to breathtaking gorges. Birding is good and crocodile, hippos, lion, elephant and cheetah are often seen.

The Sweni Trail, near Nwanetsi, is in an area of the park typified by extensive grasslands which are home to large herds of zebra, wildebeest and buffalo. Lion and spotted hyena are common here and both black and white rhino have been seen on the trails.

The Wolhuter Trail is named after two of Kruger's most famous rangers, Harry and Henry Wolhuter (father and son). The trail affords views of undulating bushveld with numerous rocky outcrops. White rhino are often seen, as are elephant, lions, leopards, buffalo, zebra and black rhino.

It can't be guaranteed, but you may see the big five on a wilderness trail in Kruger. The trails are very popular and must be booked, preferably well in advance, through the **National Parks Board**.

WHILE IN THE AREA

Companions who do not wish to walk can stay in one of the many camps at Kruger and do the usual vehicle-based safaris. The whole Mpumalanga/Northern Province area is well endowed with game destinations. Those looking for a very upmarket, luxurious game experience can contact **Conservation Corporation Africa** and enquire about one of their many private game reserves in the area. There are also interesting caves (see chapter 17), mountain bike trails (see chapter 8) and climbing routes (see chapter 18).

LAPALALA WILDERNESS WALKS

Although they also do conventional vehicle-based safaris, Lapalala Wilderness, in the Waterberg area of the Northern Province, specialise in walking safaris from Rhino Camp, on the banks of Kgogong River. It is a pleasant, small tented camp with en suite ablutions and flush toilets.

You are likely to see black and white rhino, buffalo, many species of antelope, giraffe, zebra, wildebeest and, if you are lucky, maybe wild dog or cheetah. There are a number of interesting archaeological sites, including rock paintings, which form a part of the walks. This is one of the few malaria-free big-game areas in southern Africa.

Booking is through the Johannesburg office of **Lapalala Wilderness**.

WHILE IN THE AREA

Equus Luxury Horseback Safaris, based at Lapalala, operate multi-day safaris across this and neighbouring reserves. See chapter 16 for further details.

Northern Cape

The Augrabies National Park is home to a great deal of small game species as well as a few black rhino which you stand a good chance of seeing on an escorted drive. This is usually on the second part of the Black Rhino Trail, the first part of which consists of an inflatable boat ride in the gorge. Booking is through the **National Parks Board.**

WHILE IN THE AREA

See chapter 6 for details of the Augrabies Rush and the canoe trip on the lower Augrabies, chapter 7 for the Klipspringer Trail and chapter 16 for the Kameeldoring camel trail. Walkers on the Wild Side, a subsidiary of Walker's Canoe Trails (see chapter 6), do escorted trips into the desert of Bushmanland.

North-west Province

Pilanesberg is probably the best known of the excellent wildlife destinations in this area. See chapter 11 for information on balloon safaris.

THE RUSTENBURG TRAIL

There are two two-day trails running through the Rustenburg Nature Reserve. They are mostly scenic but, if you are slow and careful, you can get quite close to game. As well as zebra and giraffe, a number of large antelope species occur here, most notably eland, red hartebeest, sable, kudu and blesbok. Black wildebeest and smaller antelope such as oribi, klipspringer, duiker and mountain reedbuck may also be seen.

The birding is excellent, with a number of the colourful bushveld species, such as lilacbreasted roller, Meyer's parrot, paradise flycatcher and crimson boubou.

Booking is essential and is through the **Rustenburg Nature Reserve**.

Botswana

Botswana's wildlife is the basis of its considerable tourism industry. The Central Kalahari Game Reserve, Khutse Game Reserve and the Mabuasehube Game Reserve are remote reserves in the Kalahari. The National Gemsbok Park, also deep in the Kalahari, is contiguous with the Kalahari Gemsbok Park in South Africa. Most of the active adventures in Botswana, though, are centred on the Okavango Delta or the Makgadikgadi Pans.

The government has made a policy decision to aim for low-density high-cost tourism, so nothing in Botswana is cheap, but the experience is worth the cost.

Botswana is best known for the Okavango Delta and the delta is best known for mokoro safaris. A mokoro (plural mekoro) is a traditional dugout canoe and is the most efficient way of getting around the delta when it is flooded.

The Okavango Delta was formed aeons ago when the Okavango River, which rises in the highlands of Angola, ran across a shallow rift valley which may be a western extension of the Great African Rift Valley. The valley has, over the ages, filled with windblown and waterborne sediment and is now almost impossible to discern. The river flows slowly into the valley and then backs up against the far fault line, forming an inland delta of about 13 000 km^2.

The flood, as it is locally called, usually arrives about June or July when the water spreads out to form countless pools, channels and lagoons. Waterlilies bloom on the surface and countless aquatic creatures, ranging in size from frogs to hippos, frolic in the crystal clear water. The surrounding area is dry, so many species of game congregate in this huge, verdant oasis, spending most of their time on the many islands or the sand tongues, which are long spits of higher land that do not flood.

A leisurely float along the limpid channels between colourful waterlilies, towering palms and bright green banks of papyrus, interspersed with short game-viewing walks on the islands, is an experience of a lifetime. The silence is like nothing else and you could imagine yourself part of the first community on earth as you watch a typically bright orange Delta sunset.

Mokoro trips are operated in the flood season, from about June to September in the seasonally flooded areas and all year in the permanently flooded areas near the top of the delta.

OKAVANGO MOKORO SAFARIS

There are a number of different companies operating these trips. Other than the Island Safaris trip described below, these will start with a flight from Maun to the delta in a light plane. The flight is a good game-viewing experience in itself as you get a chance to see game from the air, and also to get an impression of the complexity of the channels and lagoons. From the airstrip you will be transferred to camp, usually by vehicle. After being settled in, fed and briefed you will have a good night's sleep in a comfortable safari tent or reed chalet and then start your mokoro trip the next morning. This may be a multi-day excursion or just a series of short trips from your luxurious camp. It is quite tough deciding which company to travel with; there are many and they all offer excellent service. Walking and vehicle-based safaris are usually a part of the package.

ODDBALLS

Oddballs stands out from the crowd only in that it concentrates on making the deep delta experience a little more affordable. It is close to Moremi and Chief's Island, which is an excellent area for game. Oddballs is not a full-service, luxury camp. Just for starters, you walk from the airstrip to camp (only about 20 minutes, and you should see some game). You may bring your own tent and camp, or you may rent a tent. Although they have a kitchen and do meals, you can bring your own food if you like. Ablutions consist of hot showers and flush toilets and are communal, except for the treehouse and the two four-bedded chalets, which have their own ablutions. You need to bring your own soap, towels and sleeping bags. Their mokoro trips are excellent and you save money by erecting your own tent and cooking your own food. You can choose not to enter Moremi, in which case you will save the considerable park fees and probably still see good game, but one day in the park might be worth the expense. Because of its price structure, Oddballs tends to attract a younger, more sociable crowd.

Booking is essential and is through **Okavango Tours and Safaris**.

OKAVANGO DELTA PARTICIPATION SAFARIS

The first night is spent at Island Safari Lodge, just outside Maun. You are then transferred to the delta, either by four-wheel-drive vehicle, motorboat or a combination of the two. You then spend the next two days doing game walks and being poled about in your mokoro by your guide/poler. You are not waited on hand and foot on this trip. You put up your own tents, help to cook and clean up afterwards and generally look after yourself. Your guide is there to ensure your safety and to point out and interpret various aspects of the environment. You do not enter the Moremi Game Reserve on this trip, as the fees are very high. The reserve is not fenced, though, and the animals are not particularly concerned about such niceties. Your chances of seeing game are therefore pretty good.

This trip is run by **Island Safari Lodge** and booking is essential. They also run luxury trips, at a somewhat higher price.

ELEPHANT EXPEDITIONS

This trip is run from Xudum Camp, deep in the delta. You fly in from Maun, are met at the airstrip and are transferred to the rather luxurious, but very rustic, Xudum Camp. You are accommodated in huge safari tents on platforms and your en suite bathroom has a hot shower and a flush toilet.

You are driven to a spot near the elephant camp and are escorted on foot to meet the three trained African elephants: Moremi, Thembe and Jabu. After a short briefing, you wander off into the bush in the company of the elephants while your knowledgeable guides explain what they are doing and why. By the end of the day, you will have a deeper understanding of elephant physiology and behaviour. Riding the elephants is a small part of the safari, as you learn more on the ground and if for some reason the guide considers it unsafe to ride, you won't. This is unlikely and will only happen if the elephants, which are very sensitive, intelligent creatures, are feeling a bit off colour or have taken a dislike to you. This is a very luxurious, full-service trip. The minimum stay at Xudum is three days and you can spend the others going out in a mokoro, walking or doing game drives.

This trip is run from the beginning of March to the middle of December. Booking is essential and is through the **Legendary Adventure Company**. Another elephant trip is run by **Elephant Back Safaris** from Abu Camp.

WALKING SAFARIS FROM XUDUM

After being flown into the delta from Maun, you are met by your ranger and expert river Bushman tracker and are transferred to Xudum. After a briefing and light refreshments you set off for your first overnight camp, or you may choose to spend the first night at Xudum.

You are supplied with a daypack in which you carry water, a few snacks (all supplied) binoculars, camera, bird book and other necessities. The walk is across the islands and floodplains in the dry season and across the islands in the flood season. In the flood season you cross the lagoons by canoe, which you paddle yourself. After a long day's walk during which you are likely to see much game, such as zebra, wildebeest, tsessebe and others, you arrive at your overnight camp. The camps each have their own character but they are all quite rustic and set on islands with a view over the lagoons or, in the dry season, the floodplains. They consist of tents or raised, covered sleeping platforms, each sleeping two people in beds with all bedding and mosquito nets. The ablutions are mostly communal and consist of a pit toilet and bucket shower.

Like any walking safari, the main advantage of this trip, apart from the excellent game-viewing opportunities, is the extent to which you can study the minutest aspects of the environment. Your guide and tracker are both very knowledgeable and, if encouraged, can wax lyrical about the plants, animals and physical structures of the delta.

This trip is run from the beginning of March to the middle of December and is subject to a minimum stay of three days. Booking is essential and is through the **Legendary Adventure Company**.

WHILE IN THE AREA

Another very exciting way to experience the wildlife of the delta is from the back of a horse (see chapter 16 for details of horseback safaris). While in the Okavango Delta you may fish, although the fishing is better higher upstream in the Panhandle (see chapter 6). See also chapter 17 for information about other attractions in the general region, bearing in mind that in Botswana distances are significant.

QUAD BIKE SAFARI

The Makgadikgadi Pans are a vast, game-filled expanse of flat seasonally inundated land. When they fill with water after the rains they host countless migratory birds, most notably huge flocks of flamingoes and other waders. After the water has dried up, the birds leave and the game returns. It takes a while for the surface of the pans to harden sufficiently for them to support motor vehicles. Quad bikes, which are much lighter than conventional safari vehicles and have wide tyres, are the ideal vehicle for exploring this unique environment, especially as they do not leave deep tracks like a conventional four-wheel-drive vehicle. The trips are run from the rather luxurious **Jack's Camp**.

WHILE IN THE AREA

You can visit other sections of the pans, such as Sowa Pan, where the bird-watching is excellent, even in the dry season (contact **Nata Lodge**), or do a mokoro safari in the delta.

Swaziland

For such a small country, Swaziland has conservation areas covering a surprising number of different biomes. In the far north is the rolling montane grassland reserve of Malolotja (see chapter 7), Mlilwane in the midlands and Mkhaya and Hlane in the hot, subtropical lowlands. Mlawula encompasses lowland areas and also extends into the Lebombo Mountains on the Mozambique border.

MLAWULA

This is one of Swaziland's most interesting reserves covering, as it does, a number of vegetation types, including open grassland and dry and moist woodland. You may walk in the reserve, with or without a guide. Game likely to be seen includes zebra, waterbuck, impala, eland, blue wildebeest and the rather rare samango monkey. Birders should enjoy this park; there are over 300 species because of the different vegetation types, and a vulture restaurant allows you a good view of these fascinating birds. There is a campsite. The park is administered by the **National Trust Commission**, which takes all bookings.

MKHAYA CYCLING AND WALKING SAFARIS

Mkhaya is a small reserve with zebra, giraffe and many species of antelope such as impala, kudu and tsessebe, but is best known for its substantial populations of buffalo, elephant and black and white rhino. As well as regular game drives, you may do a walking safari which, especially in the presence of these large animals, is an unforgettable experience. You can also do a bicycle safari (see chapter 8). When visiting Mkhaya you are met on the main road, escorted to the gate where you may leave your car in perfect safety, and are then driven through the reserve to the camp. Accommodation is in safari tents, most of which are en suite. There is also one beautiful stone cottage. If you have a tight budget, time or money-wise, consider a day visit. All visits must be booked through **Big Game Parks of Swaziland**, Central Reservations.

MLILWANE CYCLING, WALKING AND HORSEBACK SAFARIS

Mlilwane was the first conservation area in Swaziland and it has an interesting history. Once a cattle farm and even a tin mine, the land bears scars in the form of erosion gulleys (dongas) and exotic plants. It is slowly being rehabilitated, though, and there are a number of animals, namely giraffe, blesbok, nyala, impala, zebra and warthog. There are hippos in the pool near the camp.

You may do an escorted game walk or an unescorted walk if you stick to a dedicated trail. Horseback game-viewing and mountain bike trips (see chapters 8 and 16 for details), are also available. This reserve does not have the big game of Mkhaya but it is far more accessible, both because of its proximity to Mbabane and its more affordable prices. Accommodation ranges from camping and a youth hostel to self-catering chalets. There is a basic shop and a good restaurant, the Hippo Hide, which offers diners a spectacular view of the resident hippos frolicking in the pool.

All booking is through the **Big Game Parks of Swaziland**, Central Reservations.

WHILE IN THE AREA

There is much to see and do in this fascinating kingdom. The Ncwala, or first fruits ceremony, is held in late December or early January and the Umhlanga, or reed dance, is held in spring, late September or early August, both at the royal village near Mbabane. If you would like to attend either of these ceremonies, you will need to apply in writing to the **Government Information Service**. There is a Traditional Healers' Centre near Siteki, which you may visit. For the less culturally inclined, the Great Usutu River offers a wonderful one-day rafting trip (see chapter 6). If you are into arts and crafts, you'll love Swaziland's many craft shops and studios.

Zambezi Valley

Even where there are towns on the bank, the Zambezi River retains its wildness, and the Zambezi Valley is one of the continent's premier safari destinations. For example, motorists and pedestrians have to make way for elephants in the town of Kariba and landowners just sigh and put up yet another fence after the jumbos have demolished the last one.

KARIBA CRUISES

Kariba, one of the biggest dams in the world, is bounded on most sides by wilderness where the animals which once roamed the now flooded valley still exist in relative safety and peace. You can explore this area in a number of interesting ways. You can rent a yacht or a luxurious houseboat and slowly potter along the shore, checking out the inlets for game (as long as your sailing skill is up to it). Even if you stay quite far out in the middle of the dam, though, you can see quite a lot of game on the banks if you use binoculars. There are two regular ferry services from which you can see a surprising amount of game. **Kariba Ferries** run a regular comfortable overnight service between Kariba and Mlibizi, and the **District Development Fund (DDF)** run a basic, typically African ferry service from Kariba to Matusadona and to Binga, which is not quite as far up as Mlibizi. Both these ferries are worth taking for their own sake. The Kariba Ferries trips are catered and you get a comfortable lounger-style bed and blankets. The DDF ferry is an interesting cultural experience. There is no booking, no catering and you sit or sleep where you can find space. It is much cheaper. Booking for **Kariba Ferries** is essential for passengers or vehicles but you needn't book for the **DDF** ferry unless you plan to take a vehicle aboard. For sailing contact **Sail Safaris** and for houseboats contact the Kariba office of **Shearwater**.

MATUSADONA NATIONAL PARK

This park, on the southern shore (Zimbabwean side) of Kariba Dam, is a vast, untamed expanse of mixed woodland. Animals likely to be seen include elephant, buffalo, kudu, waterbuck, bushbuck and hippos and crocodiles in huge numbers. The best way to explore here is to hire a canoe and paddle slowly around the many inlets and watch game from the water. You must be very careful if you do take this option, though, and avoid the hippos and crocodiles. Don't even consider swimming here: if the crocs don't get you the bilharzia will. You can get to Matusadona any time of the year by boat but road access is only possible between May and October, and then only by four-wheel-drive. To get here by boat you can charter one in Kariba or, if you have more time and sense of adventure than money, take the DDF ferry. This will give you a chance to meet the local people and, for a while, live exactly as they do. Hire of canoes is through the **Zimbabwe Department of National Parks**.

Safari par Excellence run backpacking wilderness trails or walks between semi-permanent tented camps in Matusadona on request between April and November.

WHILE IN THE AREA

Safari par Excellence also run a one-day safari experience from Kariba — the Nyaodza Safari. This consists of a game drive in an open vehicle from your pick-up point in Kariba, a guided wilderness walk through the acacia woodland and riverine vegetation of the Nyaodza floodplain, a canoeing trip from the mouth of the Nyaodza River to Musango Bay and then a motor-boat trip back to Kariba. Lunch is served and sundowners are available on the return boat trip.

LOWER ZAMBEZI CANOE TRAILS

There are a number of options. You can choose to do the trip from the Zimbabwean or Zambian side and will also need to choose the section which you would like to paddle. You can choose between a full-service luxury trip or a participatory camping trip and a number of options in between. All the trips are fully catered and special diets can be accommodated if enough warning is given. The trips listed below are the most likely to have guaranteed departures, but there may be other options. Ask your travel agent or contact the operators.

ZAMBEZI CLASSIC

This is the trip to do if you want to get to know the river: 10 days/9 nights, starting just below Kariba and continuing to Kanyemba near the Mozambique border. It is a semi-participatory trip and you are expected to help set up camp, although you don't have to subject yourself to your own cooking. You are accommodated in tents with camping mattresses, sleeping bags with liners, pillows and mosquito nets. This trip is run from the Zimbabwean side by **Shearwater** from 1 March to 31 December. You can do a shorter option from Chirundu to Kanyemba for 8 days/7 nights.

GORGE TRAIL/SAFARI

This 3-day/2-night trail is run from Kariba to Chirundu. The scenery is spectacular but the game is not as plentiful or varied as downstream. It is a camping trip, and tents, mattresses, sleeping bags and inners are supplied. Equipment and luggage is carried to the camps in a backup vehicle and the guide and assistant set up camp and cook. The trip described above is the Gorge Trail run by

Safari par Excellence. The Gorge Safari run by **Shearwater** is identical except there is no vehicle backup. You are encouraged to help set up camp but cooking and cleaning are done by the staff. Both trips are run all year from the Zimbabwean side.

BEE-EATER SAFARI

This is a canoe trip from Chirundu to the very comfortable Rukomechi Camp on the edge of the Mana Pools National Park. The first two nights are spent canoeing and the next two at Rukomechi, where you may choose to do more canoeing, fishing, game drives or game walks. On the canoeing section you stay in tents with camping mattresses, sleeping bags with liners, pillows and mosquito nets. At Rukomechi you are pampered in en suite chalets. This trip is run by **Shearwater** from the Zimbabwean side between the beginning of April and the end of November. There is no vehicle backup on the canoeing section.

FISH EAGLE SAFARI

From Kariba to Nyamepi in Mana Pools National Park, this 6-day/5-night trip gives you the chance to experience the scenic gorge below Kariba and to see game on the Mana floodplain as you approach Mana Pools. You are accommodated in mosquito-proof tents with camping mattresses and sleeping bags with liners, and are encouraged to help set up camp, but the guides do the cooking and washing up, unless you want to. There is no vehicle backup. This trip is run by **Shearwater** all year from the Zimbabwean side.

TAMARIND SAFARI

This 4-day/3-night trip is a leisurely drift through the Mana floodplain, starting at Chirundu and ending at Nyamepi, in the Mana Pools National Park. Facilities are much the same as for the Fish Eagle Safari and you are expected to help set up camp. This trip is run by **Shearwater** all year from the Zimbabwean side.

ROYAL KINGFISHER

This 5-day/4-night trip combines two days canoeing from Kafue to Royal Zambezi Lodge with two days at the lodge, which offers luxury tented accommodation on the riverbank. From the lodge you may paddle, fish or do a walking or vehicle safari into the park.

This trip is run by **Royal Zambezi Canoeing** from 1 March to 31 December on the Zambian side. Booking is direct or through **Shearwater**.

ZAMBEZI TRAIL

This semi-participatory trip is a 4-day/3-night trail on the Zambian side. You spend the first night at Mtondo Lodge, which has attractive en suite chalets with beds and linen, and the second and third nights are spent at Chongwe, a tented camp with large, mosquito-proof dome tents with mattresses, pillows and sleeping bags with liners. Ablution facilities at Chongwe are communal and consist of showers and flush toilets. On the third day you canoe into the Lower Zambezi National Park and are driven back to camp. Camp staff are there to ensure the smooth running of the camp, but are not at your beck and call. There is no vehicle backup so, you can't go on game drives (except for the last day's transfer back to Chongwe) but you may do game walks with your guide.

This trip is run all year by **Safari par Excellence.**

THE ISLAND TRAIL

This 3-night/4-day trip from the confluence of the Kafue River to the Chongwe River is for those with more energy than money. All camping equipment is carried in the canoes and there are no camp staff, so you have to pitch your own tent at each camp, which will usually be on an island. Camping mats, sleeping bags and liners are supplied. A portable chemical toilet is carried along and all washing is done in water taken from the river. You are encouraged to help in cooking and cleaning, although you can skive off if you really want to.

This trip starts from the Zambian side and is run by **Safari par Excellence** all year round.

ZAMBEZI LEGEND

This is a 2-day/2-night trip on the Zambian side of the river from the Kafue confluence to the Lower Zambezi National Park. You are accommodated in luxury tented camps with beds, linen, showers and flush toilets. This is a full-service trip, and you can even do it if you are not able or confident enough to paddle yourself. If you give sufficient notice they will provide a guide to paddle for you.

This trip is run by **Run Wild** from 1 May to 30 November. Booking is direct, through **Sobek** or **Ubuntu Africa**.

ZAMBEZI SPIRIT

This is a 3-day/3-night trip on the Zambian side of the river, much the same as the above but longer, and you stay in three different, but equally picturesque and comfortable camps.

This trip is run by **Run Wild** from 1 May to 30 November. Booking is direct, through **Sobek** or **Ubuntu Africa**.

MUSANGU TRAIL

This is a 4-day/3-night upmarket canoe safari on the Zambian side from the confluence of the Kafue River (just downstream from Chirundu) to the Mupata Gorge. This is not a rough and ready option. You spend the first night at Mtondo Camp in comfortable chalets and the second and third at Musango Camp, which has mosquito-proof walk-in tents. In each case you sleep in a bed with sheets and blankets. Both camps have en suite bathrooms consisting of hot showers and flush toilets. Camp staff are there to see to your every need and the three-course dinners are rather elegant affairs, served by uniformed waiters. There is a full complimentary bar, including soft drinks, beer, wine and spirits, sufficient to satisfy any reasonable requirements. There is full vehicle backup so you may do game drives or walks at your stops.

This trip is run from 15 March to 15 November, subject to the weather. Booking is through **Safari par Excellence**.

MUKUYA TRAIL

This is a luxury 4-day/3-night canoe trail on the Zimbabwean side from the confluence of the Rukomechi River to Chikwenya near the Mozambique border. You are accommodated in walk-in bow tents with folding beds and linen. There are communal flush toilets and bucket showers at each camp. A full bar is available, and the catering is up to the usual excellent standard except that no fresh fruit is served, as it is not allowed in the Mana Pools National Park.

Canoeing is interspersed with game walks or drives. You stay at a different camp, with similar facilities, every night. All equipment and luggage is transported by backup vehicle.

This trail is run from 1 May to 31 October by **Safari par Excellence**.

MANA POOLS TRAIL

This is a 4-day/3-night luxury bush trail from the confluence of the Rukomechi River to Acacia Camp near Chikwenya, at the eastern end of Mana Pools National Park. Camps are comfortable, with walk-in tents, camp beds, sleeping bags with liners, portable toilets and bucket showers.

This trip is run on the Zimbabwean side by **Shearwater** and only in the dry season from 1 May to 31 October.

CHIFUNGULU CANOE TRAIL

This upmarket 4-day/3-night trail is entirely within the Lower Zambezi National Park. Unlike most river trips it is not strictly linear. You are flown in from Kariba or Lusaka to one of two camps, both of which have large en suite safari tents. You can choose your itinerary to include two or three day's paddling, game drives and game walks. You can paddle between the two camps on two entirely different routes, either the main channel or a 10 m-wide channel which runs parallel to the main channel for about 18 km, showing you a very different aspect of the park. On the last day you can paddle downstream from the second camp and be driven back or be driven upstream of the first and paddle back. This is a full-service trip.

This trip is run by **Tongabezi** all year round. Bookings are direct, through **Hartley's Safaris** or **Ubuntu Africa**.

MUPATA SAFARI

This 6-day/5-night trail goes through the wilder parts of Mana Pools National Park (Zimbabwean side), which offers excellent game-viewing opportunities, and the dramatic Mupata Gorge. All equipment is carried on the canoes as there is no vehicle backup. You are expected to help set up camp but cooking and cleaning is done by the guides. You are accommodated in tents with mosquito nets, camping mattresses and sleeping bags with liners. This trip is run by **Shearwater** from 1 March to 31 January.

WHILE IN THE AREA

Companions not wanting to do a canoe trip can stay at one of the hotels or campsites at Kariba and enjoy a sedate boat trip on the dam, stay at Mana Pools, see lots of game and await the canoe safari, or stay at Chinhoyi (see chapters 5 and 17). Most trips start and end at Kariba so you could arrange to take the ferry before or after the safari and visit Hwange or Victoria Falls.

Listings

Big Game Parks of Swaziland, Central Reservations, P O Box 234, Mbabane, Swaziland; tel: +268 4-4541, 6-1591/2/3 or 6-1037, fax: +268 4-0957/6-1594, do all the booking for Mlilwane and the Mkhaya Game Reserve walking and biking safaris.

Cape of Good Hope Nature Reserve, P O Box 62, Simon's Town 7995, South Africa; tel: +27 21 780-9100, fax: +27 21 780-9525.

Conservation Corporation Africa, Private Bag X9, Sunninghill 2157, South Africa; tel: +27 11 784-6832, fax: +27 11 784- 7667, operate Phinda in KwaZulu-Natal and a range of other upmarket reserves in Mpumalanga and other parts of the region.

De Hoop Nature Reserve, Private Bag X16, Bredasdorp 7280, South Africa; tel: +27 28 542-1126.

Disabled Adventurers, c/o Carol Schafer, Sports Science Institute, University of Cape Town, P O Box 2593, Clareinch 7740, South Africa; tel: +27 21 686-7330, ext 297, have a database of accessible adventures.

District Development Fund (DDF); tel: +263 61 2694, operates a local ferry on Kariba.

Eastern Cape Tourism Board, P O Box 186, Bisho 5608, South Africa; tel: +27 401 95-2115, take bookings for the Great Fish River Complex.

Eco-Access, P O Box 1377, Roosevelt Park 2129, South Africa; tel: +27 11 673-4533, fax: +27 11 673-6297, have listings of venues which are accessible to people with varying types and degrees of disability.

Elephant Back Safaris, Private Bag 332, Maun, Botswana; tel: +267 66-1260, fax: +267 66-1005, run a very upmarket elephant safari in the Okavango Delta.

Emfuleni Lodge, P O Box 255, Mondeor 2110, South Africa; tel: +27 11 680-2925, 83 2355850, is near the Kruger National Park and has wheelchair-accessible accommodation.

Government Information Service of Swaziland, P O Box 338, Mbabane, Swaziland, must be contacted if you wish to attend any of the traditional festivals in Swaziland.

Hartley's Safaris, P O Box 69859, Bryanston 2021, South Africa; tel: +27 11 708-1893/5, fax: +27 11 708-1569, take bookings for the Chifungulu Canoe Trail run by Tongabezi.

Island Safari Lodge, P O Box 116, Maun, Botswana; tel/fax: +267 66-0300, operate budget (and more upmarket) mokoro trips in the Okavango Delta.

Jack's Camp, PO Box 173, Francistown, Botswana; tel: +267 65-0505, fax: +267 65-0352, run upmarket quad bikes on the Makgadikgadi Pans.

Kariba Ferries, P O Box 578, Harare, Zimbabwe; tel: +263 4 6-7661/5, fax: +263 4 6-7660, operate tourist ferries on Kariba.

Lapalala Wilderness, P O Box 645, Bedfordview 2008, South Africa; operate Rhino Camp. For bookings, contact their Johannesburg office, tel: +27 11 453-7645/7, fax: +27 11 453-7649.

The Legendary Adventure Company, P O Box 411288, Craighall, Johannesburg 2024, South Africa; tel: +27 11 327-0161, fax: +27 11 327-0162, P O Box 40, Maun, Botswana; tel: +267 66-0211, fax: +267 66-0379, 13201 Northwest Freeway, Suite 800, Houston, Texas 77040, USA; tel: +1 713 744-5244, fax: +1 713 895-8753, operate walking and elephant safaris in the Okavango Delta.

Natal Parks Board, P O Box 662, Pietermaritzburg 3200, South Africa; tel: +27 331 47-1981, fax: +27 331 47-1980, takes bookings for the Umfolozi and St Lucia wilderness trails.

National Parks Board, P O Box 787, Pretoria 0001, South Africa; tel: +27 12 343-1991, fax: +27 12 343-0905, P O Box 7400, Roggebaai 8012, Cape Town, South Africa; tel: +27 21 22-2810, fax: +27 21 24-6211, take bookings for the Kruger National Park wilderness trails and the Augrabies Black Rhino Trail.

Ndabushe Wildlife Sanctuary, tel: +27 11 956-6338, is a small sanctuary near Johannesburg with wheelchair-accessible facilities.

National Trust Commission, P O Box 100, Lobamba, Swaziland; tel: +268 4-3060, takes bookings for Mlawula Nature Reserve.

Okavango Tours and Safaris, P O Box 39 Maun, Botswana; tel: +267 66-0220, fax: +267 66-0589, take bookings for Oddballs (and the more upmarket Delta Camp) in the Okavango Delta.

Olive Schreiner Grave Trail is on the farm of J J Moolman, tel: +27 481 2683 for details and booking.

Royal Zambezi Canoeing, P O Box 31455, Lusaka, Zambia; tel: +260 1 22-4334/22-3952, fax: +260 1 22-3504/22-3747, run canoeing trips on the lower Zambezi from the Royal Zambezi Lodge.

Run Wild, P O Box 6485, Harare, Zimbabwe; tel: +263 4 79-5841/4, fax: +263 4 79-5845/6, run canoe trips on the Zambian side of the lower Zambezi.

Rustenburg Nature Reserve, tel: +27 142 3-1050, administers the Rustenburg Trails.

Safari par Excellence, P O Box 108, Victoria Falls, Zimbabwe; tel: +263 13 4424/2051/3/4, fax: +263 13 4510. Zambia: tel: +260 3 32-3349/32-1432, fax: +260 3 32-3542. Johannesburg: P O Box 1395, Randburg 2125; tel: +27 11 888-3500, fax: +27 11 888-4942, operate a number of canoeing trips on the lower Zambezi, walking safaris in Matusadona National Park and the Nyaodza Safari.

Shamwari, P O Box 91, Paterson 6130, South Africa; tel: +27 42 851-1196, fax: +27 42 851-1224, is an upmarket private game reserve in the Eastern Cape province of South Africa.

Shearwater, P O Box 229, Kariba, Zimbabwe; tel: +263 61 2433. Johannesburg: P O Box 76270, Wendywood 2144, South Africa; tel: +27 11 804-6537, fax: +27 11 804-6539, offer a number of canoeing trips on the lower Zambezi.

Sobek Expeditions, P O Box 60305, Livingstone, Zambia; tel: +260 3 32-3672, fax: +260 3 32-4289, take bookings for the Zambezi Legend and Zambezi Spirit canoe safaris.

Tongabezi, Private Bag 31, Livingstone, Zambia; tel: +260 3 32-3235, fax: +260 3 32-3224, run a very upmarket canoe safari on the lower Zambezi.

Ubuntu Africa, P O Box 41809, Craighall 2024, South Africa; tel: +27 11 706-8677/9, e-mail: afmarcon @ aztec co za, take bookings for the Chifungulu Canoe Trail, the Zambezi Spirit and the Zambezi Legend.

Wilderness Wheels Africa, 117 St Georges Road, Observatory 2198, South Africa, tel: +27 11 648-5737, specialise in safaris for people with disabilities and have all their facilities adapted for wheelchairs.

Zimbabwe Department of National Parks, P O Box 8151, Causeway, Harare; tel: +263 4 70-6077/8, administer Mana Pools and Matusadona national parks.

CHAPTER 16

Ride into the sunset

Horse trails, horseback safaris and camel trails

There are horse trails in various parts of southern Africa, ranging from one or half-day excursions on the outskirts of cities and towns to long wilderness expeditions. Horseback safaris, which are distinct from horse trails, operate in a number of parks in various parts of the region. There is only one multi-day camel trail, near the Orange River on the Namibia/South Africa border, but short rides are offered in Cape Town and Swakopmund.

Getting started

Although many of the trails are suitable for beginners, you will be a lot more comfortable and confident if you have some experience. It is advisable to take a few riding lessons in your home town before embarking on a horseback adventure. If nothing else, you can get over the inevitable beginners' bruises while you have a day or two to recover before you have to get back in the saddle. Lessons are easy to organise. Simply find the nearest riding school and make the relevant arrangements.

Camel-riding lessons are a little more difficult to organise but you can try out a short camel ride in Cape Town or Swakopmund. Failing that, some experience on a horse should at least serve to toughen up the vulnerable parts of your anatomy.

Equipment and clothing

As a beginner you don't need to invest in a lot of expensive equipment but make sure you wear appropriate clothes. Jeans look great but they are not the most sensible option, unless worn with chaps. The most comfortable pants to wear (assuming you are not going to splash out on a pair of jodhpurs) would be tight-fitting, heavy-duty stretch leggings. Baggy pants will almost certainly cause painful chafing. Knee-high socks are recommended (worn outside your pants); these give extra protection to your calves and prevent chafing. Some horse trail operators supply short chaps, which are knee-high adjustable leggings made from leather or canvas. These are great as they offer excellent protection both from chafing and from prickly vegetation. Some people recommend wearing pantihose under your riding pants to protect against chafing and some men find cycling shorts under their riding pants serve to preserve their sense of humour and their manhood. Shoes should be comfortable and must have a distinct heel to prevent your foot getting stuck in the stirrup if you fall off. This is a very important precaution: neglect it and you risk being dragged. Traditional South African "velskoens" are ideal. The above clothing is recommended if you will be riding in an English-style saddle, whereas you can get away with wearing slightly more baggy pants in a good Western saddle. Whatever you choose, make sure you have a reasonable range of leg movement or you won't be able to mount your horse.

Most riding schools will insist that you wear a hard hat and some might even supply one. If they do not, or you don't fancy wearing a communal hat, you can use a cycling, paddling or lightweight skydiving helmet. Strictly speaking, you should wear a hard hat on trails as well, but this is usually left up to your own discretion and you may find a sunhat or a peak more comfortable. All women, no matter how small and firm, will need to wear a bra with good support. Most beginners will find gloves useful on a longish trail as your hands may become sunburned or even chafed if they are quite delicate. Driving, cycling or sailing gloves are excellent and even light cotton gardening gloves offer reasonable protection.

On a trail, you will find a moonbag (waistbag) invaluable for storing lip salve, sunscreen, small snacks and the like. You will probably be supplied with a small saddlebag in which to keep a water bottle, lunch, bird books and any other necessities. A daypack is not really a good idea as it tends to bounce on your back and becomes uncomfortable after a while.

Depending on the trail, you may be given the choice between an English-style or a Western-style saddle. If you have to read this section to find out which you might prefer, you will most probably be more comfortable in a Western style or McLellan saddle.

Options for people with disabilities

In Cape Town and Johannesburg, **Riding For the Disabled** offer lessons, mainly for children but also for adults. They do not organise trails but they are an excellent starting point if you would like to try a trail and are not sure if you could manage. Horseriding is most popular with people who are mentally handicapped, blind or deaf but some paraplegics have managed to do fairly advanced riding such as jumping.

Regular events

There are two hunts in South Africa, the **Cape Hunt** near Cape Town and the **Rand Hunt** near Johannesburg. Both are drag hunts, which means that nothing is killed, but the hounds follow a scented trail which is laid down by a hunt member a few hours before the start. They are, nevertheless, very formal and adhere quite strictly to the traditional format. There is usually a hunt every Sunday in season, which in the Cape is in winter, usually from early May to September, and on the Rand in summer, usually from October to April.

Competitive events are held throughout the year but there are a few annual classics. The Dunhill Derby is the biggest showjumping event on the calendar and is held in October at Inanda Club, Sandton, Gauteng. The SAPPI Horse Trials are held at Inanda Country Base in Gauteng round about the end of March, at Shongweni, KwaZulu-Natal, in September and at Vergelegen in the Cape at the beginning of November. These are the biggest eventing competitions in the country and are very popular with spectators.

Western Cape

This region includes the city of Cape Town, the Cape winelands, the scenic and stark West Coast, some glorious mountain wilderness and the renowned Garden Route. This is not the most popular region for horse trails as the weather is a bit extreme. The summers are gloriously hot and sunny, albeit a little windy, but the winters are somewhat grey and rainy, so only the brave venture out of doors for any extended period between May and August. It is probably for this reason that there are far fewer multi-day trails than one would expect in such a beautiful area so close to a major metropolitan centre.

It is possible to find horses for hire in many of the small towns, and Cape Town has many riding schools, so you should be able to find a number of day rides to complement the trails mentioned here.

WINE VALLEY HORSE TRAIL

This trail is an incredibly mellow one- or two-day amble through the vineyards of the Bottelary subregion of the Stellenbosch wine growing region. You visit one or two wineries for extensive tasting, where you may purchase wine and arrange to have it delivered to the stables for pickup on your return, and lunch is on a wine estate.

As well as the vineyards, you get to explore the surrounding hills and will be amazed at how much open space there is so near the city and in a prime agricultural area. Once you arrive at the overnight spot, you enjoy sundowners and watch the sun set over Cape Town while your dinner sizzles over an open fire on the huge patio. Next morning you are served a full English breakfast before you continue your ride back to the stables.

The trips are run all year but the weather is more dependable in summer as it may rain in winter. The new wines are released in June, though, so winter trips should offer the full selection of the year's wines.

On the overnight trail, you are accommodated in a mountain chalet with comfortable dorm accommodation, ablutions and cooking facilities. The trip is fully catered and you need only bring a sleeping bag. This is not a strenuous trip and is suitable for beginners. You may choose between Western or English saddles.

WHILE IN THE AREA

There is much to do in the general area, including other wine tastings and driving over scenic mountain passes to neighbouring towns such as Villiersdorp, Franschhoek and Paarl, all of which have beautiful restored buildings, pretty views and a plethora of guesthouses, restaurants and more wineries offering a variety of South African wines.

EQUITRAILING, PLETTENBERG BAY

The Plettenberg Bay/Knysna area offers excellent riding country, ranging from open grazing land through fynbos to tangled indigenous forests. The trails are not fixed, but will be varied to suit the time of year or the particular needs of the participants. Riding can be combined with hiking or paddling on the Keurbooms River, which has excellent birding.

This trail is particularly suitable for beginners as the horses are well trained and the operators are experienced riding instructors, but experienced riders may enjoy a good, fast ride. Saddles are English style.

When booking, you can choose the level of comfort (and corresponding price level) of your trip, ranging from cosy bed and breakfasts to camping. Fully catered trips are the norm, but self-catered trips can be arranged.

WHILE IN THE AREA

In Plettenberg Bay there is excellent diving (see chapter 5), a range of hotels, coffee shops and restaurants. In the forest there are a number of cycle trails (see chapter 8). The hiking in the forest is excellent and the nearby Otter Trail is one of the most popular in the region (see chapter 7).

K'TAAIBOS WEST COAST TRAIL

This is a relatively new trail which operates from the small coastal town of Eland's Bay. Plans are afoot to build chalet accommodation on the farm and to offer both one-day and multi-day trails. The West Coast is blessed with wonderful long beaches, spectacular flowers in spring and interesting wetlands. This trip should, therefore, be excellent.

WHILE IN THE AREA

Besides its flowers, the West Coast is renowned for its deserted beaches, fishing, windsurfing, crayfishing in season and general scenery. You can do a sea-kayak trip at Langebaan or further up the coast (see chapter 14). The birding on the Verlorenvlei and the Berg River is excellent.

KwaZulu-Natal

There are horse trails in the montane grasslands of the Drakensberg and the subtropical bush of the northern part of the region.

HOLT TRAILS, SOUTHERN DRAKENSBERG

This trail is through the Cobham Nature Reserve and traverses spectacular mountain scenery. You are likely to see many baboons and large herds of eland. In summer it is lovely and green, but you run the risk of being caught in thunderstorms. In winter it is very cold, the grass is brown and it may snow but the weather is dependable.

You can choose the length of the trail and there are plans to extend the trails into Lesotho at a later date. There is also an alternative trail leaving from Ha Makhakhe's, closer to the bottom of Sani Pass.

These are fully catered trips. All crockery, cutlery and tents are supplied. Camping is in wilderness areas, so there are no toilet or washing facilities and minimum-impact camping standards must be adhered to. There is no backup vehicle; all equipment and stores are carried on a pack horse. The saddles are all McLellans.

WHILE IN THE AREA

You may like to do a hike along one of the many paths traversing the high grasslands; rushing streams and spectacular waterfalls end in glorious pools for swimming and lounging around. You can take a four-wheel-drive trip up the renowned Sani Pass, which winds its steep twisty way up to the top of the plateau where you can have lunch and a drink and relax in the highest pub in Africa (contact Sani Tours, tel: +27 33 702-1615). The views from there are spectacular. You can do a short or multi-day horse trail at the top, but you must organise this in advance with **Sani Top Mountaineers Chalet**. In the winter, you may be able to ski near Sani Top.

HILLSIDE HORSE TRAILS

In the northern Drakensberg, one- or multi-day horse trails are run from the Hillside Camp in the Giant's Castle Game Reserve between August and May.

WHILE IN THE AREA

You can hike for miles in the Drakensberg (see chapter 7), and in winter there is ice climbing just a day's walk away (see chapter 18).

QWIBI HORSE TRAILS

The trail is based on a farm bordering the Ophate Game Reserve in northern KwaZulu-Natal. You usually meet on Friday afternoon and ride to Qwibi base camp, on the banks of the Qwibi River, on Friday night. The next morning you ride into the game reserve, where you may see many species of antelope and birds. On Sunday you return to your cars at the farm via a different route. On longer trips, you may traverse the game reserve and spend the second or third night at Maroela Camp on the other side of the reserve. This trail is unique in that all the horses are of the indigenous Nooitgedachter breed. They are particularly well suited to trailing, being hardy and level-headed. They are all well trained and are suitable mounts for novices. Saddles are English style.

Both camps sleep up to eight people in simple rooms and have a kitchen and hot shower. The camps are fully supplied and you need bring only a sleeping bag. The trips can be fully catered, with farm milk and eggs, or self-catered.

You can book through **Qwibi** or through **Jacana Country Homes and Trails**.

WHILE IN THE AREA

The monument of the Battle of Blood River is close by. On 16 December 1838 the Boers defeated a huge Zulu impi (army) through clever strategy, superior firepower and, some claim, divine intervention, as the Boers had contracted with God to keep this day, the Day of the Covenant, sacred forever after in the event of victory. In the new South Africa this day has been renamed the Day of Reconciliation, thus fulfilling the obligation, if any exists, of the original covenant while attributing to the day much more humane and Christian values. The Simunye Pioneer Settlement, not far from Melmoth, is a cultural village where you can live with a Zulu family for a day or two and learn a bit about Zulu culture and history.

Mpumalanga

Mpumalanga is blessed with some of the best scenery in the region, especially the escarpment area. Pine plantations alternate with indigenous grasslands or small thickets of indigenous forest in the kloofs.

COSMOS HORSE TRAILS

Based near Lydenburg, these trails traverse some attractive bushveld and go up on to the escarpment where you can see forever. You may visit some interesting ruins and there is a chance of seeing small game. The trips are suitable for beginners and you may choose to do a half, full day or multi-day trip.

The base camp on the farm offers comfortable beds in an attractive thatched dorm, kitchen facilities and hot and cold ablutions with flush toilets in separate buildings. The whole complex is set in an attractively landscaped lawn with shady trees. Overnight trails have minimal facilities.

You can book directly through **Cosmos Horse Trails** or through **Jacana Country Homes and Trails**.

WHILE IN THE AREA

Just a small sample of the attractions of this area include the Kruger National Park, the Blyde River Canyon and other hikes and many beautiful waterfalls (see chapter 7). The Sudwala Caves (see chapter 17), and the nearby open-air dinosaur museum are well worth a visit. The Long Tom Pass linking Lydenburg and Sabie is spectacular and climbs a dizzying 1 000 m in 18 km on one side and 670 m in 20 km on the other. It is a very popular paragliding launch site.

Gauteng

There are no multi-day trails in this area but there are a number of stables from which you can do day rides. A fun outing for relative novices is the Horseback Africa trail in the Windybrow Reserve near Cullinan, just outside Pretoria. You stand an excellent chance of seeing game such as kudu, giraffe etc. Booking is through **Affordable Adventures**.

WHILE IN THE AREA

The stables are a short drive from the Pretoria Skydiving Club drop zone at Wonderboom (see chapter 12), so non-riding companions can do a first jump if they like. You could also do a one-day or overnight hike or cycle in the reserve. Book directly by phoning +27 12 346-3550.

Northern Province

This little-known area, close to Gauteng, offers mysterious forests, the Kruger National Park and fascinating little towns to explore.

HORIZON HORSE TRAILS

You can choose between heading off on a game-viewing ride of a few days, camping rough and really getting the feel of the bush, or you can stay "back at the ranch" and play cowboys. You stay in a bunkhouse and help round up cattle, dip them and generally do the "city slicker" thing. This is a dude ranch, modelled very much on the original American idea. Cleverly, they get you to pay them for doing their work. But it is fun.

EQUUS LUXURY WILDERNESS HORSE SAFARI

Equus is based at Lapalala on the Waterberg Plateau, which is rich in game such as giraffe, white rhino, ostrich, wildebeest, zebra and many species of antelope. The horse safaris leave from the Bush Camp, which is luxurious but rustic. Further nights are spent in various camps, with equipment and supplies driven there by staff. The safari is run only between April and September and is suitable for riders who have mastered all the basic skills and can spend almost the whole day in the saddle. If you prefer you can base yourself at the Bush Camp and ride out every day. This option operates all year except November.

WHILE IN THE AREA

Lapalala also conducts walking safaris from the rustic Rhino Lodge (see chapter 15) as well as more sedate vehicle-based safaris.

Northern Cape

This is a fairly remote area, about ten hour's drive from either Johannesburg or Cape Town and about six hours from Bloemfontein, so make the most of your time here. The whole region is very arid and links up with the Kalahari in the far north. The Orange River forms a sinuous oasis through this stark region.

KAMEELDORING CAMEL TRAIL

This is a slow, relaxed amble around the farmlands of the southern Kalahari. The scenery is characterised by flat expanses interspersed with rocky outcrops. The vegetation is interesting with camelthorn trees dominating the plains and kokerbooms *(Aloe dichotoma)* the hillsides. Game likely to be seen includes oryx, springbok, dassies and hares.

Although the scenery and wildlife are interesting, most people do this trip for the experience of interacting with the camels. They are very unusual animals and, although they tolerate people and do (almost) what you ask them, they are totally independent, quite haughty and most entertaining. Don't ever let one see you laughing at it, though.

All camel tack is provided and the trip is catered, but you need to bring your own cutlery and crockery. No camping equipment is supplied so bring your own. Although it can be bitterly cold in winter, it hardly ever rains so a groundsheet, sleeping mat and good sleeping bag should be adequate.

WHILE IN THE AREA

Don't miss out on the Augrabies Falls National Park. The falls are spectacular in summer when the river is full, and the gorge is the largest granite canyon in the world. The park has plentiful game, including black rhino, and many species of birds. The Klipspringer Hiking Trail (see chapter 7), the Augrabies Rush and the Black Eagle or Augrabies Canoe Trail (see chapter 6), are well worth doing.

This trip is suitable for complete beginners and it is not necessary to be fit at all. If you prefer, you can do a "two ships" trail which involves two-and-a-half days paddling on the Orange River and a two-day camel trail (see the Black Eagle canoe trail in chapter 6). This is also an option if you want to do the camel trail outside the winter months, as full trips are run only in winter. Two ships trails are run all year.

This trip is run by **Adventure Runners** and all booking is done through their Johannesburg office.

Free State

Much of the Free State is not suitable for horse trails but the eastern part is absolutely wonderful — rolling grasslands stop abruptly at huge sandstone cliffs and clear streams tumble down from the highlands.

BOKPOORT HORSE TRAILS

There are three trails leaving from this multi-purpose adventure venue near Clarens. The scenery is spectacular with huge concave sandstone cliffs typical of the region, streams and waterfalls. Day rides explore the surrounding countryside and the adjoining game farm. You may also ride into Clarens and visit a number of art galleries, combining a bit of culture with some fresh air. The two-day Snow Hills Trail and the three-day Simply the Best Trail are suitable for experienced riders. They traverse the high grasslands of the Free State, where you may encounter snow. Ouma's Kraal Trail is not quite a granny's trail but it is suitable for beginners. It is a two-day trail across the Clarens Conservancy and you spend the night in a mountain hut high up in the mountains. All trips are fully catered and there is accommodation ranging from comfortable cottages to dormitories in a huge stone barn.

Booking is through **Jacana Country Homes and Trails**.

WHILE IN THE AREA

There are numerous hiking and mountain biking trails on the same farm and in the general vicinity. The nearby Rustler's Valley Mountain Lodge organises spectacular alternative music festivals twice a year; over the Easter weekend and the December holiday period from 16 December to just past New Year. These are definitely for the young at heart.

Swaziland

This tiny kingdom has some wonderful riding country but there is only one commercial trail, at the Mlilwane Game Reserve. There are stables in other parts of the country, though, where you can go out on a short hack.

MLILWANE GAME RESERVE

Situated in the Ezulwini Valley of Swaziland, Mlilwane is a small reserve with many species of antelopes and birds. There are no predators and it is a perfect venue for watching game from horseback. The terrain is varied and offers fun riding. At present the reserve offers only half- or full-day trips but intends to start multi-day trails. The trips are suitable for beginners. Because you are approaching game you should wear neutral colours such as khaki, brown, green or very muted pastels, and definitely not white. Mlilwane is one of the **Big Game Parks of Swaziland** and all bookings are through their central office in Mbabane.

WHILE IN THE AREA

Mlilwane offers game drives, escorted walks and mountain bike trails as well as some self-guided walks and, of course, you may watch game from your own vehicle. Mkhaya Game Reserve is not too distant and offers game drives, escorted walks and cycle trails. Hlane, in the lowlands, is one of the largest parks in Swaziland and the only one that has lions. Mlawula offers excellent hiking in the Lebombo Mountains and Malolotja, in the north of this tiny kingdom, offers some of the most spectacular montane grassland hiking in southern Africa (see chapter 7). Mlilwane has accommodation ranging from camping to self-catering chalets. There is also a youth hostel and a small restaurant. This area is renowned for innovative craft workshops and shopaholics will have a field day.

Botswana: Okavango Delta

The Okavango Delta is one of the most spectacular wilderness areas in the world. At times consisting of extensive grassland and bush, it changes character entirely when it floods with crystal clear water, forming many meandering channels and lagoons.

AFRICAN HORSE SAFARIS AT MACATEERS

Deep in the Delta, Macateers Camp is the base from which African Horse Safaris operate. You can choose to stay at the camp and go out every day to see game, or you can move to one of a number of satellite camps and thereby travel further afield. You can choose the length of your stay, subject to a minimum of three days. This is not so much a horse trail as a horseback safari, and the emphasis is on tracking and approaching game. One of the highlights is the opportunity to run alongside herds of zebra or wildebeest.

You are likely to see, as well as the above, giraffe, impala, tsessebe, lechwe, elephants, hyenas and lions. Because you are stalking game, it is important that you wear neutral colours such as green, brown or khaki or, at least, very muted shades of other colours. White is definitely out.

You may choose between English or Western-style saddles and short chaps are supplied. This trip is only suitable for riders who are confident and can control a horse at any pace as it may be necessary to gallop out of danger.

The trips are all fully catered and the camps are rustic but very luxurious, consisting of huge safari tents with en suite showers and private pit toilets. You need to bring nothing but your personal clothing, and there is a weight limit on luggage as you fly in a light plane from Maun to the delta. The trips are run from the beginning of March to the middle of December. Also see chapter 15 for details on the annual variation of conditions in the delta.

African Horse Safaris is part of the **Legendary Adventure Company**, which handles all bookings from its offices in Maun, Johannesburg or Houston, USA.

OKAVANGO HORSE SAFARIS

Okavango Horse Safaris, also known informally as "PJs", operates a similar horseback safari in the adjacent safari concession. Their main office is in Maun.

WHILE IN THE AREA

Close by is Xudum, a camp also operated by the Legendary Adventure Company. It is somewhat more upmarket than Macateers, with flush toilets, etc. They offer elephant safaris, multi-day walking safaris, mokoro safaris and canoe safaris. There are many other operators in the delta area, most of whom specialise in mokoro trips (see chapter 15).

Lesotho

This tiny country is extremely mountainous, very poor and has a rather rudimentary transport network. There are many rivers with spectacular waterfalls, caves with extensive rock art, dinosaur footprints and absolutely stunning scenery. And the best way of seeing all of it is on horseback.

All the horse trails are run by local villagers, so don't expect a slick operation with the latest and best equipment. Remember, too, that life in these mountains is harsh, so don't expect a sleek, beautifully groomed horse. Basotho ponies are rough and ready but gentle and tractable.

MATELILE PONY OWNERS ASSOCIATION

This is a cooperative of villagers who operate pony trails from Malealea Lodge. Ranging from half a day to seven days, the trails take in the spectacular mountain scenery which is so characteristic of Lesotho. You visit remote waterfalls and stay in isolated Basotho villages, thus catching a glimpse of the way of life of these hardy mountain people. The trails are suitable for beginners as they are not fast and the ponies are reliable and sure-footed. Most trails are self-catering but catered trips can be arranged. You may use Malealea Lodge as a base. It is very comfortable with self-catering cottages and a campsite, and they handle bookings for the **Matelile Pony Owners Association**. You can also book through **Jacana Country Homes and Trails**.

THE BASOTHO PONY PROJECT

The Basotho Pony Project at Molimo Ntusi offers hourly or multi-day trails through similar scenery. All trips are self-catering. There is no official accommodation at the starting point but they are almost certain to let you camp on the lawn on the night before and after your trail or you could stay at the nearby Molimo Ntusi Lodge. You can book a self-catered trip directly through the **Basotho Pony Project** or a catered trip through **Adventures Unlimited**, who will organise all bookings and catering.

WHILE IN THE AREA

See chapters 7, 8, 9 and 18 for other activities in the mountain kingdom.

OTHER HORSE TRAILS IN THE AREA

One of the most reliable modes of transport in this rugged and isolated country is the hardy Basotho pony, and the whole country is suitable for trails. You can hire ponies from almost any villager but it is usually easier to go through a third party, such as Malealea Lodge (above), who will look after both your interests and those of the pony owner.

Other lodges that regularly operate in this way are **Sani Top Mountaineers Chalet**, at the top of Sani Pass, **Fraser's Semongkong Lodge** at Semongkong, **Molumong** near Mokhotlong and the **Trading Post** at Roma. If you really know what you are doing, you could buy a pony and traverse the whole length of this tiny country, but this course of action should not be considered lightly.

WHILE IN THE AREA

The area through which you ride is also suitable for hiking, there are many trails that are ideal for mountain biking, and four-wheel-drive enthusiasts consider Lesotho a paradise of dreadful roads. The many streams offer reasonable trout fishing and very experienced hang- or paragliders can revel in the excellent ridge soaring off some of the steep slopes (see chapter 9). When travelling through Lesotho carry a camping stove, as firewood is scarce. If you really want to cook on open fires, bring a bag of charcoal.

Namibia

This huge and apparently inhospitable country offers one of the best, but toughest, horse trails in the region. As well as the Namib Trail described below, there is a shorter Panorama Trail, a shorter desert trail, a horseback safari in the Namib Rand Nature Reserve and an epic trail along the Skeleton Coast, all run by the same company.

NAMIB DESERT TRAIL

This is one of the most spectacular trails of any kind in the region. It is nine long days through the oldest desert in the world, six hard hours in the saddle every day (sometimes more), and takes you into some utterly breathtaking scenery. On some sections of the trip you will feel like the only people in the world.

You spend the first day riding on the farm near Windhoek, where you and your horse can get to know each other before you head off towards the sea. You then travel across the Khomas Hoghland, or Central Highlands, reaching a maximum altitude of 2 000 m. Still on the semidesert farms of the highlands, you cross over the Hakos Mountains, where you have to walk some of the way as the terrain is very steep. The sure-footed horses can be left to make their own way over the rocks as you just guide them to keep them on the right track. You are likely to catch a fleeting glimpse of a mountain zebra, oryx (gemsbok) or some smaller game. There are leopards in these hills but you are unlikely to see them, although you may see tracks.

Once over the mountains, the terrain changes to red sand-dunes, covered in sparse grass and supporting, as well as some game, surprisingly large herds of cattle and goats.

On your fifth day out of the farm you enter the Namib-Naukluft Park and ride through the Kuiseb River Pass, seeing vehicles and other people for the last time till Swakopmund. You are likely to see many springbok, zebra and oryx.

The next three days are spent riding straight through the ever-changing scenery of the true desert. Only at lunch breaks, water stops and night camps, do you see your backup vehicles and possibly other people.

You then leave the park and travel down the Swakop River bed, once again seeing signs of human habitation. Just before you reach Swakop, you ride through the red dunes which fit most people's idea of a real desert. And then you finally reach the sea.

This is a full-service trip. All meals, cutlery, crockery, etc., is provided. Cold drinks (including beer and wine) are available throughout, to your account. You are supplied with spacious tents, camp beds, duvets and pillows, but it is still advisable to bring a sleeping bag as the nights can be very cold indeed. There is a hot shower (yes, in the desert!) but no toilet facilities. Two backup vehicles carry all your personal gear, camping equipment, horse feed and water. You spend the first two nights in comfortable accommodation on the farm and the last night in chalets in Swakopmund. The trip ends in Swakopmund and if you want to return to Windhoek, you must find your own way.

The trips are run from February to September as the summer months are simply too hot. There are no trips during May as the possibility of sand storms is high. Although midwinter is the coolest and therefore a good time to do the trip, there is still a slight chance of sand storms in June or July from day eight of the trip. If this happens, the horses (and people) will be trucked out of the desert. Although some novices have done this trail, it is definitely recommended only for experienced riders who are reasonably fit. As you can imagine, the horses need to be very fit and in good condition to manage the trip and therefore may be a bit of a handful. Even very experienced riders find themselves saddlesore after a few days.

The trip is operated by **Reit Safari** who are based just outside Windhoek. They handle all bookings, but be patient if trying to contact them by phone or fax as the farm is remote and they operate on a party line. It's worth the hassle, though, so persevere.

WHILE IN THE AREA

Swakopmund is a picturesque seaside town with excellent fishing. You may do a one-day camel trail from just outside the town: enquire at the publicity association offices. The Namib/Naukluft National Park is worth a visit to see the dunes at Sossusvlei or visit Sandwich Harbour. There is a four- or eight-day unescorted hike in the park (see chapter 7), and a balloon flight over the park (see chapter 11). The nearby dunes are among the highest in the world; Alternative Space Backpackers, tel: +264 6431 2713, in Swakopmund offer dune-boarding excursions.

Zambezi Valley

The Victoria Falls/Livingstone area is is one of the most popular tourist destinations in southern Africa. Many people travel here just to see the falls, but the region has also become the adventure travel capital of Africa.

CHUNDUKWA HORSE TRAILS

The trails go through magnificent teak forests, along the river bank upstream from Livingstone on the Zambian side and through game-filled mopane forests. Besides getting the opportunity to see game, you can learn much about the birdlife and trees from your experienced guide. You start off at Chundukwa River Camp, which consists of attractive reed and thatch en suite chalets perched on stilts on the riverbank. There is a swimming pool and a comfortable thatched boma overlooking the river. All equipment is supplied and the trip is fully catered. You spend the night in a tented camp on the banks of the Zambezi.

The saddles are mostly McLellans. Because you are approaching game, you should wear neutral colours such as khaki, brown, green or very muted pastels, and definitely not white.

The standard trip is two days and is only suitable for competent riders. You can, however, arrange to do a half-day, one-day or longer trail. Less experienced riders or beginners may do a short, scenic trail along the river where there is very little chance of encountering dangerous game.

WHILE IN THE AREA

Chundukwa also offers walking safaris into Kafue National Park and canoe trips on the upper Zambezi. The area around Victoria Falls and Livingstone offers numerous other attractions: see chapters 6, 9, 11 and 13.

ZAMBEZI NATIONAL PARK GAME RIDE

The Zambezi National Park runs along the banks of the Zambezi above Victoria Falls on the Zimbabwean side. This ride is more a horseback safari than a horse trail. You keep very quiet and, under the watchful eye of an experienced guide, slowly approach the animals, allowing your horse to graze and so appearing very natural. In this way you can get very close to large herds of buffalo and even walk amongst impala and other antelope.

Because of the real risk of an animal charging you, you must be a competent rider to do this trip. You wouldn't want to fall off while galloping away from an irate buffalo. Most trips are half- or full-day but overnight trips are run from time to time and can be specially arranged if there is sufficient demand. Because you are approaching game, you should wear neutral colours such as khaki, brown, green or very muted pastels, and definitely not white.

Saddles are mostly English style, but you can choose a Western saddle if you prefer. The trip is operated by Zambezi Horse Trails and all booking is through Safari par Excellence or one of the other Victoria Falls booking agents.

OTHER HORSE TRAILS IN ZIMBABWE

There are horses for hire in the Matobo National Park and the Nyanga National Park. These are mostly for day trips. Mopane Lodge near Kwekwe also offers day rides if you happen to be in the area. Carew Safaris offer luxurious horseback safaris in the Mavuradonna Wilderness. They range from 2 to 6 nights, overnighting at a luxurious, but rustic, base camp or a comfortable fly camp. Experienced riders can do an even wilder safari.

Listings

OPERATORS

Adventure Runners, P O Box 31117, Braamfontein 2017, South Africa; tel: +27 11 403-2512/339-7183, fax: +27 11 339-4042, run camel trails in the southern Kalahari.

Adventures Unlimited, P O Box 2323 Rivonia 2128, South Africa; tel/fax: +27 1205 5-1246, organise catered pony treks through the Basotho Pony Project.

Affordable Adventures; tel: +27 11 465-9168, fax: +27 11 705- 3203, take bookings for the Horseback Africa trail.

Basotho Pony Project, P O Box 1027, Maseru 100, Lesotho; tel: +266 31 4165, run pony treks in Lesotho.

Big Game Parks of Swaziland Central Booking Office, Mlilwane Wildlife Sanctuary, P O Box 234, Mbabane, Swaziland; tel: +268 4-5006, fax: +268 4-4246 (o/h); tel: +268 6-1591, fax +268 6-1594 (a/h), offer escorted game-viewing rides through Mlilwane Game Reserve.

Carew Safaris, Private Bag 295A, Harare, Zimbabwe; tel: +263 58 2358, operate horse safaris in the Mavuradonna Wilderness in Zimbabwe. They can also be contacted through Livingstone Safaris, tel: +263 4 73-5920, fax: +263 4 79-5301.

Chundukwa Adventure Trails, tel/fax: +269 3 32-4006, offer one- or two-day trails along the banks of the Zambezi River in Zambia.

Equitrailing, P O Box 1373 Plettenberg Bay 6600, South Africa; tel: +27 4457 30599, offer one- or multi-day trails through the coastal fynbos and the forests.

Equus Horse Safaris, 36 12th Ave, Parktown North 2193, South Africa; tel: +27 11 788-3923, fax: +27 11 880-8401, run horseback safaris on Touchstone Game Ranch in the Northern Province of South Africa.

Frasers Semongkong Lodge, P O Box 243 Ficksburg 9730, South Africa; tel: +27 5192 2730, can organise one- or multi-day trails, including one to Maletsunyane Falls, near their lodge in Lesotho.

Hillside Horse Trails, tel: +27 363 2-4435, operate in the Giant's Castle Game Reserve in the northern Drakensberg of KwaZulu-Natal.

Holt Trails, P O Box 18 Himeville 3256, South Africa; tel/fax: +27 33 702-1030, offer trails through Cobham in the southern Drakensberg in KwaZulu-Natal.

Horizon Horse Trails, P O Box 301, Vaalwater 0530, South Africa; tel: +27 15352 ask for 2141, operate horseback safaris in the Northern Province as well as offering guests the opportunity to experience a working ranch environment and round up cattle on horseback.

Khotso Pony Trails, P O Box 19, Underberg 3257, South Africa; tel/fax: +27 33 701-1502, run one-day or multi-day trails in the southern Drakensberg.

K'Taaibos, P O Box 26, Redelinghuys 8105, South Africa; tel: +27 263 684, offers one- and multi-day trails on the West Coast.

The Legendary Adventure Company, P O Box 411288, Craighall, Johannesburg 2024, South Africa; tel: +27 11 327-0161, fax: +27 11 327-0162P O Box 40, Maun, Botswana; tel: +267 66-0211, fax: +267 66-0379. 13201 Northwest Freeway, Suite 800, Houston, Texas 77040, USA; tel: +1 713 744-5244, fax: +1 713 895-8753, operates horseback safaris at Macateers in the Okavango Delta.

Marquard Cherry Trail, P O Box 140, Marquard 9610, Free State, South Africa; tel +27 51 991-0126, is a general booking agent for a number of horse trails (and other trails) in the eastern Free State.

Matelile Pony Owners Association operates in conjunction with Malealea Lodge, P O Box 119, Wepener 9944, South Africa; tel/fax: +27 51 447-3200 and tel/fax: +27 51 448-3001, cell phone: +27 82 552-4215, e-mail: malealea @ pixie.co.za. They offer trails of up to seven days into the remote hills of Lesotho.

Molumong Tours, P O Box 44, Underberg 3257, South Africa; tel: +27 33 701-1490, +27 33 702-1050 (a/h), will organise pony trails or the hire of ponies with local villagers in Lesotho.

National Parks and Wildlife of Zimbabwe, Central Booking Office, P O Box 8151, Causeway, Harare, Zimbabwe; tel: +263 4 70-6077/8, should be able to give information and take bookings for the one-day horse trails in Matobo and Nyanga national parks.

Okavango Horse Safaris, Private Bag 23, Maun, Botswana; tel: +267 66-0822/3, fax: +267 66-0493.

Qwibi Horse Trails, tel: +27 3545 2817, operate in the Ophata Game Reserve, northern KwaZulu-Natal.

Reit Safaris, P O Box 20706, Windhoek, Namibia; tel: +264 628 ask for Friedendal 1111, fax: +264 61 23-8890, operate a number of trails in Namibia. (The fax is some distance from the farm.)

Sani Top Mountaineers Chalet, tel: +27 33 701-1466, can arrange the hire of ponies from villagers at Sani Top in Lesotho.

The Trading Post, P O Box 64, Maseru, Lesotho; tel: +266 34-0202 (o/h), 34-0267 (a/h), can arrange the rental of ponies near Roma.

Wine Valley Horse Trails, tel: +27 21 981-6331 or +27 83 226- 8735, offer one- or two-day trails in the winelands of Stellenbosch, near Cape Town.

ACCOMMODATION

Most of the horse trails are on farms or game reserves with accommodation; those listed below are the exceptions.

Holt Trails at Himeville

See listings at the end of chapter 8.

Kameeldoring Trail at Augrabies

See listings at the end of chapter 6.

Zambezi National Park Game Rides, Victoria Falls

See listings at the end of chapter 6.

CLUBS AND SOCIETIES

Cape Hunt and Polo Club, tel: +27 21 96-3968

Natal Horse Society, tel: +27 331 43-3912

Rand Hunt Club, tel: +27 11 464-1344

SA Riding for the Disabled, Johannesburg; P O Box 1171, Fourways 2055, South Africa; tel: +27 11 708-1974. Cape Town; P O Box 235, Constantia 7848; tel: +27 21 794-4393.

South African National Equestrian Federation (SANEF), tel: +27 11 701-3062, is the national body controlling the provincial horse societies.

Transvaal Horse Society, tel: +27 11 702-1659

Western Province Horse Society, tel: +27 21 981-2409

Zimbabwe Horse Society, tel: +263 4 753-9015

RETAIL OUTLETS

A C Smith Saddlery, Durban, tel: +27 31 306-0935

Cape Pet-O-tel Saddlery, Cape Town, tel: +27 21 73-1004

Dee's Saddlery, Johannesburg, tel: +27 11 465-1253

Horseland, Johannesburg, tel: +27 11 468-2790

Horseman's Haven, Johannesburg, tel: +27 11 787-2436

Laird's Leatherware, Cape Town, tel: +27 21 797-8336/511-5008

CHAPTER 17

Go underground

Caving

If you have never gone caving, you may find it hard to understand the lure of the heart of darkness. Part of the attraction is the fact that it's hard to get into caves and you can go where no, or at least few, people have gone before. But the main reason cavers love their sport is because caves are so beautiful. Huge, glistening stalactites and stalagmites abound, tiny delicate crystal structures reflect the light of your lamp, iridescing with every colour of the spectrum, and the silence is broken only by the steady "drip drip" of yet another spectacular natural sculpture continuing its thousand-year formation. Cave interiors are magic places. They are also extremely difficult to preserve. The very act of entering a cave, opening it up to the atmosphere, breathing in it and bringing light into it (albeit artificial and for a short duration) will dull the spectacular sheen and, inevitably, some of the delicate crystal structures will be destroyed. But, some might argue, what is the use of having caves if no one ever sees them.

The more logical and pragmatic among those responsible for the conservation of cave environments have, however, come up with what seems a reasonable compromise. Some caves are open to the public and tours are conducted to introduce people to the spectacular beauty of these places. In most cases the guides also point out, with examples, how the very presence of hordes of tourists has degraded the cave. Other caves are only open to experienced cavers, usually as part of an official expedition, either as a policy decision or as a result of remoteness or general inaccessibility. And still others are closed completely, except maybe for one or two very well-planned expeditions. This policy ensures that at least some cave environments will survive intact.

Getting started

Caving is relatively safe if you follow all the rules, know what you are doing and use the right equipment. Just wandering off into an unknown cave to see what's there, though, is extremely hazardous.

If you want to cave, the only way to do it safely is to join one of the clubs; either one of the two branches of the South African Speleological Association (SASA) or the Cave Research Organisation of South Africa (CROSA). Most cavers are friendly and knowledgeable, so you will get ample opportunities to learn the necessary skills. It is not formalised, but the clubs usually have training evenings where you learn skills such as single rope technique (SRT), which is essential for getting into and out of some caves. You may join club outings to relatively easy caves and will be invited to more technical ones as your skill level increases. It is a small community and anyone who is really keen will be welcomed.

Equipment

Probably your first encounter with a cave will be on an escorted trip into one of the commercial "tourist" caves; just wear comfortable clothes and reasonable walking shoes. All caves, even tourist ones, are dirty, so don't wear your newest and favourite designer gear.

Once you get into slightly more serious caving, you will need to be better prepared. Some of the caves mentioned below can be explored (but relatively superficially) with just the aid of a hand-held torch, and you could wear any comfortable clothes which you don't mind ruining. Serious caves, though, demand serious equipment such as a real caving lamp (very much like a miner's lamp), overalls, waterproof suit, maybe even a wetsuit, helmet, climbing harness and climbing gear. You can rent much of this from the clubs when you start and eventually buy your own.

Options for people with disabilities

CROSA have taken a number of blind people into caves, and SASA have had people who are dependent on crutches at a few of their meets and were impressed at how well they managed. When you understand what caving entails, this is not so surprising. A certain amount of walking is required to get to the cave and also in the more roomy sections. However, a lot of the time is spent crawling along on your belly, using your arms to propel yourself.

The access to Cango Caves is not good. Sudwala is relatively easy to get in and you pay half price if you are in a wheelchair. They do not have special toilets, but the ones they have are usable by disabled people. There is one step to the toilets and one to the restaurant. Neither the Wonder Cave nor Sterkfontein is easily accessible.

Western Cape

The Cape has a number of sandstone caves, especially in the Peninsula Mountain Chain (Cape Town). They are very different in origin to the more usual limestone caves as they are formed by erosion of moving water, whereas limestone or dolomite caves are formed almost exclusively by solution of the rock. This has two effects on the eventual appearance of the cave: sandstone caves are usually not quite as smooth and rounded and they don't have spectacular crystal structures or stalagmites and stalactites. There are a few limestone caves as well in this region; De Kelders is described below and there are also some little-known limestone caves in De Hoop Nature Reserve (see chapters 8 and 15). Of course, the Cango Caves on the eastern extreme of the region are well known.

MUIZENBERG CAVES

These caves, above the picturesque fishing village of Kalk Bay, are very popular and are often visited by groups of schoolchildren. Don't be fooled by this, though. You can wander in with just a torch, but keep careful note of your route. Just because they are easily accessible does not mean they are trivial. There are some very tricky sections and a number of people have been lost, trapped or injured in them. If you use your common sense, though, you can explore the shallower sections.

Before exploring the caves, contact **SASA (Cape)** for guidance. There is a well-worn path to the caves from Boyes Drive.

WHILE IN THE AREA

There are lovely walks across the mountain and the walk to the caves is worth doing for its own sake. The village of Kalk Bay is one of the most picturesque areas of Cape Town. There is a fishing harbour, many interesting restaurants, pubs and shops. The surfing is great when conditions are favourable (see chapter 14), and in winter there is excellent diving in the bay (see chapter 5).

TABLE MOUNTAIN

Table Mountain has numerous interesting sandstone caves, many of which are quite extensive and very complex. Many are also in rather inaccessible areas of the mountain and, despite the fact that it is in the middle of a city, Table Mountain is a real mountain with all the attendant risks, such as astonishing weather changes, mist and hidden ravines. Contact **SASA (Cape)** if you want to explore these caves.

WHILE IN THE AREA

When you're tired of Cape Town, you're tired of life. Why not take advantage of the windy weather and go fly a kite. Visit the Kite Shop in the Victoria and Alfred Waterfront for top-of-the-range high-tech kites. And after your purchase, do the tourist thing in the Waterfront. Watch the concerts in the Agfa amphitheatre, support the buskers (look out for the sax-playing gorilla), shop till you drop and eat and drink to your heart's distress. And then, if it's windy, take your kite out to Bloubergstrand and fly. See also the Cape entries in chapters 5, 7, 8, 9, 14, 15 and 18 for further information on the Cape Town area.

DE KELDERS

This is a pretty limestone cave near De Kelders Hotel, just outside the small town of Gansbaai. It is right on the beach and has a crystal clear ice-cold freshwater pool, just a metre or two above sea level. There is a locked gate but you can usually get the key from the hotel for a small fee. This connects up to quite an extensive system, so don't go wandering too far if you don't know what you're doing. You should be able to find a local who knows the way if you enquire at the hotel.

WHILE IN THE AREA

There is good diving in nearby Hermanus and Gansbaai (see chapter 5). In winter and spring, you can stand on the cliff above the cave and watch southern right whales frolicking in the sea.

CANGO CAVES

This huge and impressive limestone cave system near Oudtshoorn is probably the most spectacular in southern Africa. Cango 1 is open to the public from 8 am to 5 pm in season (December/January and March/April South African school holidays) and from 9 am to 3 pm out of season. Guided trips are offered hourly in season and every two hours out of season. You may not explore on your own. The caves need to be lit in order to facilitate the tours, but this is highly destructive as it allows the growth of algae and other plants. A partial solution is to use coloured lights. So if you find the fanciful lighting a bit kitsch, remember it's not just a whim.

There are full ablutions, a restaurant and a real tourist trap of a curio shop. It is not necessary to book cave tours.

OTHER CAVES IN THE AREA

Cango 2 and 3 are (evidently) exquisitely beautiful extensions which are not open to the public. Of the many other interesting caves in the area, Emerald Pool and the North-west Passage are firm favourites with local cavers. They are probably all part of the same system and one day the connections may be found.

Emerald Pool has a unique entry. Cavers, like anyone else, like a bit of drama and it's fun to kit up in full wetsuit and then clamber down a hole in the middle of the road in full view of passing motorists.

The North-west Passage has become a bit of an obsession to some local cavers. It is a cold, wet, very cramped cave, but there is no accounting for taste. Every year they go a little deeper and further into it and still haven't reached the end or a connection with another system.

The Cape branch of **SASA** visits this area annually.

Gauteng

The Gauteng area is riddled with interesting dolomite caves, but most of the more accessible ones have been destroyed. During the Boer War, the importation of cement (from England) was stopped so the locals mined the caves for lime in order to make cement. There were plenty that weren't found, though, and Gauteng, Mpumalanga, the North-west and the Northern Province together (the old Transvaal province) are the mecca of caving in southern Africa, boasting hundreds of dolomite caves.

As well as the sheer number of caves, this area also boasts the largest cave yet discovered in the region, Apocalypse Pothole. Most of the caves in this area are on private property. Contact **SASA (Transvaal)** who have all the connections to get access.

WHILE IN THE AREA

If you feel a deep need to descend into the bowels of the earth and there are no available caving excursions, you may do so courtesy of the Chamber of Mines. They offer visits to a working gold mine on Tuesdays, Wednesdays and Thursdays. Telephone Johannesburg (011) 838-8211 for more details. It's not caving, but it is interesting.

STERKFONTEIN CAVES

Although this cave is not as spectacular as, for example, Cango or Sudwala, at least not in the area open to the public, it is one of the more interesting. It is the site of the discovery, in 1936, of the first fossil of *Australopithecus africanus*, our delicate little ancestor. It is this evidence which lends credence to the theory that Africa is the cradle of humanity. To date, no evidence has come to light that contradicts it, so a visit to Sterkfontein is a visit to your roots. Sterkfontein is part of a sizeable cave system, most of which is off-limits to tourists, including a beautiful crystal clear pool which leads to a complex submerged network. There is an interesting interpretive centre and a small restaurant.

The caves are open to the public Tuesday to Sunday from 9 am to 5 pm. The last tour leaves at 4 pm, so if there is no tour then, they close. Booking is not necessary.

The nearby Krugersdorp Game Reserve is a tiny park with an interesting variety of habitats. You can join a guided interpretive walk and will have the chance of seeing blesbok, roan and sable antelope, kudu, nyala, giraffe and many other species of antelope, all of which have been reintroduced into the area.

WONDER CAVE

This is a huge single chamber with beautiful cave formations. You enter the chamber by a lift which goes through a hole in the roof of the cave. This cave is open to the public daily from 8 am to 5 pm. Tours are conducted hourly from 8.45 am to 3.45 pm.

WHILE IN THE AREA

The nearby Rhino and Lion Park is worth a visit, especially if you are really keen to get photographs of these animals, as they are enclosed in relatively small spaces and are not too difficult to find. For a totally different experience, fly over the park in a balloon (see chapter 11).

Mpumalanga

Besides the many dolomite caves in this region, the most extensive quartzite caves in southern Africa can be found here. They are all on private property and in order to gain access you will need to contact **SASA (Transvaal)**.

SUDWALA CAVES

These huge and spectacular caves are open to the public from 8.30 am to 5 pm every day. They are part of a typical dolomite system and have many stalagmites, stalactites and other pretty cave features, as well as some fascinating fossils. You may only explore on a guided tour. Tours do not leave at set times but depart when there are sufficient people — you are not likely to wait longer than 20 minutes, though. The last tour leaves at 4 pm. To see the best, though, book a "crystal tour", which is conducted on the first Saturday of every month. This involves a tour into the deeper chambers which are protected from tourist pressure the rest of the time. This tour will also be run for groups on request.

There is a dinosaur park nearby, with life-size models of these creatures. There is also a shop and restaurant. The area boasts a number of scenic walks.

WHILE IN THE AREA

This area offers many scenic drives through thick forests, along tumbling streams, up onto the escarpment and to spectacular waterfalls. Trout fishing is very popular, especially in the Dullstroom area, and the Fanie Botha Trail, Blyde River Canyon and many lesser known hikes are not too far away. Waterval Boven has some of the best rock climbing in the country (see chapter 18). The small town of Pilgrim's Rest was a working mining town until the 1970s (albeit at a vastly reduced level compared to its heyday in the gold rush era of the last century.) When mining became totally unprofitable, the whole town was sold off to the provincial authorities who have turned it into a living museum. Most of the buildings are still used for their original purpose. See chapter 7 for hikes in this area.

Northern Province

The Wolkberg Mountains (see chapter 7), have a number of interesting and beautiful dolomite caves. The best-known, Wolkberg Cave, rivals Cango for scenic splendour. It is well worth trying to join a trip there — contact **SASA (Transvaal)**.

WHILE IN THE AREA

See chapter 7 for the excellent hiking in the area. There is some wonderful climbing (see chapter 18), and horse trails, safaris and horseback safaris in the Northern Province (see chapters 15 and 16).

Botswana

There are a number of relatively unknown caves in the Lobatse area. **SASA (Transvaal)** conduct expeditions there periodically. Contact them if you are interested in joining one.

DROTSKY'S CAVES

This is a huge system of dolomite caves, surprisingly set in an almost imperceptible outcrop of rock in an extensive sea of sand, the Kalahari. To get there you need a four-wheel-drive vehicle. There are absolutely no facilities. Bring all your own food, water, fuel, etc., and make sure you are totally independent and self-sufficient. There are two entrances to the caves and it is possible to go from one to the other. In the past, some generous traveller left a string to mark the way but it has deteriorated and in some places is missing entirely. It is not a bad idea to use your own piece of string here if you intend doing any extensive exploring. Also make sure that your light source is reliable: it is a good idea to have a back-up. Don't be tempted to follow any very narrow passages unless you are an experienced caver and have planned a proper penetration. Remember, you are a long way from anywhere.

You can obtain a map of the caves from the **National Museum of Botswana** in Gaborone. If you would like to do an escorted trip to the cave, you can organise one at **Drotsky's Cabins** in Shakawe.

WHILE IN THE AREA

Travelling anywhere from here involves quite an expedition, but there are a number of interesting destinations. It is not that far to the Okavango Delta (by Kalahari standards of distance measuring). See chapter 15 for details of interesting safaris in the delta. The Okavango Panhandle, which offers excellent fishing and birdwatching, is a lot closer. You could stay at Shakawe Fishing Lodge or Drotsky's Cabins, both of which organise fishing excursions and have comfortable accommodation and a campsite (see chapter 6). You can head off further into the Kalahari. It's not too far to Ghanzi, which is a remarkable town. Known as the Wild West of Botswana, it is the centre of a huge cattle-ranching area. On the way, stop at the brightly coloured shop in the middle of the tiny town of D'kar. It is the retail outlet of the Kuru Development Trust, which has encouraged a whole new generation of San artists. Their work is like nothing you have ever seen before; it is most definitely not a slavish imitation of primitive rock art, as one might imagine.

Namibia

The sinkholes Otjikoto and Lake Guinas are evidence of the extensive karst system which exists in Namibia, but only one cave is open to the public. There are a number of caves which are known to serious cavers, though. (And, obviously, to local tribespeople and the farmers who own the land.) The most spectacular of these is Dragon's Breath, near Tsumeb. It is entered through a tiny opening, then there is a long free abseil into total blackness onto a tiny piece of dry land at the edge of the biggest underground lake in the world. There have been two expeditions here to date, both of which involved extensive planning and preparation. The lake was dived to a depth of 93 m and there was no sign of the bottom at that point.

If you are a serious cave diver, you probably know about this spot from the literature already and, if you would like to dive it, you will have to raise vast amounts of money and mount an expedition. Contact **SASA** or the **Cave Diving Club of Southern Africa** for further information.

Other interesting caves in Namibia include Gaub, near the town of Tsumeb. It is a national monument and is the second largest known cave in Namibia. (It is not open to the public but you can get further information about it from the **Tsumeb Museum**.) Harasib Cave, on the same farm as Dragon's Breath, is spectacular. There is a 150 m shaft to a crystal clear lake which has been dived to a depth of 105 m. It is not a cave for casual ramblers. In order to visit it you will need to organise an expedition: contact **SASA** or the **Cave Diving Association**.

ARNHEM CAVE

About 130 km east of Windhoek, near Gobabis, this is the biggest cave known in Namibia and is the only one which is open to the public. It is situated on the farm Arnhem, guided tours are conducted and you may camp on the farm. Booking is essential.

Zimbabwe

There is a significant karst system near Chinhoyi, and many caves which are not open to the public. **SASA (Cape)** have done expeditions here and have a pretty good idea who to contact. The Chimanimani Caves have also been the scene of three serious expeditions to date.

CHINHOYI

Chinhoyi, formerly called Sinoia, is a deep limestone cave whose roof has collapsed, leaving it open to the sky. It is filled with beautiful crystal-clear aquamarine water and, unlike many other water-filled caves, you may walk right down to the edge of the pool and even swim. The local branch of the BSAC (British Sub-Aqua Club) dive here very often. If you are a reasonably experienced cave diver and would like to join them, see chapter 6 for contact details. The best view of the cave is probably from the top, especially if there are divers, as you can see them getting smaller and smaller before they disappear under the overhang. It is interesting to stand at the bottom and imagine the roof before it collapsed. Local legend has it that evildoers were put to death by being hurled into the pool from the top of the cliff.

There is an attractive, shady National Parks campsite and a motel right next to the cave. The cave itself is administered by the **Zimbabwe Department of National Parks** and there is an entrance fee.

WHILE IN THE AREA

There is excellent birding in the campsite; you don't even have to leave your deckchair, and the motel is a pleasant place for a drink or a meal. The cave is about halfway between Harare and Kariba or between Harare and Mana Pools, so it is a good stopover. Mana Pools is one of the best game parks in Africa (see chapter 15 for details). If you are travelling along this road, look out for the "zorse" between Chinhoyi and Karoi. It is a cross between a zebra and a horse and lives in a paddock on the left-hand side of the road (if you're heading towards Karoi) with a lot of real horses. Its mother may also be there (she's a zebra).

CHIMANIMANI

There are a number of extensive sandstone cave systems in the Chimanimani Mountains on Zimbabwe's eastern border. Many of the caves are very deep and require ropes to enter. SASA has mounted three expeditions here to date as they believe that these are the deepest sandstone caves in the world, but to date have only proved them to be the second deepest. These caves are not suitable for casual rambling, but if you would like to join one of the future expeditions, contact **SASA (Cape)**. See chapter 7 for details of the interesting hiking in this spectacularly beautiful wilderness area of montane grassland.

Listings

OPERATORS, CLUBS AND SOCIETIES

Arnhem Cave, tel: +264 628 1430, for booking cave tours and camping.

Cango Caves, tel: +27 443 22-7410, fax: +27 443 22-8001.

Cave Diving Club of Southern Africa, P O Box 2411, Cresta 2118, South Africa.

CROSA (Cave Research Organisation of South Africa), P O Box 51219, Raedene 2124, Johannesburg, tel: +27 11 640-4394.

Drotsky's Cabins, Private Bag 13, Maun, Botswana; tel: +267 66-0351, organise escorted trips to Drotsky's Caves.

National Museum of Botswana, P O Box 00114, Gaborone, Botswana; tel: +267 37-4616, can be contacted for a map of Drotsky's Caves.

SASA (Cape), P O Box 4812, Cape Town 8000, South Africa.

SASA (Transvaal), PO Box 6166, Johannesburg 2000, South Africa; tel: +27 11 976-5124 (a/h).

Sudwala Caves, tel: +27 13 733-4152.

Sterkfontein Caves, tel: +27 11 956-6342.

Tsumeb Museum, tel: +264 671 2-1538, should be able to give information about the near-by Gaub Cave.

The Wonder Cave, tel: +27 11 957-0106, fax: +27 11 957-0344.

Zimbabwe Department of National Parks, P O Box 8151, Causeway, Harare, Zimbabwe; tel: +263 4 70-6077/8, administer the Chinhoyi Caves and the adjacent campsite.

CHAPTER 18

Off the wall

Climbing and abseiling

Most of the climbing in the region is centred on the Western Cape, Gauteng and Mpumalanga in South Africa. There are route guides available for the more popular spots, and novice climbers should be able to organise escorted climbs without too much trouble.

Basic information

Adventure, or traditional, climbing is probably what most non-climbers consider climbing to be. It involves making your way up a rock face using various non-permanent methods of anchoring the rope to the rock. Usually this will be on quite a long pitch or even more than one pitch. Sport climbing, on the other hand, consists of using a number of pre-set and permanent bolts to climb. In both cases the rope is there just as a safety precaution — you don't haul yourself up on it. Many sport climbing venues have a number of routes on the same face so you can choose one to suit your level of expertise.

Abseiling is the technique climbers use to descend after climbing a face. To do this you wear a harness clipped into an abseiling device, which controls your rate of descent on the rope. This can be done down a steep face, in which case you put your feet against the rock and "walk" down, or from an overhang through thin air in which case you just dangle. Commercial abseiling has taken off in South Africa and you can now do just this aspect of climbing under supervision with one of the many guiding companies.

Southern Africa uses the Australian numerical grading system which runs, theoretically, from 10 to 30 (below 10 is not actually climbing). As the sport develops, though, harder and harder routes are being opened up so there are some climbs that are graded higher than 30. Grades 10 to 13 are quite easy — not too steep and with nice big handholds reasonably close together; 14 to 16 may be a bit steeper with very small overhangs, but the holds are still good; and 17 to 19 are quite a bit steeper, with smaller holds further apart. Grade 20 seems to be a big barrier, especially for climbers using natural gear, and grades 20 to 24 are for quite skilled climbers. Grade 25 and above is serious stuff. These grades take no account of exposure, so even a grade 10 or 11 climb may be very high and exposed.

Getting started

If you have no idea whether you will enjoy climbing, the best way to decide is to go out for a day's simple climbing with a professional guide/instructor. You can enquire from the **Mountain Club of South Africa** (MCSA), which will give you a list of qualified guides. If you decide you really like the sport, get some training. The South African Mountaineering Development and Training Trust (MDTT) was started by the MCSA in order to standardise training for rock climbing and hiking. Basic, intermediate and advanced rock climbing courses are run by the MCSA and by any number of private organisations, but all under the auspices of the MDTT. They also oversee the training and registering of mountain guides, for both climbing and hiking.

A climbing course usually consists of a few evenings of lectures where you will learn about equipment, general safety techniques, different types of rock and different types of climbing. This will be followed by practical sessions, initially on really easy rock faces or artificial climbing walls, progressively advancing to more challenging routes. During the course, it is emphasised that the most important qualities a climber should have are a love of the outdoors, a desire to clamber around on rocks and a respect for mountains. Strength, skill and stamina, although useful, are secondary. You are taught to climb safely at whatever level you feel comfortable. If, for example, you never want to do more than be led up relatively easy routes, this will be respected and you will be taught to do so safely. So although your instructors are bound to be very skilled climbers, they won't be mindless machos who will try to throw you off a cliff if you don't measure up. You will also be surprised to hear that many rock climbers started climbing to overcome their fear of heights. Don't be intimidated: the mountains belong to all who love and respect them.

Options for people with disabilities

I don't know of any climbers who have severe disabilities but, if you really want to climb, you will find a way. Ask the MDTT who they recommend.

Equipment

If you are just going on an experimental climb to see how you enjoy the sport, you can borrow or hire everything you need. Just wear comfortable clothes, stretch leggings or tracksuit pants and the thinnest pair of non-slip canvas tennis shoes or running shoes you have. They're not ideal, but they'll do for a first time. If you decide to continue, you should get your own harness, screwgate, belay device, and climbing shoes. Get your instructor to help you choose shoes, as you are bound to buy them a size too big. They need to be very tight-fitting. If you are doing serious rock climbing or are on a course, you must wear a helmet. Once you go climbing on your own, of course, you can choose whether or not to wear it. You will need your own chalk bag at some stage, but they are relatively inexpensive. Once you get serious and start leading climbs you can buy ropes, nuts, friends and all the expensive hardware. Climbing gear is very specialised so ensure you buy yours from a shop with knowledgeable salespeople, preferably climbers.

Before you open new routes

Sport routes are generally equipped with stainless steel, 10x70 mm or 10x90 mm bolts and Petzl-type hangers. If you plan to open your own routes, please follow this precedent. Please also note that South Africa has a zoning approach to bolting, so it is only allowed in certain, pre-negotiated areas. Bolting in other areas may lead to prosecution of the perpetrator, at best, and, at worst, the banning of all climbing in the area concerned. Please ensure that you get the latest information about access: consult local climbing shops or the MCSA.

Western Cape

This is climbing heaven. The rock is of two distinct types: Table Mountain sandstone, which yields steep to overhanging climbing on positive edges, and granite which gives technical face climbing. Beginners in the Cape can contact **The Leading Edge**, **The Cape Town School of Mountaineering**, **Orca Industries**, **High Adventure** or **GAIA** for escorted climbs or courses. The MCSA also has its headquarters in Cape Town so you can enquire whether they are running a course. There are MCSA route guides for Table Mountain, Muizenberg, the Four Apostles, Du Toit's Kloof and a guide by G Holwill to the sport crags of the Western Cape.

CAPE TOWN

There are about 18 developed sites on the Peninsula Chain, most of which are within 15 to 30 minutes' drive of the city centre. The climbing ranges from big naturally protected multi-pitch routes to short, bolted sport crags. Major sport crags include the Mine (19 to 30), Silvermine (15 to 27) and the Hole (24 to 29). Lion's Head Granite (10 to 23) is one of the few climbs in the Cape Town area which is not on sandstone. It offers good slab climbing with up to three pitches. The Ledge (14 to 30), on the upper buttress of Table Mountain, offers steep walls with up to seven pitches. Muizenberg (12 to 22) offers up to five varied pitches. It was in Cape Town that commercial abseiling first took off. This is great fun and really gets the adrenalin flowing. If you would like to give it a try, contact any of the organisations listed above or **Abseil Africa**.

WHILE IN THE AREA

Table Mountain has loads of wonderful day walks: see *Table Mountain Walks* by Colin Paterson-Jones (for more details see "Further reading" at the end of chapter 7). Lion's Head is particularly popular as it is very easy, has attached chains for the last scramble, and there's a magnificent 360-degree view from the top. Take the family and a picnic lunch, especially on a clear night at full moon (but not during the holiday season, when it is invariably crowded). See the Cape Town section in the other chapters of this book for more information on what to do in this exciting city.

PAARL ROCK

This huge granite pluton is a favourite sport climbing venue and it also has some interesting naturally protected climbs ranging from 10 to 29. The town Paarl, which means "pearl" in Dutch, gets its name from this almost perfectly round rock, as it shines like a pearl in the sun after the rain.

WHILE IN THE AREA

The Paarl wine route is as rewarding to explore as the Stellenbosch one. The farm Fairview, besides having a wide variety of wines, makes goatmilk cheese, which you can taste and buy. You may also visit the goats and watch the cheesemaking process. There are lovely walks in the mountains and the town of Paarl has a number of pretty restored buildings, coffee shops and craft shops.

DU TOIT'S KLOOF

This is a very popular traditional climbing venue, offering long alpine climbing (minus the snow and ice) with up to 22 pitches. Grades range from 14 to 24.

MONTAGU

The Montagu Crags are the newest and hottest climbing venue in the Cape. There are a number of high-grade sport climbs, Neuromancer (23), Burning Chrome (28) and the Activist (30). The climbing is within the surrounding kloofs and there are 17 different crags. Most offer single-pitch bolted sports climbs from grade 15 upward. Walk-ins are generally short and the pleasant town nearby makes it a popular winter weekend getaway for Cape Town climbers.

WHILE IN THE AREA

You can pop in to the Montagu Springs to relax those pumped-up muscles after a long climb by lounging around in the mineral-rich 43 °C water. The local wineries are renowned for their sweet fortified wines, such as muscadel, and are well worth a visit.

Eastern Cape

The excellent climbing in this huge and diverse province is not well known and sites are far apart. Many routes were opened in the seventies and eighties but descriptions were only published in mountain club journals. Good areas include Tarkastad, Queenstown, Graaff Reinet, Hogsback, the Cockscomb range and Lady's Slipper near Port Elizabeth. The best contacts are the two climbing shops **Berg Sports** and **Camp Trails**.

GRAHAMSTOWN

Grahamstown has a number of good sport climbing areas close to the town and, right in town, some excellent bouldering in the botanical gardens where you can usually find a number of students practising on weekday evenings. There is an excellent route guide to the climbs around the town.

WHILE IN THE AREA

During the first week in July the annual Festival of the Arts dominates the town completely. The Great Fish River Complex Conservancy is one of the largest conservation areas in the Eastern Cape. Animals likely to be seen include black rhino, kudu, buffalo and many other smaller species (see chapter 15). The nearby coastal town of Port Alfred has excellent diving and surfing (see chapters 5 and 14). Also see those entries for other attractions.

MORGAN BAY

Near the town of East London, Morgan Bay has the closest to sea cliff climbing that southern Africa has to offer. The steepish cliffs just above the sea provide some very enjoyable climbing.

WHILE IN THE AREA

East London has some excellent diving and surfing (see chapters 5 and 14), and great hiking (see chapter 7).

KwaZulu-Natal

There are a lot of excellent sport climbing venues in KwaZulu-Natal, most of which are listed in *A Climber's Guide to Natal Rock*. Some of the more popular include Monteseel, Kloof Gorge and the formidable Wave Cave near Shongweni. The last-mentioned is reputed to have the highest concentration of hard climbs in the country, with over 20 routes ranging from grade 19 to 30.

DRAKENSBERG

The Drakensberg, although offering excellent hiking, consists of rather friable basalt. Despite this, many people still climb there as it offers truly spectacular routes, some on huge, free-standing spires. It usually involves a day or two of hiking to get to any climbable spots and so is not particularly popular except with pretty hard-core climbers or in winter.

In most years the waterfalls in the Loteni region freeze solid for about six weeks in June and July and may be climbed then. For climbers from the northern hemisphere who will understand this, it is more like Scottish than Alpine ice climbing. It takes about a day to hike to the frozen falls and it is a little shorter from Giant's Castle than from Loteni.

WHILE IN THE AREA

See chapters 7 and 16 for more information on hiking and horse trails in this scenic area.

Mpumalanga

Not far from the densely populated Gauteng region, this area is a favourite weekend and holiday destination for climbers and non-climbers alike.

RESTAURANT AT THE END OF THE UNIVERSE

This is one of the most popular sport climbing venues in the region with about 500 bolted routes ranging from 12 to 33. There are two route guides available, one published by Southern Rock and one by the National Bolting Fund, both of which may be purchased from the nearby campsite or climbing shops. If you like social climbing (in the literal sense), this is a great place to spend the weekend.

WHILE IN THE AREA

This pretty area has no lack of attractions. Lovely day walks, hikes, trout fishing, mountain biking and horse trails are on offer on many private farms. Not too far away are a number of game farms and some interesting caves which are open to the public (see chapters 7, 8, 15, 16 and 17).

Gauteng and Northern Province

There are a number of sport climbing venues close to the major cities. The best known are Baviaanpoort, about half an hour's drive north of Pretoria, Strubens Valley in Roodepoort and North Cliff, all of which are bolted and are suitable for top roping. **Sanga Outdoor** in Johannesburg and **Ntaba Mountaineering** in Pretoria take escorted climbs to these and other areas on request.

MAGALIESBERG

Close to Johannesburg, this has long been a favourite climbing destination. There are some bolted climbs at Fernkloof but the rest are naturally protected. Route guides are available from most climbing shops. You may bush camp in the area. Most of the mountain is private property and access is strictly controlled. Contact the Transvaal section of the **Mountain Club** for permits. If you need accommodation in the area, the Mountain Sanctuary Park (tel: +27 142 75-0114) offers camping and chalets.

WHILE IN THE AREA

There are a number of hiking trails, kloofing and lovely rockpools around which to languish. You could start the day off with a balloon ride (see chapter 11), and then wander off for a climb after breakfast.

CLIMB INN

There are 66 different routes on 500 m^2 of wall in this indoor climbing gym. Situated in Kya-Sand Industrial Park, about half an hour's drive from

Johannesburg, this is definitely not pristine wilderness, but it's a great place to be when it's raining. The gym is open from 9 am to 1 pm on Monday, Tuesday and Wednesday, from 1 pm to 10 pm on Thursday and Friday and from 10 am to 7 pm on weekends.

ARCADIA CLIMBING WALL
This wall, in the Arcadia Shopping Centre in Pretoria, is 12 m high and has about 20 routes ranging from grade 12 to 24. It is open from 2 pm to 10 pm Monday to Thursday, 12 am to 10 pm on Fridays and from 10 am to 10 pm on weekends, public holidays and during school holidays.

BLOUBERG
This remote spot in the Northern Province has lots of naturally protected big wall climbing on nice solid rock. Most of the climbing is on private land, but you can organise permits and permission to camp through the **Mountain Club**.

Free State

Most South Africans from other provinces think the Free State is one huge flat maize farm with a few gold mines in between. They have obviously never been to the eastern part of the province.

MOUNT EVEREST RESORT
About 20 km on the Johannesburg side of Harrismith is the Mount Everest Resort. There are 15 bolted routes in sandstone, ranging from easy to 30.

WHILE IN THE AREA

The hiking is spectacular, and there are beautiful sandstone walls which glow in the sunset, giving the name to the nearby Golden Gate National Park. Clarens offers scenic horse trails (see chapter 16), deadly mountain bike trails (see chapter 8) and fun hiking. Music lovers should plan a climb here around Easter or in the December holidays. That's when Rustler's Valley, not too far away in the Ficksburg district, hosts huge concerts — definitely the place to hear the best of South Africa's indigenous music.

Lesotho

This mountainous country has surprisingly few known climbing spots. This may be partly because it is totally unexplored but is also due, to a large degree, to the friable nature of the rock in most areas. The only known area is near Katse Dam, where there are about eight bolted routes ranging from about 24 to 30.

Swaziland

There are some exposed granite domes at Mlilwane. Nyonyane, meaning "little bird" and otherwise known as Execution Rock, looks quite promising, offering only naturally protected climbing. The name "little bird" is descriptive of a condemned offender being hurled to death from the summit, a tradition which is no longer practised.

WHILE IN THE AREA

The Great Usutu River is raftable (see chapter 6), there is good mountain biking on Mlilwane and biking safaris on nearby Mkhaya (see chapter 8). There are a few paragliding launch sites, most of which have been discovered only recently (see chapter 9), and great game watching nearby (see chapter 15).

Namibia

Besides Spitzkoppe, described below, there is not much climbing in Namibia. There are mountainous regions with numerous day walks, such as the Waterberg and the Brandberg. You are bound to find a boulderable spot and possibly even a climbable face in one or both of these areas.

SPITZKOPPE

This huge granite outcrop has some excellent natural and sport climbing ranging from about a grade 14 to 24 with pitches of up to 200 m. The scenery is spectacular as it is the only relief in a vast flat plain. It is not necessary to pre-book or to get a permit, but you must pay a small entrance fee at the gate. There is a small campsite at the base of the rock.

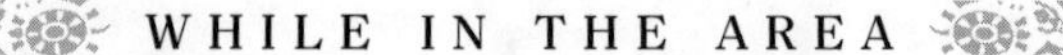

WHILE IN THE AREA

Spitzkoppe is miles from anywhere but non-climbing companions need not be bored. The scenery is spectacular, with the rock changing colour at different times of day. The birding is excellent and there are interesting rocks; the local children sell topaz crystals which they collect on the mountain.

Listings

OPERATORS, RETAIL OUTLETS AND CLUBS

Abseil Africa, tel: +27 21 25-4332, do commercial abseiling in the Cape Town area.

Arcadia Climbing Wall, tel: +27 12 323-0815, is a commercial climbing wall in Pretoria.

Berg Sports, tel: +27 41 51-1363, is a climbing shop in Port Elizabeth.

Camp Trails, tel: +27 41 35-2098, is a climbing shop in Port Elizabeth.

Cape Town School of Mountaineering, tel/fax: +27 21 61-9604, offers guided climbs and tuition in the Cape Town area.

Climb Inn, tel: +27 11 462-4919 or +27 83 266-6224, offers a commercial indoor climbing wall.

Drifters Adventure Shop in Sandton City, tel: +27 11 783-9200, sells climbing gear and has knowledgeable sales staff.

GAIA (Guided Ascents in Africa), tel: +27 21 761-9900 or +27 82 494-9635, offers guided climbs and tuition in the Cape Town area.

High Adventure, tel: +27 21 680-7158, offers guided climbs and tuition in the Cape Town area.

The Leading Edge, tel: +27 21 797-3386, offers guided climbs and tuition in the Cape Town area.

Mountain Club of SA, 97 Hatfield St, Gardens 8001, South Africa; tel: +27 21 45-3412 (Cape Town).

Mountain Club of SA, Transvaal section, P O Box 1641, Houghton 2041, South Africa; tel +27 11 786-8367.

Mount Everest Resort, P O Box 471 Harrismith 9880, South Africa; tel: +27 5861 2-1816, fax: +27 5861 2-3493.

Ntaba Mountaineering, tel: +27 12 323-2428, is a climbing shop in the Arcadia Shopping Centre in Pretoria. As well as selling all gear, they run courses and will take guided climbs on request.

Orca Industries, corner of Bowwood and Herschel Rds, Claremont, Cape Town; tel: +27 21 61-9673, sell a full range of climbing gear and other adventure equipment, offer escorted climbs in the Cape and do climbing and hiking leadership training under the auspices of the MDTT.

Outdoor Centre, tel: +27 331 45-2528, is a general outdoor store in Pietermaritzburg that also stocks climbing gear and has reasonably knowledgeable staff.

Sanga Outdoor, 8 Ameshof St, Braamfontein, 2001, P O Box 32924, Braamfontein 2017, tel: +27 11 3393374, fax: +27 11 339 3460, sell all equipment and run training courses under the auspices of MDTT.

FURTHER READING

A Climber's Guide to Natal Rock, Roger Nattrass, Mountain Club of South Africa, Natal Section, 1994.

The route guides mentioned in the text should be available from all climbing shops or, if you can't find them, you could try the MCSA.

Cape Rock, Julian Fisher, Julian Fisher, Cape Town, 1996. This is a guide to sport and natural climbing in the Cape and should be available from most climbing shops or the mountain club.

Index

D

K

L